AF251298

The Legacy of a Master Potter

The Legacy of a Master Potter

Nampeyo
and Her Descendants

by Mary Ellen and Laurence Blair

Treasure Chest Books
Tucson

Treasure Chest Books
P. O. Box 5250
Tucson, AZ 85703-0250
(520) 623-9558

ISBN 1-887896-06-6
This book is set in Minion, Eurostile, and Bellevue types.

Front cover and title page photograph: Nampeyo storage jar.
Originally a gift from Georgia O'Keeffe to Tom and Margaret Pack
Bahti. Now in the collection of Henry and Margaret Pack McKinley.
7½ by 15 inches. W. Ross Humphreys, photographer.

Back cover photograph: Nampeyo by Edward S. Curtis

Editorial Consultant: *Barton Wright*
Editors: *Linnea Gentry and Patricia Shelton*
Editorial assistant: *Natsuki Yokokura*
Designer: *Simpson & Convent*
Printed in Canada

Contents

❸

Pottery Making, Nampeyo Family Style... 121

❹

Continuing the Legacy: The Nampeyo-Lesou Progeny... 167

Foreword

When first asked to provide an introduction for a book concerning the history and art of the Native American ceramic artist Nampeyo and her descendants, I hesitated. After spending time with the Blairs during their frequent research trips to the Hopi Reservation, however, my viewpoint gradually changed. As I became more familiar with their endeavor, the country around me began to assume a new grandeur, and its history became more impressive. My Native American friends and neighbors with whom I had grown up assumed a new stature. I began to reminisce about the role they played in my childhood and to recognize the profound effect they still exert on me and, to a lesser extent, on the entire Hopi population.

The life of the remarkable Englishman Thomas Varker Keam, who well over a century ago founded the trading post that would provide my livelihood and feed my deep interest in Hopi and Navajo art, has now become my avocation. The grave just a short distance across the road from the trading post is no longer simply the location of the remains of a person whose headstone reads "Alexander Stephen." It now holds greater meaning to me as the resting place of someone who came to this country seemingly out of nowhere and became the chief recorder of Hopi and Hopi-Tewa history in the few short years remaining to him. Stephen was more responsible than any other outsider, before or since, for preserving their rich heritage.

I soon realized that it would be both a pleasure and an honor for me to express my thoughts and feelings about a most noble Tewa-Hopi lady, Nampeyo, and her descendants and about their pioneer contributions to Native American art in almost all of its forms. Most of my life has been spent on the Hopi reservation. As a youngster, I went to school with Nampeyo's descendants, some of whom were playmates and classmates. Many times Fannie and Nellie were my baby-sitters, and I came to know their firm but affectionate discipline. My parents also shared a close and fond relationship with members of the Lesou family in business and church affairs over a long period of time.

Almost all of Nampeyo's descendants are talented perfectionists when creating and decorating the ceramic art forms which are sought after by both museums and private collectors worldwide. As Nampeyo set the artistic example, her descendants have set examples in turn for their children and on to the succeeding generations. The inherited artistic talent was not limited to clay forms, and there are noted artists and sculptors now included in the ranks. In addition, many adopted by the family through marriage have become recognized in the artistic world. Just as Nampeyo's work was fresh and innovative when compared to her predecessors, so is the work of many of her successors when compared to hers. She inspired innovation.

This book is a landmark in providing insight into the art, inspiration, and lives of this remarkable group of people and is based on comprehensive and meticulous research. The Blairs undertook the project from a background in technical and artistic research, as well as longtime experience in recording observations and data. Over a thirty-year period, they spent much time at Hopi, developing long-term relationships with the residents, and spent much time in Europe as well, investigating those whose lives intertwined with Nampeyo and her family. I am delighted to see that this long overdue reference is finally a reality.

—*Wm. Bruce McGee*

Preface

Biano [a respected Taos Indian] expressed his contempt for all whites, and concluded: "We think that they are mad." Jung [Carl Gustav Jung, noted psychologist] asked why he thought so.

"They say that they think with their heads," Biano replied.

"Why, of course. What do you think with?" Jung asked in surprise.

"We think here," the Indian said, indicating his heart.

Jung was stunnded. "I fell into a long meditation....This Indian had struck our vulnerable spot, unveiled a truth to which we are blind."

C. W. Ceram, The First American *(1972)*

Like many people who grew up on the East Coast of the United States, we mistakenly thought that United States history began with the landing of the Pilgrims on Plymouth Rock in 1620 and covered nothing west of the Mississippi River until the acquisition of land by various means enlarged our territorial boundaries. Eastern Native Americans had been subdued, and we rarely heard or saw them mentioned.

In 1957, with three weeks' time at our disposal, we decided to drive as far west as possible, returning when either money or time was half expended. We investigated intriguing points of interest on maps, many of them national monuments dedicated to preserving the works and culture of prehistoric Indians. Then we departed.

What an eye-opening experience it was to see that people had built remarkable cultures in this country long before the arrival of the Pilgrims and that their progeny continued to struggle to preserve their heritage! How unexpected it was for us to drive through the bi- and trilingual settlements of the Rio Grande Valley with widely different language bases—an Indian language, a Romance language, and a Germanic language—a situation existing in only a few places in the world! What a shock it was to find ourselves in the minority, where we often did not understand a word spoken. We discovered Southwest cuisine and had our first taste of chile. We discovered Spanish and Indian art forms, that were scarce in the East and appeared only as small samples in museum exhibits. We were stunned to meet the creators of these arts and crafts and to realize that they had such a long and unique inheritance. Our interest in pottery started then.

We spent more than our alloted time examining the impressive, unfamiliar structures built by ancient civilizations at Mesa Verde. Ignoring advertised delights of towns and tourist traps, we then devoted our time to the pueblos and their people in the Rio Grande Valley. We fell farther behind schedule as we worked our way down. Days evaporated while we visited with John Valesquez, the Cochiti drum maker, and the potters Andrea Garcia of Santo Domingo, Virginia Duran of Picuris, and Juanita Bernal of Taos, whose last pot was made in 1965.

From then on, there was no quenching our thirst for knowledge about these Southwestern cultures. The sustaining remedy was to return at least once a year, until we moved to Denver to be closer to the area. We must confess that at the end of five years we considered ourselves "experts." But, of course, the more we learned about the native peoples, the greater the realization that our knowledge was sparse and would never be complete.

In 1963 our interest began to accelerate with concentration on pottery: we bought thirteen pieces that year, most of them directly from the makers. Included were a Maria and Santana Martínez bowl (cost $20), an unsigned Margaret Tafoya piece for $10, and our first Hopi-Tewa pottery from what seemed like a remote village, Hano. Following our westward move in 1971, we spent more time in Indian country and gradually made friends with Indian families and with traders such as the McGees of Keams Canyon, Tom Woodard, then of Gallup, and Joe and Belle Becker of Española, New Mexico. All had the confidence and trust of Indian artists and dealt fairly with them. As our visits became more frequent, we built closer relationships with the families in the Tewa communities of New Mexico and Arizona. We were privileged to observe pottery-making procedures from beginning to end and, at times, to assist in such menial chores as hauling manure or searching for pottery kiln furniture.

Our early retirement in 1979 provided the time to undertake a study of the art and technology of the Indian potters we had come to know, applying our professional backgrounds in ceramic engineering and art with our avid interest in this intriguing subject. We began with Margaret Tafoya, since hers was the first family we had come to know well. She was at that time a relatively unpublicized pottery artist equally as skilled as the famous Maria of San Ildefonso but less inclined toward studio demonstrations and public appearances. Her clear memory supplied us with information about the great Santa Clara potters of the past, including her mother, Sera Fina (spelling by Margaret Tafoya), aunt Santana, and sister Tomacita.

We began our research on Nampeyo and her family in 1984. Every minute was enjoyable, beginning with research in libraries and museums, and interviewing family members, traders, private collectors, and others whose paths had crossed those of Nampeyo and her family. At first our main focus was on Fannie Polacca, who as the only surviving daughter of Nampeyo at the time was credited with doing much to perpetuate the Nampeyo tradition. Our time with her ran out too soon; she passed away in 1987—but not before she and her family made a large contribution to this book.

Our first meeting with Fannie was inauspicious, a fault due entirely to ourselves. A few years later, however, we were properly introduced to Fannie by her sons Ellsworth and Thomas. It was through the services of Ellsworth that we were able to propose writing a book about Nampeyo and her successors. Fannie carefully considered our proposal before she agreed. Soon we came to understand that what appeared to be gruffness in Fannie was a combination of shyness and difficulty in communicating in anything but the Hopi and Tewa languages. When she smiled, which was often, the area seemed to light up, and her laughter was contagious. We belatedly thank this remarkable lady for her patience and cooperation.

There are now so many members in the large Nampeyo family that interviewing each one personally was impossible. Time and space were simply not available. However, many of Nampeyo's descendants all hosted us and cooperated in supplying information. Many of the other descendants, outstanding potters, artists, and carvers also, must be left for future studies.

Acknowledgments

Grateful acknowledgment is given to the following individuals and institutions for their cooperation, contributions, and encouragement. Those who provided multiple illustrations are identified in the captions by the initials indicated here.

Albany Institute of History and Art, Albany, NY

Alexander Anthony, Adobe Art Gallery, Albuquerque, NM

American Museum, Bath, England

American Museum of Natural History, New York, NY (**AMNH**)

American Philosophical Society, Philadelphia, PA

Arizona Historical Foundation, Hayden Library, Arizona State University, Tempe, AZ

Arizona Historical Society, Tucson, AZ (**AZHS**)

Arizona State Museum (**AZSM**)

Bowers Museum, Santa Ana, CA

Brooklyn Museum, Culin Archival Collection, Brooklyn, NY (**BMB**)

California Historical Society, Los Angeles, CA

Cambridge University, Museum of Archaeology and Anthropology, Cambridge, England

Central Public Library, Edinburgh, Scotland

Chicago Historical Society, Chicago, IL

Church of Jesus Christ of Latter-day Saints, Museum of Church History and Art, Salt Lake City, UT

Clarkson University, Potsdam, NY

Colorado History Museum, Denver, CO

Colorado School of Mines Research Station, Golden, CO

Colorado Springs Fine Arts Center and Taylor Museum, Colorado Springs, CO (**CSFAC**)

Cornwall Record Office, Truro, Cornwall, England

Denver Art Museum and the Douglas Library, Denver, CO (**DAM**)

Denver Museum of Natural History, CO (**DMNH**)

Dillingham, Rick, Santa Fe, NM (**RD**)

Edinburgh University Library, Edinburgh, Scotland

Enchanted Mesa, Albuquerque, NM

Etnografisk Museum (Ethnographic Museum), Universitetet I Oslo, Oslo, Norway (**EMOs**)

Etnografisk Samling Nationalmuseet, Copenhagen, Denmark

Field Museum of Natural History, Chicago, IL

General Registrar Office and New Register House, Edinburgh, Scotland

Gilcrease Institute of American History and Art, Tulsa, OK (**GIAH&A**)

Grammer, Maurine, Albuquerque, NM (**MG**)

Hamburgisches Museum fur Volkerkunde und Vorgeschichte, Hamburg, Germany

Hanging Tree Gallery, Albuquerque, NM

The Heard Museum, Phoenix, AZ (**HMPx**)

Heriot-Watt University Library, Edinburgh, Scotland

Hood Museum of Art, Dartmouth College, Hanover, NH (**HMA**)

Hubbell Trading Post National Historic Site, National Park Service, Ganado, AZ

The Huntington Library, San Marino, CA

Keams Canyon Arts and Crafts Collection (**KCAC**)

Kenwyn Parrish Church, Truro, Cornwall, England

Maxwell Museum of Anthropology, University of New Mexico, Albuquerque, NM (**MMA**)

The McGee Family, Keams Canyon Arts and Crafts, Keams Canyon, AZ

The Middle American Research Institute and the Latin American Library, Tulane University, New Orleans, LA (**MARI/LAL**)

Mennonite Library and Archives, Bethel College, North Newton, KS

Milwaukee Public Museum, Milwaukee, WI (**MPM**)

Musee de l'Homme, Paris, France

Museum fur Volkerkunde, Vienna, Austria

Museum of Man, San Diego, CA (**MMSD**)

Museum of Mankind, British Museum, London, England

Museum of New Mexico: Anthropology Laboratory, History Library, Museum of Indian Art and Cluture, and Photographic Archives, Santa Fe, NM (**MNM**)

Museum of Northern Arizona, Flagstaff, AZ (**MNAZ**)

The Nampeyo Family Descendants

National Anthropological Archives, Smithsonian Institution, Washington, DC (**NAA-SI**)

National Museum of the American Indian, Smithsonian Institution, New York, NY (**NMAI-SI**)

National Museum of Natural History, Smithsonian Institution, Washington, DC (**NMNH-SI**)

Peabody Museum of Archaeology and Ethnology, Harvard University, Cambridge, MA (**PMAE**)

Philbrook Art Center, Tulsa, OK

Phoebe Hearst Museum of Anthropology, Univerisity of California, Berkeley, CA

Pitt Rivers Museum, School of Anthropology and Museum Ethnology, Oxford, England (**PRMOx**)

Public Record Office, Kew-Richmond, Surrey, England

Royal Cornwall Museum, Royal Institution of Cornwall, Truro, England

School of American Research, Santa Fe (**SAR**)

Scotts Bluff National Monument, National Park Service, Scotts Bluff, NE

Seaver Center for Western History Research, Natural History Museum of Los Angeles County, Los Angeles, CA (**SCWHR**)

Southwest Museum, Los Angeles, CA (**SWMLA**)

Barbara and Michael Stanislawski, Santa Fe, NM

Suomen Kansallismuseo (National Museum of Finland), Helsinki, Finland

Tay Valley Family History Society, Dundee, Scotland

United States Department of the Interior, United States Geological Survey Photo Library, Denver, CO

University of Arizona Library, Tucson, AZ

University of Colorado Museum, Boulder, CO

University Museum of Archaeology and Anthropology, University of Pennsylvania, Philadelphia, PA

University of New Mexico Zimmerman Library, Albuquerque, NM (**UNM**)

The Warburg Institute, University of London, London, England

Wheelwright Museum of the American Indian, Santa Fe, NM

Woodard, Tom, Santa Fe, NM

Recognition is also due our daughter Joanne Blair who provided photography and assembled some of the art work. Unless otherwise noted, she was the photographer.

Many thanks also to the collectors who graciously shared material and knowledge but preferred to remain anonymous.

The Legacy of a Master Potter

History of the Hopi-Tewa People

Bands of Homo Erectus undoubtedly took advantage of every favorable opportunity offered by the environment, but the fundamental reason for their success in globe trotting was within themselves and not outside.

R. E. Leakey and R. Lewin, Origins: The Emergence and Evolution of Our Species and Its Possible Future

Researchers have expended a great deal of effort to establish the origins and migration patterns of artist Nampeyo's prehistoric ancestors, the Anasazi people who lived in the Southwest, roughly where the states of Colorado, Utah, Arizona, and New Mexico now meet. The Tewa group was an outgrowth of a population known as the Eastern Anasazi of the Four Corners area, dating from approximately A.D. 575.[1] Although the Eastern Anasazi culture reached its peak about 1200, during the next century most people had begun to migrate. The reason can only be imagined. Had drastic climatic changes occurred? Had they been struck by an epidemic, or had there been a breakdown of strong social and religious ties, or was it that they moved at every opportunity afforded by a favorable environment?

Migration Period: 1200–1525 A.D.

Groups of different sizes gradually abandoned the area, possibly beginning before 1200, and moved toward the east and south along the headwaters of the San Juan and down into the Chama and Rio Grande river courses. Oral tradition says that during their migration something happened in the prehistoric village of Tehauiping (fig. 1.1). As a result of either an unknown discontent or an intrusion of other people into the area, the population of the Tewa separated into the northern and southern branches. According to early ethnologist John P. Harrington, the site of Tehauiping is at the geographic center of all of the prehistoric and historic Tewa pueblos: "The Tehuas claim that this pueblo marks the center of the range of their people, and that the division into two branches, of which the Tewas became the northern and the Tanos (at times called the Hanos and now known as the Southern Tewa) the southern, took place there in very ancient times. Certain it is that in the sixteenth century the Tewas already held the Tesuque Valley ten miles south of Pojoaque and still hold it today."[2]

The motives for this smaller independent group of Tewas to continue to relocate is a matter of conjecture, but move they did. Unfortunately, this time they would find that the ancient belief of their people—those who would prosper would ever move south—had exceptions. The boundary of their new land provided little protection against either a hostile Old Woman Earth and Old Man Sky or the pillaging nomads. The land was difficult to farm and lacked dependable water resources. One of the largest pueblos of the area, Arroyo Hondo, has been exhaustively studied by the School of American Research and was found to have been abandoned twice because of drought and resulting famines.[3] The fate of Arroyo Hondo was typical of many other Southern Tewa settlements.

Worse than drought and famine were the raids by nearby nomadic tribes. Though the hostile people were not mounted on horses as yet (the Spanish had not arrived to provide this swift form of transportation), the raids were devastating. According to early Spanish sources, a massive raid took place about 1525 when four of the seven Southern Tewa settlements were destroyed. The pueblos that survived were San Marcos, Galisteo, and San Cristóbal. It was inevitable that even the inhabitants of these miserable sites would eventually be forced to evacuate.[4]

The first Spanish colonists to arrive in the area found a decimated population inhabiting a land that could neither support its people nor be defended from a military standpoint.[5] There were too few souls in the area for the newly arrived padres to proselytize profitably. Except for the erection of the small missions in the vicinity of San Marcos and Galisteo, between 1617 and 1680 the Spanish all but turned their backs on the wretched scene.[6]

In summary, the two decades between the great raids of 1520 and the arrival of the Spanish were a time when the Southern Tewas were forced to face unpleasant facts: they had not moved far enough south, they had not gone in the right southerly direction, or the ancient law of their people was not infallible. During this short period the native population in the area moved little. With the Spanish came ideas of landownership that further restricted Native American groups to fixed areas. Had the Europeans not arrived on the scene, who knows what part of North America the Tewas might occupy today or where the Southern Tewas might be living.

How had the art of Tewa pottery making fared during these many moves? The pottery quality and type depended more on the

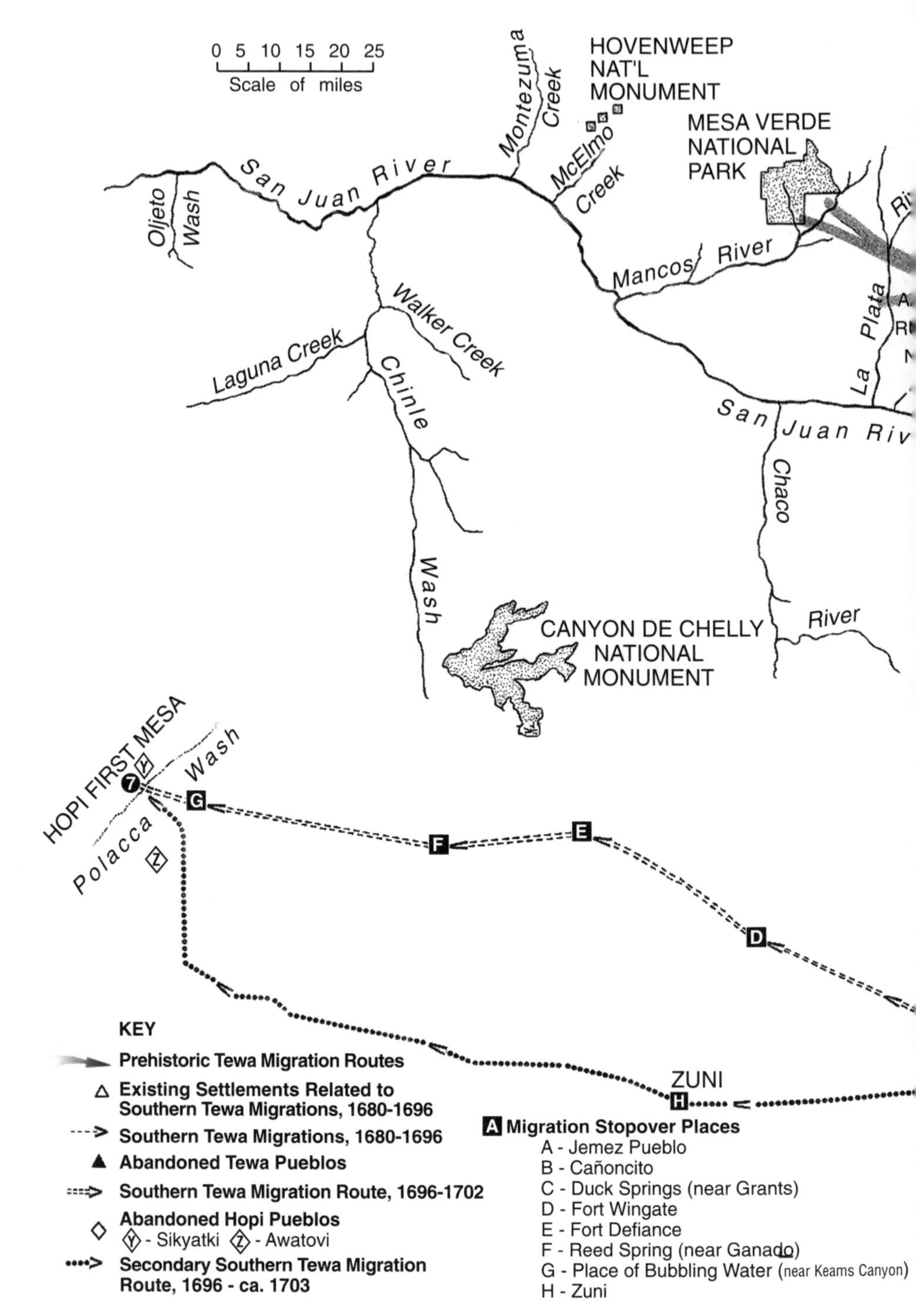

Fig. 1.1. Possible prehistoric and historic Southern Tewa migration routes.

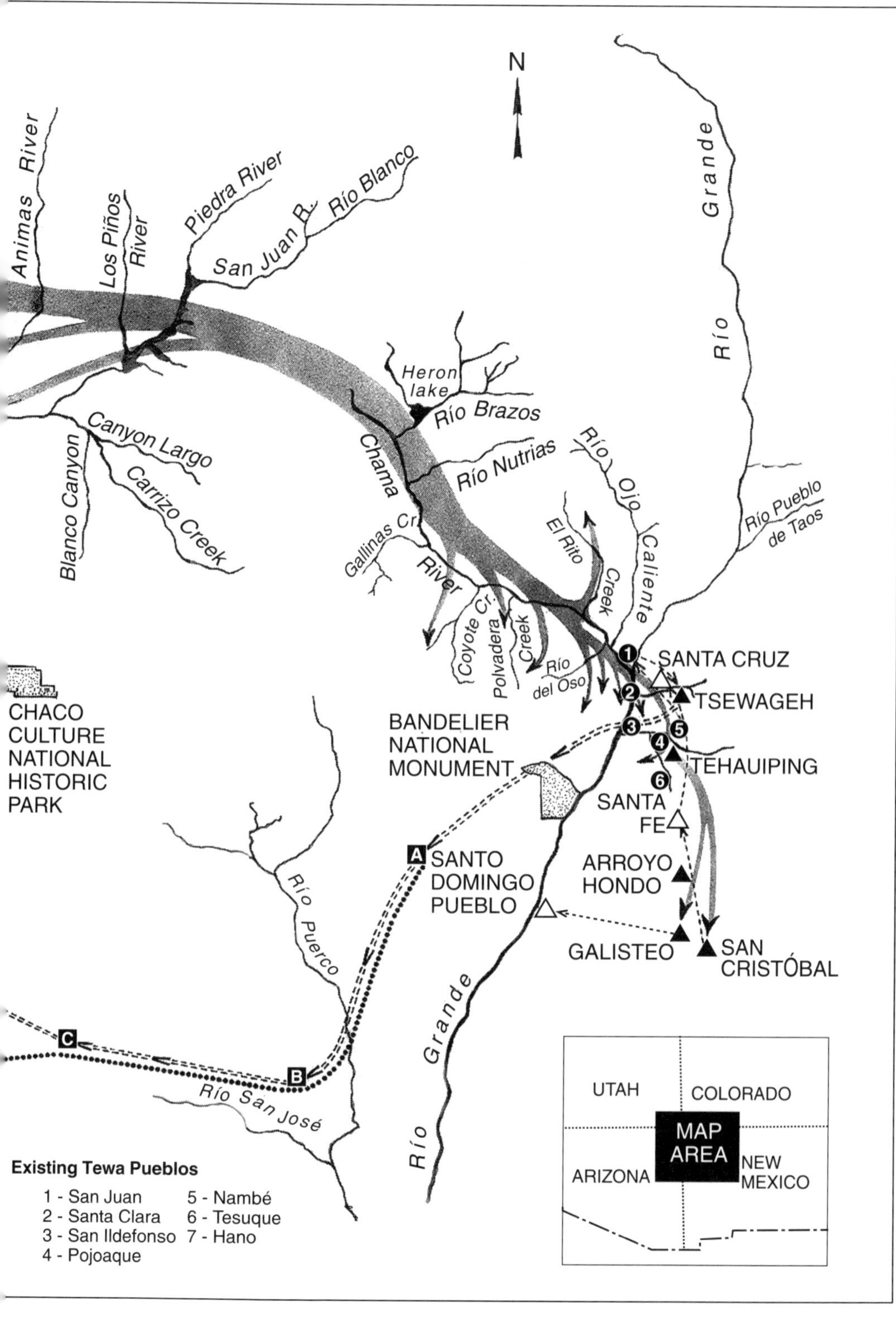

N
Animas River
Los Piños River
Piedra River
San Juan R.
Río Blanco
Río Grande
Canyon Largo
Blanco Canyon
Carrizo Creek
Heron lake
Río Brazos
Chama
Río Nutrias
Gallinas Cr.
River
Coyote Cr.
Polvadera Creek
Río del Oso
El Rito
Río Ojo Caliente
Creek
Río Pueblo de Taos
CHACO CULTURE NATIONAL HISTORIC PARK
BANDELIER NATIONAL MONUMENT
1 SANTA CRUZ
2 TSEWAGEH
3
5
4 TEHAUIPING
6
SANTA FE
ARROYO HONDO
GALISTEO
SAN CRISTÓBAL
A SANTO DOMINGO PUEBLO
Río Puerco
Río San José
Río Grande
B
C
UTAH
COLORADO
MAP AREA
ARIZONA
NEW MEXICO
Existing Tewa Pueblos
1 - San Juan
2 - Santa Clara
3 - San Ildefonso
4 - Pojoaque
5 - Nambé
6 - Tesuque
7 - Hano

available raw materials than on most other factors. The clays and tempers of the Four Corners area had allowed for the production of thin-walled vessels, very often stone polished to a high luster. Designs were well organized and integrated. The clays found in the Rio Grande area were very different, requiring different skills, and the design work was cruder, perhaps due to the disruptive influences on the lives of the people. A superior piece owed much of its beauty to the quality of the ingredients, as well as to the skill of the artist.

Fig. 1.2. *Tewa pottery sherds from the vicinity of the Santa Cruz River, Española, New Mexico. The decoration is somewhat cruder than that applied by the potters of the late Mesa Verde period.*

With the Tewas who moved to the south, pottery forms and decorations changed, and the execution became cruder. Raw materials were not as suitable and required different working techniques. Fine temper, not available in their new locations, was replaced by a coarse material produced from local igneous rocks known as "andesites." The available clays contained a higher percentage of impurities, had different firing properties, and did not burn to as light a color (figs. 1.2 and 1.3). Techniques for proper forming of the new clays and insertion of tempers were never developed. Even so, raw materials were adequate and pottery production was not too different from that of their Tewa neighbors to the north.[7]

Southern Tewa potters were quick to discover that they could

Fig. 1.3. *Restored Glaze III, Pueblo IV jar from the Rio Grande Valley. A classic example of Southern Tewa pottery (9¾ in. high by 13 in. diameter). Jemez Pueblo artists in recent years have rediscovered glaze paint decoration. A 1986 photograph. No. 140, DAM.*

partially mask crude forms by painting them with a glaze decoration made by suspending finely ground local lead ores in fluid mediums. Then, as now, the ores were obtained from an area near the present town of Cerrillos, New Mexico. Considering the information that has been amassed about volatility, toxicity, and the cumulative poisonous nature of lead compounds, one might conclude that the lifespan of a potter of that era was short and that death was unpleasant.

The Exodus, 1525–ca.1704

Although the Southern Tewas may have realized as early as 1525 that their land was virtually uninhabitable, it was not until 1680 that the restraints put upon migration by the Spanish were broken in the great Pueblo Revolt. As the beaten, confused Spanish retreated from Santa Fe into Mexico, the Southern Tewas divided into three groups, each abandoning wretched living areas to seek more hospitable environments.

The Galisteo inhabitants moved to Santa Fe after the town was abandoned by the Spanish and became its principal occupants until reoccupation by de Vargas in 1692. General de Vargas, remembering the aggressive nature exhibited by the Native Americans during the revolt, spent little time in ousting them from his capital and forcibly relocating them to the site from whence they had come—Galisteo. The group lost seventy warriors in the struggle with de Vargas. Starving and unprotected from Apache and Comanche raiders, as well as being victims of a smallpox epidemic in 1794, the now decimated band of people realized that they must vacate Galisteo or perish. Without Spanish permission, they received asylum from the Santo Domingo people who lived some twenty-five miles west. Within a short period they were assimilated, although in 1908 John Harrington did locate a frightened older woman who spoke a few words of Tewa to him. He writes: "…her fears soon got the best of her and she commanded me to leave the house lest she be flogged by the governor for giving me information; the door was locked during the rest of [my] stay at Santo Domingo."[8]

Simultaneously, the Southern Tewas who resided in the devastated pueblos of San Lazáro and San Cristóbal bypassed Santa Fe and settled in the Santa Cruz River valley. The San Lazáro people settled on the north bank near the present village of Santa Cruz, while those from San Cristóbal chose a location known as Tsewageh (Wide White Gap), five miles east of Española, New Mexico, on the south bank of the Santa Cruz River. At this time the Southern Tewas began to produce pottery similar to that made during their settlement three centuries earlier (fig. 1.2).

De Vargas, after promising the Indians that he would not remove them from the land grants previously allotted them by the King of Spain, broke his word. Wishing to build a church on the site of their village, he forced the San Lazáro and some Santa Clara people to vacate their homes on the Santa Clara grant and move eastward toward Chimayo and Tsewageh. Hatred and mistrust of the Spanish continued to develop after their repeated failures to keep promises, coupled with memories of cruelties and injustices inflicted by Spanish politicians and church officials during their rule before the revolt. These broken promises goaded the Southern Tewas into playing a prominent role in the second, but unsuccessful, rebellion of 1692. Joining the people of Santa Clara, they engaged in a prolonged battle that churned around a spectacular lava plug (Black Mesa) located between the pueblos of Santa Clara and San Ildefonso.

De Vargas, unable to dislodge the Indian warriors from the mesa summit after several costly attempts, broke up the conflict by holding the children of Santa Clara hostage and threatening to kill them all unless the Indian warriors surrendered. A treaty was finally signed on 4 September 1692; it included promises—promises the Indians should have known would not be kept.

Deceived, defeated, frustrated, and blinded by hate and rage, the Southern Tewas seized the first opportunity to vent their wrath by striking out at the Spanish Catholic church. On 4 June 1696 they murdered two priests, Fray José de Arbizu and Fray Antonio Carbonel. No matter the justification, one fact was clear: To avoid harsh retaliation by de Vargas and his army, they must vacate their homes and land immediately. The killing of the priests may not have been the spontaneous act that it first appeared to be; it could have been a final, carefully planned act of defiance and revenge against their tormentors.

The long journey to the land of the Hopi would be the final and longest segment of the Tewas' great exodus (fig. 1.1). The Southern Tewas and the Hopis have different versions of why the Tewas chose the domain of the Hopis as their destination. The Hopi version as presented by Marah Ryan emphasized that the Tewas requested asylum:

> Te-hua is the keeper of the Gate Way, the Gap. The Te-hua people belong to a different lingual group, but ages ago they migrated from the Rio Grande and sought to live with the powerful Walpis. Our people said, "Yes you are welcome; there is room, but you build your village where the pass is, and you guard the Gate Way against the Apache and the Navajo—thus may you live here." So they did and they put the shrine at the Gate Way to help them guard it, and so it has been ever since![9]

The Tewas' reason for choosing the land of the Hopis as their destination has been passed by word of mouth in their kivas for three centuries. Taking countless hours in the telling, it consists of more than two hundred stories detailing the great escape.

An abbreviated Tewa account of the story has been written by native historian Albert Yava. The Hopis wanted to use the Tewas as mercenaries to repel the raiding Utes and Navajos as well as the Spanish should they return to First Mesa to reestablish their churches. As compensation, the Tewas would be awarded land on which to settle, build their homes and kivas, and raise their crops. The negotiations required several years to complete and included guarantees to the Tewas. The Tewa version omits mentioning a request for asylum but avers that they were offered land as a part of the contract.[10]

Accounts of the long journey are limited to verbal accounts available from the Hopi-Tewa descendants of the San Cristóbal and San Lazáro people. They detail how badly the Tewas were treated by both the Spanish and the Hopis. They tell of the hardship suffered after their arrival, but for some reason they seldom tell of the fight with the Utes. Investigators such as Jesse Walter Fewkes and Albert Yava have published short versions of the flight. Barbara Freire-Marreco in her unpublished notes (1913) added more detail, stating that the Corn Clan ancestors of Nampeyo played an important role in the Southern Tewa exodus. "This Corn Clan man said that when the people left—they went to Zia [near the stop mentioned by Fewkes]. They stopped there and some of the ladies had babies and were left behind there… and the others started without them. So when these came on afterwards, they came by the Zuni road; but the first lot came by the straight road, stopping, living awhile, cooking provisions and starting again."[11]

A Hopi-Tewa informant claimed that the Corn Clan people accompanied the main body who traveled via Keams Canyon, acting as trailblazers and also fulfilling their ceremonial duties by blessing the path with corn meal. Later, an old Corn Clan woman volunteered to meet the splinter group from Zuni in order to properly escort them to their homes. The Hopi-Tewa refer to those who came via Zuni as those "from the bottom." This is difficult to rationalize because the Corn Clan people are not supposed to lead, for as seed people they are the most carefully guarded clan. Other more recent versions of the story say that the people did not stop to build permanent homes on the way but lived instead in caves and natural shelters.

The flight began shortly after 1696, following the killing of the two priests at Tsewageh. An old Indian "saw many people descending from the mountains of the Tanos with their horses loaded with clothing, and crossing the Rio Del Norte [Rio Grande] in the vicinity of the Pueblo of Santa Clara."[12] The mass movement went undetected by the Spanish. Several years would pass before the Spanish learned that the Tanos were living with the Hopis just three hundred miles west of their starting point.

The Spanish were ignorant of the movements of the Southern Tewas for many reasons. To the Indians the land was familiar; to the Spanish it was not. They were hidden in pueblos hostile to the Spanish, such as Zia and Jemez. Their trek took them through rugged unpatrolled lands, and the army of de Vargas was forced temporarily to abandon the chase in order to extinguish other revolts larger and nearer to Santa Fe. Confrontation was postponed but not abandoned, as the Spanish authorities could not allow the killing of priests to go unpunished. They feared such laxness would encourage further uprisings.

Nearing the end of their flight, the Indians paused at the Place of the Bubbling Water (Kwalalata or Pawsaiyeh) in Keams Canyon in Arizona. This beautiful site was later used by Kit Carson to rest his troops while on a foray against the Navajos; still later it became the site of Thomas Varker Keam's first trading post. Their final stop was located at Coyote Spring near present-day Polacca, Arizona. Versions differ according to which legend one accepts. The Tewas claim they were there by Hopi invitation and awaited the land promised them atop First Mesa; Hopi tradition states that the Tewas were running from the Spanish and asked the Hopis for sanctuary.

In either case the new arrivals were restricted to the land below First Mesa, a small area near Polacca called Tcewadi. According to Yava, the Walpi hosts acted in an unusual manner: "They contacted the Utes and challenged them to make an attack on Walpi. They said, 'We've got some real fighters here now. Why don't you come and try to drive them off?' If this story is true, then it must be that the Hopis had a change of heart and really wanted to get the Tewas out before they had a chance to settle, or maybe they just wanted to test them."[13]

A Ute raid was unsuccessful against the superior military strategy of the Tewa. Under attack, the Utes were forced to retreat and took refuge in a rock shelter. They fought until only a few warriors were left. The survivors were spared their lives and told to return home and warn their people never to attack the Hopis again.

Following this impressive display of the Tewas' capabilities as warriors, the Hopis undoubtedly felt compelled to give them residence on the mesa top at the edge of the large gap from which Walpi gets its name; here the Tewas have maintained a shrine. The Tewas were also given farmland east of the north-south line through the Gap (Wala) and across the valleys on either side of First Mesa. The Hopi retained the land west of this line and in the foothills area. These boundaries are still generally observed when building homes, burying the dead, or working farm plots. Due to the absence of written descriptions, occasional land disputes still erupt. The descendants of Tom Polacca, Nampeyo's brother, were involved in a dispute as recently as the 1970s.[14]

In assimilating the Tewas into their culture, the Hopis sought to establish control over them. The Tewas in turn fought to retain their tribal identity and shrewdly chose language as a way to keep themselves autonomous. However, intermarriage with the Hopis, who were greater in number, slowly transformed the social systems of the Rio Grande people. Such was the case with the marriage ritual. When a man marries, he moves to the abode of his wife and remains there as long as the marriage lasts. Thus, if a Hopi man marries a Tewa woman, he moves to his wife's Tewa village; when a Tewa man marries a Hopi woman, the Tewa man moves to his wife's Hopi village. Consequently, as children belong only to the mother's clan, each group retains a lineage that is either Hopi or Tewa; neither can be termed pure-blooded.

Santa Clara Tewa scholar Edward Dozier maintains that no Tewa child is ever allowed to forget the events of their migration.

> Whenever I went to see Thete [a Tewa clan grandfather] he made me sit beside him and told me the Tewa migration legend which I had heard countless times from his lips. I knew the story so well that I could probably relate it better than he. Thete would start from the beginning repeating all important events four times, as is the traditional pattern in all legends. His voice would become charged with emotion when he spoke of the injustices the Tewa suffered from the Hopi, and he always ended the legend by telling me that we Tewa must never forget this story, but must always tell it to our children as he had related it to me. I became so tired of the story that I would try to invent some excuse so that I would not have to listen to it again. Sometimes I went to sleep while he was telling me the story, and

then he would shake me gently and tell me that I must not sleep, that the story was very important, and that I must learn it well.[15]

One of the most important events in the agreement between Hopis and Southern Tewas was the assurance that the Tewas would retain their separate language and that it would not become a common property with the Hopis. Yava gives the following version of the event:

> After that [the battle between the Tewas and the Utes] the Tewa leader said, "Another thing, my brother, we want you to know that we are going to remain Tewa forever. No matter what you do we will follow our own ways." He took a small ear of corn and handed it to the Hopi chief. He said, "Chew it up but do not swallow it." The Hopi chewed the corn. The Tewa chief said, "Now give me what you have chewed." The Hopi chief spat the corn into his hand. The Tewa chief took the chewed corn, put it into his mouth, and swallowed it. The Hopi chief asked, "What is the meaning of this?" The Tewa chief answered, "It means that we will take from your mouth the language you speak. We will speak Hopi." The Hopi chief said, "It is good that you will speak Hopi. Now you chew us some corn and give it to me." The Tewa chief chewed some corn, and the Hopi chief put out his hand to receive it. But the Tewa chief did not give it to him. He had his people dig a deep hole in the ground, and he spat his corn into the hole. They filled the hole with earth and covered it with heavy rocks. The Hopi chief asked, "What is the meaning of this?" The Tewa chief answered, "It means that you will never have our language in your mouths. We will speak Hopi and Tewa, but your people will never speak the Tewa language."[16]

The language barrier thus established still exists. The speech of the Tewa village is Southern Tewa, while the neighboring villages of Sichomovi, located only a few feet from Hano, and Walpi are Hopi.

Dozier offers the following explanation of the effectiveness of this prohibition:

> The inability of the Hopi to learn the Tewa language in the initial contact period can probably be explained in terms of the numbers involved. The original migrants may have totaled no more than 400 or 500, whereas the Hopi population must have been ten times as large. [This is an interesting exaggeration of numbers; it is doubtful that the population of Walpi ever reached 1500, and Sichomovi did not yet exist. Still, his thesis is correct.] Under these circumstances it would have been easier for the Tewa to learn the Hopi Language. This explanation is difficult to accept for the more recent period. Intermarriage with Hopi and the matriarchal residences custom bring Hopi husbands to live at Hano (the old name for the present Tewa village). It is remarkable that in such unions the Hopi husband does not speak Tewa, even though in many cases he may have spent the major portion of his life at Hano and in his Tewa wife's household where Tewa is the preferred language. In such unions the children are, of course, conversant in both languages since husband and wife speak to one another in Hopi and a child must respectfully speak Hopi to his Hopi father but Tewa to his mother and his Tewa kinfolk at Hano. The Hopi men currently married at Hano do not speak Tewa; most of them surely understand it, but none of them will venture to speak it…[and] although a Hopi may understand everything said in Tewa he cannot utter a Tewa word.[17]

The descendants of Nampeyo state that the verbal history of the Tewa migration and arrival in Hopi country is kept alive during the Hopi-Tewa ceremonies held near the end of each calendar year. Also, once in every decade, a group of the Hopi-Tewa people retrace the route taken by their ancestors, much of it by motor vehicle except for the more rugged portions around Mt. Taylor, which they cover on foot.

A Hopi-Tewa who visits distant Rio Grande relatives hears a much-altered language, spoken at a rapid pace. Both the speed with which the altered language is spoken and its changes through the influence of the Spanish language increase from the northern Tewa pueblo of San Juan to the southern pueblo of Pojoaque. But under some circumstances, the differences in language are not a barrier. Following a visit to Santa Fe in 1977, the well-known Hopi-Tewa potter Grace Chapella, then said to be more than one hundred years of age, visited Margaret Tafoya, herself a seventy-three-year-old Santa Clara potter. The two women understood each other well because, in Margaret Tafoya's words, the language they spoke was "the old language of the ceremony and the kiva."

With the exception of language, the Hopi-Tewas seldom have any sense of relationship to their eastern kin. Descendants of Nampeyo have friends at many pueblos, but direct blood relationships, other than those between clan members such as Margaret Tafoya and Nampeyo, are not recognized.

The Period of Consolidation, 1705–1856

The period between the Tewa settlement at Hopi and the birth of Nampeyo was a time when the Hopis experienced few outside intrusions and, with the exception of the effects of natural disasters and disease, were free to determine the course of their lives. Their culture would not be disturbed until the arrival of the United States government representatives about 1860.

Despite the arrival of the Tewas to assist the Hopis, the move engendered bickering between the two groups, bickering which continues to this day with arguments about promised rights never delivered. Simmering disputes erupt and then quiet down only to erupt again, sometimes unexpectedly. Similar quarreling may also occur between the progressive and conservative factions of both groups. Different, confusing, and entangling arguments can arise at any given time. Should an outsider attempt to intervene, however, all sides will temporarily join forces and will resume the debate only when the outsider's interruption is suppressed.

Since their entrance into the Hopi domain, the Tewas have occupied the position of the first line of defense. According to the customs of the Hopis, any group joining them must assume the most vulnerable position until someone or some other group arrives. Among the Tewas, the Chakwaina people first occupied the defensive location at the Gap, but when they returned after a brief hiatus, they lived in Walpi while their relatives, the Asa people of Tewa, built their homes in the exposed position of Hano.[18] Apparently due to their more aggressive nature, the Tewas were better suited to the defensive role than were the Hopis; even today there is a higher percentage of Hopi-Tewas hired as police, rangers, and truant officers.

Although the Spanish under de Vargas had succeeded in quelling the rebellions of the Rio Grande pueblos, neither time nor resources were available to punish the unmanageable Hopis and Tewas, although several unsuccessful attempts were made to capture and bring back some of the refugees. The last effort under Gov. Don Pedro Rodríguez Cubero in 1701 also failed; he was unable to reduce them, especially since the "Moquis had with them the Tanos Indians, who after committing outrages, had taken refuge among them and had risen at their command."[19]

Gov. Felix Martínez engaged in two brief skirmishes with small Hopi parties near First Mesa but was unable to entice any Hopis to go to the Tewa village and request representatives to descend from the mesa top to negotiate. All Hopis suggested that, should the Spanish wish this done, they do it themselves. Next the governor suggested that the Walpis deliver up the Tewas, but with the battle against the Utes fresh in their minds the Walpis declined. Discretion being the better part of valor, Martínez elected to forego the climb up the mesa. He settled for burning a few cornfields, feeling by this action that he had somehow taught the Tewas a lesson. Two years later the Spanish took a less belligerent approach by peacefully inviting the Tewas to return to the Rio Grande river valley. The invitation was never acknowledged.

For the next sixty years Spanish priests and brothers of the cloth made periodic forays into Hopi country in attempts to Christianize the Hopis or to lure the recalcitrant Tewas back to the Rio Grande. In 1732 Fray Francisco Techungi returned to Isleta with five Tewas and established them there. Ten years later Fray Carlos Delgado and Pedro Ignacio de Piño persuaded 441 "Hopis" to return and settle at Isleta. Both men felt that they could have brought more Tewas back had they been given more assistance. It is very unlikely that these people were truly Hopis and far more likely that they may have represented a number of various Pueblo refugees. Eleven years later Padre de la Torré spoke at Hopi. Even so, whenever he appeared to be making progress, the elders would interrupt and effectively talk against him. Despite all the inducements given to the Hopis to persuade them to listen, the religious sermons and appeals had no impact.

In 1776 two more Catholic fathers made their way to the land of the Hopi. Coming from the west, Father Francisco Garcés was left to sleep in the streets of Oraibi and was unable to speak to anyone. Conversely, during that year the remarkable explorer Father Silvestre Veléz de Escalante was welcomed for the second time in two years at the Hopi villages at the end of a long and daunting trip, but only with the stipulation that he not mention the subject of religion to the people. About the visitation, Escalante noted:

> In the month of June I entered Moqui, where I remained for a week, well attended by those wretched infidels, obstinate in their foolish libertinism, especially those who govern, who impede with terrible threats the conversion of their inferiors and subjects because they fear that they will be abused and almost enslaved [by the Spaniards] if they submit. A falsehood in which the demon succeeds in holding them by some sadly undeniable truths. I pointed out for them the good for which they were created and the eternal evil to which their infidelity is leading them, but for my great sins I achieved the sorrow of leaving them in their obstinacy, although I did succeed in my intentions in other matters.[20]

The year 1777 marked the beginning of the Great Drought. Usually able to store enough food for three years at a time, the Hopis found their reserves depleted by 1779. To avoid starvation many took refuge with other groups, such as the Havasupais and the Zunis. No one knows whether the Tewas participated in these flights, but common sense would dictate that they must have in order not to starve. Some scholars believe the evidence suggests that almost two hundred Hopis went to the Rio Grande in 1780 in a flight to survive. The events of the next year almost wiped them out. In 1781 a small-pox epidemic killed many of the inhabitants on the mesas. Most of the new infectious diseases transmitted to the Hopis by whites had catastrophic consequences, just as they did for all American Indians without the benefit of natural immunity.

Some small benefits accrued from these disasters; immigrants who fled to escape starvation or disease were exposed to different cultural influences. The Hopi and Tewa pottery designs reflect strong influences from the Zunis and Acomas. Not too long after the outbreak of smallpox, the deities of the Hopis heard once again their prayers made through their rituals and dances. Rains began to fall, and the Hopi and Tewa refugees returned to the mesas.

Between 1781 and about 1840 contact with the Spanish diminished rapidly, while raids by marauding Navajos and Apaches became more frequent. From 1821 until 1846 the Mexican government ruled the Hopi territory in absentia—the mesa dwellers were barely aware of their existence. Anthropologist and historian Edward Spicer notes:

> The Hopis and the Zunis experienced relatively few contacts with the whites during the years that the American Southwest was part of Mexico. Not only were there vast differences between the villages of the western pueblos and the government at Santa Fe, but the widespread warfare which took place with increasing frequency during those years between the settled pueblos and the far ranging, marauding Navajos and Apaches—and which the Mexican troops were unable to prevent—virtually stopped all travel in the northern area. Neither the Hopis nor the Zunis felt the touch of

Mexican political authority. Both groups were visited occasionally by Anglos, parties of trappers, and soldiers with early Anglo-American military expeditions—but it was well into the American period before Hopis and Zunis came into frequent contact.[21]

Probably the first citizen of the United States to visit the Hopis, in defiance of Mexican law, was James O. Pattie in 1826, but "Old Bill Williams," who visited some time later, receives the credit. A worse ambassador from the new republic than Williams could not have been found had it been the devil himself. Kit Carson once said of the renegade Baptist minister, "In starving times no man that ever knew him would walk in front of Bill Williams."[22] Williams had two encounters with the Hopis. He lived with them for a short period, taking advantage of their hospitality, and then returned six years later, presumably guiding the Frapp-Jarvais party led by mountain man Joe Meek. The party of over a hundred men was accompanied by a large herd of horses, cattle, and dogs, all stolen from the Spaniards of California. They plundered the Indian's corn and melon fields, and when the Hopi men protested, twenty of them were shot.

Three years after the United States wrested the New Mexico–Arizona Territory from Mexico, James Calhoun was appointed Indian agent. During his tenure he alienated the Hopis by not visiting the mesa country. Hopi historian H. C. James notes:

> Traditional Hopi hospitality has only too often been sadly taken advantage of. In many instances it has been grossly abused. Yet the Hopi continue to welcome visitors in accordance with their long-established way of life.
>
> The Hopi had no opportunity to demonstrate this traditional hospitality to the first government agent whose official responsibilities included the Indians of Tusayan. It seems ironical that he [Calhoun] never found it possible to visit the Hopi villages during his term in office.[23]

Calhoun was hard-working, sincere, and intelligent, though intemperate, with a true interest in the welfare of Indians. He struggled to prevent pillaging by warlike tribes who preyed on peaceful pueblos, but his hands were tied. He was totally handicapped by the absence of military support. For this reason he never visited the Hopis. His requests for a military escort were never honored. He wrote: "I am extremely anxious to visit these Indians; but it would be unsafe to do so, without a sufficient escort, as the Apaches are upon the left and the Navajos on the right in traveling from Zuni to the Moquis."[24]

Although Calhoun was unable to visit the Hopis, they called on him in Santa Fe. The Indians were both eager to learn the aims and views of the new government and to complain bitterly about Navajo raids. The leader of the delegation to meet Calhoun was a Tewa from the village of Tanoquevi. Unfortunately, Calhoun died in 1852, and it was seventeen years before another Hopi agency was established. The new office, known as the Moqui Pueblo Agency, was situated at Fort Wingate, far to the east of the mesa country. After that, the offices were moved to Fort Defiance in Navajo country. The final move to Keams Canyon was made in 1873. Sometime during this period of shifting political controls and unrestrained Navajo raids, Nampeyo was born.

Time for both the Hopis and Tewas is not measured in years but rather by events such as wars, raids, droughts, and epidemics. Details of these events are passed down verbally, and unless they can be correlated with the modern calendar, they are not easily assigned a date. As a case in point, Fannie Polacca, Nampeyo's daughter, recalled an event that took place in her life a few years after a great flood, but she did not know the year of the flood.

Although Indian agent Calhoun was hampered by hostilities in 1852 and found it impossible to visit the Hopis, by 1870 Maj. John Wesley Powell, the one-armed explorer of the Colorado River, was able to reconnoiter much of the mesa country. Accompanied by Mormon missionary and explorer Jacob Hamblin as a guide and friend to the Hopi, Powell visited their villages. Without the services of Hamblin, Powell would probably have experienced great difficulty in reaching the Hopis from his position in remote southern Utah.

Despite the arduous trip, he collected outstanding examples of Hopi pottery on his explorations, pottery which he donated to Illinois Wesleyan University in Bloomington, the institution that had sponsored his first Colorado River expedition.

Powell, both an explorer and a visionary, planned to return to the mesa country, but it would be his appointees who would complete the research projects he had envisioned. He had an uncanny ability for getting the best men into key positions in his organizations, and it was some of these men who contributed to Nampeyo's career by introducing her art to the world.[25]

The Synergistic Trio, 1880–1894

From time to time throughout history humans of vastly different backgrounds and talents cross paths, and their associations profoundly influence both their own lives and those with whom they come in contact. Their combined accomplishments often exceed the sum of their individual contributions. So it was for Thomas Varker Keam, Tom Polacca, and Alexander McGregor Stephen during the fourteen-year period of their acquaintance (fig. 1.4). In addition to exerting a profound influence on the families of both Nampeyo and Tom Polacca, they were a moderating influence in what promised to be a violently disruptive showdown between a Hopi-Tewa alliance and the United States government over Hopi land adjustments and educational policies.

Thomas Varker Keam, 1842–1904

He was something of a paradox: a squaw man equally at ease, and voluble in an Arizona hogan as in calling upon a Washington bigwig: disliked and feared by some officials of the Indian Office; generous host or informed friend to stray wayfarers and scientists; an outspokenly honest and intelligent partisan of Indians, a foe of self-serving political humbuggery.

Frank McNitt, The Indian Traders

Fig. 1.4. The trio of men who contributed to the cultural preservation and acculturation of the Hopis and Navajos near the turn of the twentieth century are, from the left, Alexander M. Stephen, shown here at Keams Canyon in 1890; Thomas Varker Keam in 1904 after he had returned to England; and Tom Polacca in 1901 while part of a delegation to Washington, D.C. Stephen photograph No.8392 courtesy of Special Collections, University of Arizona Library; Keam photograph from Journal of the Royal Cornwall Museum; Polacca photograph by A. C. Vroman, SWMLA, No. 4660.

Thomas Varker Keam was born Thomas James Keam on 6 August 1842 to Grace and Thomas Varker Keam, a mariner from the county of Cornwall, England. Thomas James Keam probably adopted the middle name Varker, for it was customary for Cornish men to use a middle Christian name (usually that of an ancestor) other than the name bestowed at birth.

British census records show that Thomas was eight years old and living with his mother, sister, and brother in 1851 while his father was at sea. His youth was happy and secure, despite his family's lack of wealth and the prolonged absences of his father. Truro, then as now, was the center of social and trading activities for the county of Cornwall. It enjoys a warm, pleasant climate not found in many other parts of England. Keam's two childhood homes and the home in which Keam died were well situated and located within a stone's throw of each other, close to the center of town.[26]

Ties to his youth remained strong throughout his life. He formed lasting friendships, especially with one Nathaniel Bullen, who later became mayor of the city of Truro. During Keam's years in Arizona, he maintained a close association with the Royal Cornwall Museum and was aided by the efforts of his friend Bullen.[27]

During this period of English history, restless young men often sought fame and fortune on distant horizons. Keam joined the British Merchant Marine, which provided his passage to the United States via Australia. Jumping ship in San Francisco, he enlisted in Company C of the First California Cavalry on 22 January 1862. The end of the Civil War found him in Santa Fe, New Mexico, where he reenlisted in the First New Mexico Volunteer Cavalry, commanded by the famous Indian fighter Kit Carson. His final tour of duty lasted eighteen months, and during this time he planned his future. While in the field, he made note of, and eventually homesteaded, a spectacular piece of real estate located in northeast Arizona. This was an area where the cavalry bivouacked, a beautiful canyon known to the troops as Peach Orchard Springs Canyon and to the Hopis as the Place of Bubbling Water. Soon the area would be given another name, the one by which it is known today, Keams Canyon. Keam's enlistment expired in 1868, about the time the Navajos were being released from Bosque Redondo and were permitted to return to their homeland in northeastern Arizona. Keam had now developed an empathy for Indians, and he understood their problems. His aptitude for language led to his first civilian position as Spanish interpreter for agent F. T. Bennett.[28]

For Keam the two decades following his discharge were times of growth in his understanding of Indians, of material gain, and of overall accomplishment, although he also experienced bitter frustration at times. He opened an unsuccessful trading post on the Ute Reservation, acted as clerk and interpreter at Fort Defiance, Arizona, and was appointed special agent to replace James H. Miller, who had been killed in a skirmish with Indians. In 1868 or 1869, Keam married Grey Woman in a Navajo ceremony at Fort Defiance. She bore him two children, Thomas Keam Jr. (Hosteen Dedesa'hi or Mr. Painted) in 1870 and William Keam (Hosteen Bindithohih or Fuzzy Face) in 1872.

For nineteen unsuccessful years Keam set his sights on securing an appointment as Indian agent to the Navajo tribe. Although the appointment he requested was endorsed by influential and knowledgeable men such as the Speigelbergs and the Ilfelds, respected merchants and bankers of Santa Fe who agreed to bond Keam's trading post, Keam's honesty and the unorthodox manner in which he handled many situations so infuriated the civilian Indian agency employees that the assignment was never awarded to him.

One enemy of Keam was W. F. M. Arny, civil servant and hack politician whose ambitious plans for self-advancement at the expense of the Native Americans seemed to be continually thwarted by Keam. Conversely, Arny successfully blocked Keam's appointment by citing Keam's Navajo marriage as an example of the sinful act of "promiscuous cohabitation with Indian women."

While acting governor of New Mexico Territory, Arny began to lay the groundwork for Indian exploitation. In a report to Washington he wrote:

> It has often become patent to every person who is at all acquainted with the territory, that the greater retarding influence to the development of this vast and rich section of our country, has arisen from the hostility of the Indians who, heretofore claimed the right to roam over a large portion of it. This, however, I am glad to say is being corrected by the wise policy of the government by which the Indians are being placed on reservations, where it is proposed to civilize, Christianize and make them self-sustaining and thus open for settlement and development large tracts of very valuable public land and other lands, which are being held by grants.[29]

A year after this publication Arny was to conceive a most ambitious land-grabbing scheme and then have it thwarted by Keam. Arny had duped the Navajos into sending a delegation of their own to Washington to present a plan to President Grant that would propose an exchange of valuable mineral and farm lands in the north of their reservation for parcels of land of less worth on their east and west boundaries. Keam, learning of this plan, made his way to Washington, located the delegation, and succeeded in getting the Indian representatives so drunk and disorderly that most of them were thrown in jail. This was Keam's way of preventing Arny's delegation from meeting with the president. Arny was infuriated, but his plans for a meeting with Grant never materialized. In the words of McNitt: "From every point of view but Arny's, theirs was a salubrious condition. A white man, for once, had gotten Indians drunk—and entirely and unquestionably for their own good."[30] Keam, on the other hand, waited in vain for his expected appointment; he finally lost interest in government assignments and became more involved with personal pursuits. In retrospect, it was fortunate for the Hopis and their Tewa neighbors that his attempts for appointments were doomed to fail.

Increasingly, Keam spent less time at his post and more time exploring the country surrounding his future home. He began to establish binding relationships with people such as the trader and territorial representative John Lorenzo Hubbell at Ganado, Tom Polacca at Tewa, and the native residents in the vicinity of Peach Orchard Springs. More and more visitors, including prospectors, scientists, educators, and other interested people, were making their way into the area. Although he never allied himself with any group, he was ever willing to contribute his time and resources to their causes.

In 1873, Keam brought his twenty-seven-year-old brother William to America and obtained a temporary clerk's position for him at the Fort Defiance Indian agency.[31] William, as well as Hubbell, acted as ears for Thomas, keeping him advised of all agency activities, particularly those involving Arny. On 31 August 1875, about the time he became an American citizen, Thomas obtained a license to trade with the Hopis. William moved to Peach Orchard Springs to work as clerk and help open a trading post on the land that Thomas had been homesteading.

The following year William operated the Peach Orchard post while Thomas returned to Truro after learning of the illness of their mother. He remained in Cornwall for more than a year, so long in fact that Grey Woman divorced him. Upon his return, Thomas opened a second trading business at Fort Defiance, hiring one

William Leonard as clerk. He eventually abandoned this venture and permanently installed himself at Keams Canyon. In the meantime, William assumed all of the responsibilities of the operation of the post that had now grown into a settlement (figs. 1.5, 1.6).

In 1880 the character of the Keam establishment changed, due first to the death of Thomas's brother William on 15 November at Fort Wingate, New Mexico, and second to the arrival on the post of Alexander M. Stephen. The close relationship between Keam and Stephen was possibly the result of Keam's need to fill the void left by his brother's death.[32]

Fig. 1.5. The original trading establishment owned by Keam, 1879. J. K. Hillers, photographer. No. 463, USGS.

Fig. 1.6. William Keam, Hopi trader and interpreter. This photograph was taken from the roof of Nampeyo's Corn Clan home in 1875. J. K. Hillers, photographer. No. 1003, USGS.

Alexander M. Stephen, ca. 1845–1894

Sometimes I feel sure that we have fame... and such temporal glory at hand... and again I am plunged in the deepest... blackest despair. But at any rate we shall write only the truth... and some reward always comes to the honest laborer... if but only the placid stretch of his backbone... when he evens that out with a satisfactory grunt at the end of his toil.

Letter dated 15 June 1893. Alexander Stephen to Jesse Walter Fewkes, National Anthropological Archives.

The name of Alexander Stephen first appears in the 1851 census records of Dundee, Scotland. Alexander, then age five, was reported to be the youngest son of James Stephen, born in 1811, and Betsy Cree Stephen, born in 1812. James Stephen's occupation was that of a joiner (furniture maker or inside carpenter). At the time of Alexander's birth the family lived in the parish of Dunan, Forfarshire. (About 1970 Forfarshire became the county of Angus, which surrounds the city of Dundee.) Alexander was the youngest of three children. His sister, Mary, was five years his senior, while his brother, William, was nine years older. The next word of the family appears in marriage records of 1859 where William was wed to a Betsy Allan. The records show that both of Alexander's parents were still living. Census records of 1861 list Alexander, then age sixteen, as a lodger at Dudhope, Wynd, and show his profession to be that of millwright.

Although Elsie Clews Parsons, quoting Frederick Dellenbaugh who was well acquainted with Stephen, says that Alexander was trained in metallurgy at the University of Edinburgh, Stephen probably never attended a university in Scotland. Dellenbaugh possibly made the claim in an attempt to add legitimacy to Alexander's assaying efforts while at Keams Canyon. A search of the records at the University of Edinburgh and other nearby universities failed to produce proof that he attended any institution of higher learning. His United States Army records note that when he enlisted on 4 January 1864 he was only eighteen years old, which would also cast serious doubts on his having earned a degree.

Stephen enlisted at Potsdam, New York, under the name of Alexander M. Stephen. He gave Dundee, Scotland, as both his birthplace and residence, his trade as mariner rather than millwright. (These records are the first documents to be located that hint of a middle name.[33]) It appears that he served with distinction. Eleven months after enlisting in the 96th Regiment of the New York State Infantry he was promoted to sergeant and then later to lieutenant. After a period of service in the Confederate territories, he was mustered out in February 1866.

Between Alexander's discharge from the army and his arrival at the canyon, there is a fourteen-year gap. As a self-styled metallurgist, he may have wandered through as he searched for mineral wealth. John Bourke is the first person to mention that Stephen was "a metallurgist and mining prospector."[34] Stephen had come from Nevada in 1880 during the height of rumors of great silver and gold deposits on what is now the Navajo Reservation. That Keam and Stephen were interested in mining is evidenced by Bourke's comments on the contents of the house as having "chemical reagents, test tubes, and blow pipes" in it. Again, Keam and Stephen are mentioned as prospecting along the Echo Cliffs, where they located a large copper deposit. The inference is that Stephen came out of the Nevada silver camps with some knowledge of assaying and that he was looking for a bonanza and ended up being grubstaked by Keam. He soon abandoned prospecting and his dreams of mineral wealth; for the remaining fourteen years of his life, he became so engrossed in the area and its inhabitants that he devoted himself to recording their way of life. He took a wife, Talahonsi of the Bear Clan, who long outlived him;[35] and he spent his last years on First Mesa at their home in Walpi.

Like Keam, Stephen was short in stature, light-complected, blue-eyed, and fair-haired.[36] The size of these two men was a definite advantage in dealing with the Hopis, who were also small and felt ill at ease with large people. As Keam's artifacts and pottery collection grew, Stephen began to study, classify, and catalog them. He soon became recognized as an authority on the subject of Hopi artifacts.

Stephen built strong and long-lasting personal relationships with the Hopis by locating sources of clay, decorating materials, and fuel for firing pottery. He assisted them in their work and medically treated their ills. In return he was made privy to their innermost activities. Some have said that after Stephen settled at the canyon, he became a parasite, living off Keam. Records prove otherwise. After William's death Keam required Alexander's assistance and companionship.[37] Stephen's work on the Keam collection alone was invaluable. In addition, Stephen had other sources of support.

On 12 March 1883 a post office was established and named "Keam's Canyon in Apache County." Stephen was appointed its first postmaster, a position that he held until his resignation on 6 June 1888.[38] Other steady or temporary incomes were at his disposal as well. From 1891 until his death in 1894, he received a stipend of fifty dollars a month from the second Hemenway expedition, under the direction of Jesse Walter Fewkes, for services that provided Fewkes with source material for many publications for which Fewkes credited Stephen only superficially. But more on this later.

Previous commitments prevented Stephen from accepting the position of Hopi census director in 1890, though he and Tom Polacca were advisers and interpreters for those who did take on the responsibility. The census record reads more like an illustrated technical discourse on Hopi life and traditions of the time than a list of population statistics.[39] It includes pen-and-ink drawings of Tom Polacca and his home, which was considered quite commodious by visitors (fig. 1.7). It was fifty-six-feet long and almost as wide, with walls fifteen to twenty-two inches thick.

Fig. 1.7. A. J. Scott's pen-and-ink sketches of "Pueblo of Walpi, First Mesa, Arizona, 1890. Tom Po-la-kis house at base of Mesa" and insert of "Tom Polaki of Walpi, Arizona." Drawings reproduced from illustrations in Donaldson's 1890 United States Government Hopi Census Report. MNAZ.

Stephen was also recommended for the position of clerk and doctor at the Canyon Indian School, this despite his lack of formal medical training.[40] The records do not show that he ever assumed the position, but in view of Keam's disrespect for the school superintendent and of the fact that Stephen and Fewkes were accused by school officials of impeding the progress of the Hopis, it seems doubtful that he did.[41] In 1892, when he had finished ethnographic work on the Hemenway collection, Stephen moved his abode from Keams Canyon to First Mesa, where he lived the rest of his life.

Tom Polacca, ca. 1853–1911

> Polacca and Nampeyo shared one important characteristic: they were both traditional Tewa, participating in the ceremonies, working parties, and food exchanges of the community. In this respect Polacca and Nampeyo were little different from other Tewa, and they were not considered to be deviants or outstanding persons by the inhabitants of Hano. The fame of these two is due almost completely to their popularization by American friends. Polacca and Nampeyo, in adhering to the traditional pattern of life, became submerged as individuals in the society. The fruit of their economic success was shared, however, by all of the inhabitants of First Mesa through the system of exchange of food and services.
>
> *E. P. Dozier,* Hano: A Tewa Community in Arizona, *1966*

How Tom Polacca acquired the name Tom is not known for sure; the Hopi and Tewa people of that day were known by one Indian name, and none adopted foreign first names unless those names were conferred on them by white associates. His surname, Polacca, was originally spelled Polaccaca. According to his descendants, Polaccaca, which meant "Butterfly," was shortened through time to Polacca.[42]

Polacca, a part-time cattle trader, was a self-taught, farsighted man with a facility for learning a variety of languages. He learned white ways, both good and bad, not only from Stephen and Keam but from the many white visitors who stayed at his home. He continually tried to distinguish the best of the white people's ways so that he could encourage his people to select the best ways from the Indian and white worlds.

Together Polacca, Stephen, and Keam sought out the outstanding potters of the Keams Canyon region and encouraged them to enhance their work by using shapes and designs found in the best examples of their ancestors. Nampeyo was an outstanding member of this group. Both Keam and Stephen became well acquainted with Nampeyo and her husband Lesou through Tom Polacca, her brother. Keam employed Polacca and Lesou as guides and as hosts who were responsible for arranging room and board in their homes for outside visitors (fig. 1.8). Keam, Polacca, and Stephen explored the area, locating many of the historic and prehistoric ruins and shrines that were part of the heritage of the Hopis.[43] Pottery and other artifacts uncovered from these sites, as well as specimens obtained by trade or purchase from the Indians, were placed either in Keam's personal collection or in the inventory of the trading post for eventual sale or trade.

Fig. 1. 8. A. L. Groll made this pen-and-ink sketch of Nampeyo and Lesou's home in Polacca during the Stewart Culin expedition of 1905. BMB.

From 1881 to 1887 Keam was engaged in trading-post activities and school-building programs, while Stephen was occupied with his anthropological studies of the Hopis and the Tewas. During this interval Tom Polacca encouraged the people of First Mesa to cooperate in the establishment of educational and agricultural reform programs. Polacca's proposed policies, unlike those imposed on many Native American cultures, were designed to strengthen the culture rather than weaken it; nevertheless, he was opposed from all sides.

By 1882 the tracks of the Atlantic and Pacific railroad, later to be incorporated as the Atcheson, Topeka, and Santa Fe railroad system, moved west from Gallup, New Mexico, to Holbrook, Arizona, a point approximately sixty miles south of Keam's trading post. Prior to the arrival of the railroad at Holbrook, it could take from five days to two months to haul goods round trip from either Fort Defiance or Fort Wingate, the closest eastern railroad station. Travel time depended on the weather and on the promptness of the overland supply wagons arriving from Santa Fe. The slow-moving wagons required an overnight stop, which was made at the house of Charlie Cohen who ran a small trading post at Bidahochi, Arizona.[44]

The Hopis' World Expands

Keam soon developed a relationship with the Fred Harvey Company, which built, operated, and maintained hotels and restaurants at important railroad stations. Harvey was interested in stocking native crafts for his customers, and the demand for goods gave Keam an outlet for the merchandise he acquired from the Indians. Unfortunately, the materials were considered trade items for quick sale rather than works of art. Harvey company records of transactions with the Indians are practically nonexistent.[45]

Keam was a trusted trader to both Indians and whites. His shelves were overstocked with items for which he had bartered—Navajo rugs and silver and turquoise jewelry; Hopi weaving, baskets, kachina dolls, and most important to the Polacca and Nampeyo families, pottery. As Keam's fortunes rose, so did those of the Polaccas and

Nampeyos. With the arrival of the railroad, the path to Keam's door was shorter and easier to travel. Keam was soon to host a wide assortment of military personnel, scientists, geologists, geographers, artists, photographers, and sundry other people interested in controlling, studying, observing, or generally intruding upon the Indians of the Southwest.

One of the first visitors to show an interest in Hopi pottery and in methods by which the pottery could be classified was William H. Holmes, artist and recorder for the second Grand Canyon expedition of Maj. John Wesley Powell. Much of his research was on specimens found in the Keam collection. Although his attempts at classification were crude, his illustrations were excellent. These works of graphic art still provide a precise picture of the artifacts he drew, including in many instances, their structure. Today it is next to impossible to locate any of the kinds of pottery artifacts he so vividly illustrated.

Of all Keam's guests, none was more aggressive or resented by the Hopis than Matilda Coxe Stevenson, a well-known and overrated anthropologist of her time. Much to the horror of both the Indians and Stephen, "Tilly" intruded on the privacy of many Hopi families and forced her way into their kivas, all the while ignoring the protests of unhappy Hopi priests.[46] Stephen once commented about her: "How can anyone who has ever been in the field have the impudence to offer hearsay as a scientific contribution of any value whatever.... I have no grudge against Tilly... barring that devilish commissary chest that defied my efforts to steal her brandy... but she has been guilty of much ethnologic villainy."[47]

As much of an embarrassment as Tilly must have been to both Stephen and Keam, they undoubtedly bore their burden in silence. Tilly's husband, Col. James Stevenson, an ethnologist with the Smithsonian Institution, was a friend and staunch backer of Keam. He defended the trader's unorthodox actions in Washington and did all he could to promote Keam's request for the Indian Agent appointment. Under the directive of John Wesley Powell, Stevenson amassed a collection of Hopi articles from Stephen and Keam for the national museum. Under his supervision countless artifacts were removed from their context to the archives in Washington, DC, some of which were later traded to overseas museums. (The Southwest American collection of the Musée de l'Homme in Paris achieved its start from the Indian artifacts presented to them by the Smithsonian Institution in 1885.) One interesting observation is that both Powell and Stevenson, it seems, almost compulsively insisted on imprinting their names on the specimens they collected.

Among the first European scientists to use the Keam establishment as a base while doing field studies and collecting artifacts was the Dutch physical anthropologist H. F. C. Ten Kate. His first visit to the canyon in 1885 was followed by a return visit as a member of the second Hemenway expedition. His collections, purchased by the museum of Leiden, The Netherlands, were initially placed on exhibit in Paris, where the European public was first introduced to the beauty of Hopi art.

The most outstanding contributions of the time to the field of archaeology and to the preservation of Southwest Indian ceramics were those of Gustaf Eric Nordenskiold, son of Finnish parents residing in Stockholm.[48] In 1891 he came to the United States, where he visited an exhibition of artifacts in Denver that the Weatherill brothers had removed from the prehistoric Anasazi ruins of the Mesa Verde area of southwest Colorado. The exhibit inspired Nordenskiold to join another excavation being conducted at Mesa Verde at the time.

Like other shirt-sleeved archaeologists before him, the young Finn traveled via narrow gauge railroad and then horse and buggy to reach his destination. Once on the site, he rolled up his sleeves and began work with a terrible sense of urgency. Those already involved with the project excavated without plan or direction, but Nordenskiold introduced new scientific methods of unearthing and preserving artifacts, methods that are now standard practice. He accomplished a great deal in a few months of concentrated effort.

Nordenskiold left Mesa Verde in November 1891 to begin an arduous horseback journey across northern Arizona where he met Keam, Stephen, and Polacca. He hired Tom Polacca as guide, host, and translator on his first visit to First Mesa. In the *Journal of Arizona History*, M. S. Fletcher noted: "Near the base [of First Mesa] Jack [Nordenskiold's guide from Mesa Verde] took them to a small house and introduced them to Tom Palatka—also called Polacca—who was to be their host on First Mesa. They were taken into a roomy open square with a series of rooms on three sides and a wall completing an enclosure on the fourth, a rather large house for that location." The visitors were each assigned a separate room, and after unloading their pack animals, they transferred their baggage inside. Fletcher goes on to say:

> Tom and his fat wife and a whole group of naked children occupied two large rooms across the patio. Also residing somewhere in the recesses of the ample house was a young man whose entire face was painted a bright red.
>
> Tom Palatka, 'a remarkable man,' was a seasoned veteran among the various tribes of the region, having learned nine or more dialects plus passable English, Spanish, and Navajo. Many objects of American origin… wooden floors, glass windows, cooking stoves… contributed to this unusual home, while blankets, woolen goods, and pottery all of their own manufacture provided very comfortable quarters.[49]

During Nordenskiold's stay, he photographed the Hopis and collected artifacts consisting mostly of pottery, much of which he obtained from Keam. The most complete collection of his Hopi photos, as well as those of Mesa Verde and the Rio Grande Pueblos, is located at the Swedish State Museum in Stockholm. His Mesa Verde and Hopi pottery collections, which may include unidentified pieces by Nampeyo (fig. 1.9), were sold to a Dr. Antel, a Finn then living in Paris. Antel willed his collection to the National Museum of Finland at Helskinki. Gradually, Hopi art was making its way around the world.

Fig. 1.9. Hopi Polychrome jar. Despite its age and travel record, this large jar is in fine condition. The shape, excellent decoration, and workmanship indicate that it may well be the work of Nampeyo. It was collected by Gustaf Nordenskiold from Thomas Keam in 1891. 7 in. by 13$^{3}/4$ in. L. Blair, photographer, 1985. Catalog No.4834.462, Finland National Museum.

Nordenskiold helped improve methods of recovering and preserving American Indian artifacts in three ways. He introduced excavation methods that minimized damage to the objects during excavation; he developed unique photographic techniques that recorded the artifacts in situ with the Indians themselves; and he was a catalyst (through his large-scale removal of artifacts) for the enactment of legislation preventing the removal of artifacts from the country that were associated with the heritage of the United States. Concerned people had become alarmed at the large number of artifacts that Nordenskiold took back to Europe, and they endeavored to block such export. When appropriate legislation was found to be nonexistent, binding laws were enacted to prevent future drains of Native American artifacts to foreign countries.

Of all those who called on Keam and Stephen for hospitality and assistance, none was more famous in his field or more controversial than Jesse Walter Fewkes. Fewkes was appointed to replace the ailing leader of the first Hemenway expedition, Frank Hamilton Cushing. Fewkes, who had no formal anthropological training, began his career by investigating the possibility of using the phonograph to record the songs and folklore of the Indians of Maine. Then he led the second Hemenway expedition west, first to Zuni and then to Hopi in 1891. At Hopi he met Keam and hired Stephen to assist him. At the direction of Mary Hemenway, the wealthy Boston socialite and philanthropist who sponsored the expeditions, he supervised the purchase of much of the Indian art and artifacts that Keam had amassed. The collection, including Nampeyo's pottery, consisted of approximately three thousand ceramic pieces that sold for $10,000, or roughly $3.30 per item.

As Keam and Stephen were cataloging and packing the Hemenway collection, they were also merchandising material to such European institutions as the National Museum of Finland and the Ethnological Museum of Berlin, Germany.[50] A lesser Keam collection was acquired later by the Field Museum of Chicago at an average price of $1.69 per piece, a bargain when compared to the prices paid by Mrs. Hemenway (fig. 1.10). In retrospect, the amount of material collected and distributed over a brief period of time staggers the imagination.

RAILWAY AND TELEGRAPH STATION, HOLBROOK, ARIZONA.

Keam's Canon, Arizona, ___________ 18___

MATS AND SADDLE BLANKETS.
TEXTILE FABRICS.
RUGS, BLANKETS, AND PORTIERES.
CEREMONIAL GARMENTS.
BASKETRY ——— POTTERY.

To THOMAS V. KEAM, Dr.

DEALER IN

NAVAJO PRODUCTS, JEWELRY, AND MOKI PRODUCTS,

TUSAYAN TRADING POST, KEAM'S CANON, APACHE COUNTY.

Memorandum of Keams Collection

Orange Ware	Cream Coloured	Blk Lines	Red	Corrugated & Indented	Total
25 peices	65 peices	80 peices	10 peices	180	360

Stone Axes	Celts	Arrow Points Beads & Amulets	Pihuis
95	7	Several hundreds	100

Modern Pottery   200 peices

Ancient Pottery	700 00
Stone Axes & Celts	75 00
Arrow Points Amulets Beads &c	100 00
Modern Pottery	150 00
Baskets	300 00
Pihuis	125 00
Sashes Kilts & Blankets	75 00
	$1525 00

List of Pottery & Implements from Ruins in vicinity of Keams Canon Arizona

Cream & Orange Coloured Ware				Red Ware				Black & Line Ware				Corrugated & Indented Ware		
Bowls	Jars	Ladels	Other forms	Bowls	Jars	Ladels	Other forms	Bowls	Jars	Ladels	Other forms	Bowls	Jars	Cantd
205	46	29	10	7	3	2	From Ruins of Awatubi							
							3	13	11	16	37	6	10	2
81	30	18	6	8	6	5	From Ruins of Coor-wa-ash-ka-koo							
							5	17	16	10	18	1	4	1
60	18	15	18				From Ruins of Coo-wry-kal							
							5	8	2	1		2	3	
14	7	6					From Ruins of Ancient Shumopavi							
							10	50		12		5	5	3
	107	68	84	15	9	7	8	45	65	28	68	14	22	6

Stone Implements Tablets Beads &c

Totals			Axes	Celts	Arrow & Spear Points	Stone Tablets	Stone & Other Ceremonial Emblems	Amulets Beads &c
420			110	12	About 1000 (perfect & in fragments)	6	2	
261								

Modern

Totals			Baskets	Pihuis	Pottery Bowls	Jars	Water Bottles	Other forms	Pipes Kuiku & Ceremonial
149			100	100	30	20	10	40	6
70									

Thomas V. Keam

Fig. 1.10. Keam inventory and price list for the last of his collection sold to the Field Museum of Chicago. Keam was known for his meticulous record keeping and beautiful handwriting. *Courtesy of the Field Museum of Natural History.*

From the time of his first meeting with Stephen, Fewkes began to absorb for personal benefit the vast fund of ethnologic information Stephen had accumulated in the previous eleven years. One of many examples of Fewkes's publishing Stephen's information without giving credit was sarcastically discussed by Dr. Washington Matthews, army physician at Fort Wingate, in a letter to his friend Frank Cushing.

> You may expect soon a great work on the Moqui snake dance from the hand of the learned ethnologist [J. W. Fewkes] who has recently been there. He pumped poor Steve and promised Steve, (so the latter told me, poor fool!) that he would give him credit for all. But I see, in the last number of the Anthropologist, an article by him on "Tusayan Pictographs" Now this has been for years Steve's specialty and all of his information must have been derived from Steve. Yet he only mentions Steve in the most indirect way and in a footnote and then gives his name incorrectly. But he will prosper! All frauds do and get ahead of honest men.[51]

Fewkes began to disassociate himself from the Hemenway project after the death of Mrs. Hemenway in 1904. The reputation of the group had become tainted when a scandal arose concerning the credibility of Frank Cushing, director of the first expedition.

The manner by which the second expedition was disbanded has undergone just criticism. In addition to wasted effort, valuable written material was lost, and the collection was buried from public view for many years. Stephen's system of classifying Hopi pottery was lost and has only recently been recovered. Consequently, the system was never incorporated into the current system devised by Harold Colton, improved by Eric Reed, and further defined by Francis Harlow. One unhappy member of the second expedition was the group's historian, Adolph Bandelier, who angrily wrote in a letter to his friend Prof. Charles Norton of Harvard University: "From the Hemenways I expect nothing. Their last letters show that all that is wanted is a hasty winding up. None of my disinterested (unbiased) suggestions have been accepted. The monographs I sent in are not even spoken of any longer. They seem to have been thrown away. ...As for the material accumulated, I consider it as good as lost. It will most likely have to be sent to Boston. I wish them joy to it. It is gain to them, and a serious, perhaps irreparable, loss to me."[52]

At the request of the Queen of Spain, Mrs. Hemenway had agreed to exhibit the Keam collection at the Hispanic-American Exposition in Madrid. Using the data provided by Stephen, Fewkes published a catalog, *Catalogue of the Hemenway Collection in the Historico-American Exposition of Madrid*, in 1895. Adding insult to injury, he erroneously stated that Keam had collected ceramics by purchasing them rather than by discovering them himself in the field. In addition, while attending the exposition, Fewkes either sold, traded, or donated some items to at least one European museum. The Swedish Museum acquired some artifacts as a gift from Mrs. Hemenway. A letter from museum curator Staffan Brunius told the authors: "Also the Swedish archaeologist, Gustav Nordenskiold, who conducted surveys and excavations in Mesa Verde in the early 1890s received vessel fragments from Miss Hemenway. I am not sure if this transaction took place in the USA or in Madrid. The original list of contents for 1893.1.1–27 seems to have been made in Madrid, 1893, interestingly enough by J. Walter Fewkes."[53]

Fewkes next returned to Hopi country to conduct a cursory excavation of the early village of Sikyatki, located at the foot of First Mesa, east of the Gap (fig. 1.11). His excavation methods were primitive compared to those of Nordenskiold. The clumsiness of the dig is attested to in Fewkes's own words:

> The method of excavation pursued in the cemeteries was not so scientific as I had wished, but it was the only practicable one to be followed with the native workman....It was with great difficulty that the Indians were taught the importance of excavating to sufficient depth and even to the end of the work they refused to be taught not to burrow. In their enthusiasm to get the buried treasure they worked very well as long as objects were found, but became at once discouraged when relics were not forthcoming and went off prospecting in other places when our backs were turned. A shout that anyone had discovered a new grave in

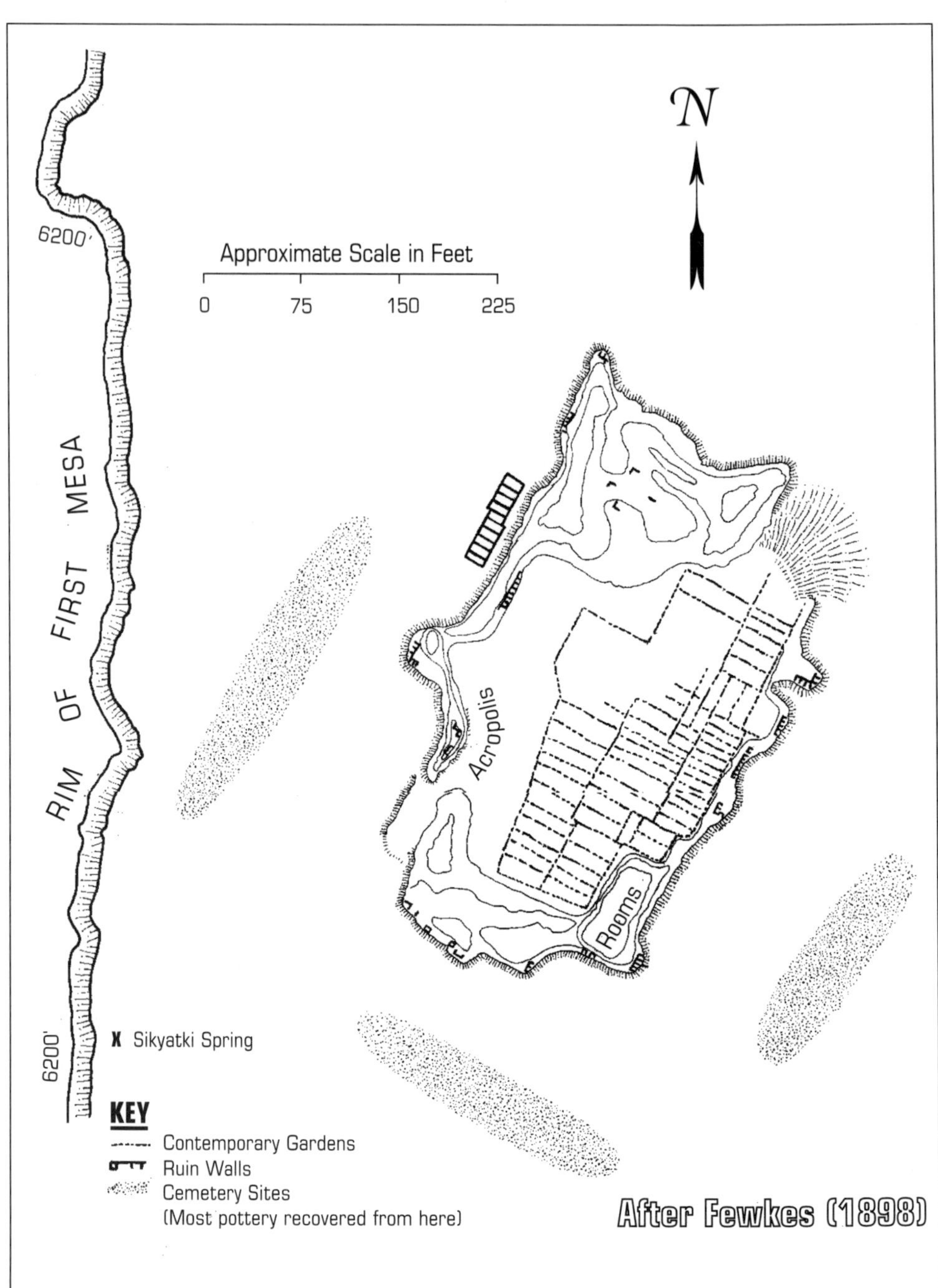

Fig. 1.11. *Map of Sikyatki ruin. The locations of garden plots (denoted by the dotted lines in the center of the ruin mound), established after the site was abandoned, remain visible. Numerous pottery sherds litter the ground. (After Fewkes, updated 1987)*

a trench was a signal for others to stop work, gather around the place, light cigarettes and watch me or my collaborators dig out the specimens with knives. This we always insisted on doing, for the reason that in their haste the Indians at first often broke fragile pottery after they had discovered it, and in spite of all precautions several fine bowls and jars were thus badly damaged by them.

No rule could be formulated in regard to the place where the pottery would occur, and often the first indication of its presence was the stroke of a shovel on the fragile edge of a vase or bowl.[54]

While writing of this work at Sikyatki, Fewkes made false statements about the origins of Nampeyo's work. These statements would be so often quoted that they would become accepted as fact, even by some Nampeyo descendants. Fewkes wrote:

Much of the pottery offered for sale by Harvey and other dealers in Indian objects along the Santa Fe Railroad in Arizona and New Mexico is imitation prehistoric Hopi ware made by Nampeyo. The origin of this transformation was partially due to the author who, in the year named was excavating the Sikyatki ruins and graves. Nampeyo and her husband, Lesou, came to his camp, borrowed paper and pencil, and copied many of the ancient symbols found on the pottery vessels unearthed and these she reproduced on pottery of her own manufacture.[55]

Fig. 1.12. This large black-on-cream water jar by Nampeyo is one of her earliest documented works. It was acquired by J. W. Fewkes for the Bureau of Ethnology from Thomas Keam ca. 1896. 16^1/2 in. high. No. 80-3733, NAA-SI.

Reports of Fewkes's earlier activities at Hopi would prove that Keam and Stephen, not Fewkes, first introduced Nampeyo to the world. Between 1891 and 1896, Fewkes transferred a black-on-cream Nampeyo jar from the Hemenway to the Smithsonian collection (fig. 1.12). Dr. Walter Hough of the Smithsonian Institution had written on the base of this work: "Cop. of an ancient jar in the Hemenway coll. by Nampeo."

Nagging questions remain as to why a scientific recorder such as Fewkes would make patently false claims and take credit for the work of others, such as Stephen's. It seems obvious that he practiced plagiarism. It is also possible that he saw competition between his limited discoveries and an endless supply of "copies" made by Nampeyo for sale by Keam. Again Fewkes comments:

> From that time [in 1895, when Nampeyo visited Sikyatki] all pottery manufactured by her [Nampeyo] was decorated with modified Sikyatki symbols, largely to meet the demand for this beautiful ancient ware. The extent of her work, for which there was a large demand, may be judged by the great numbers of Hopi bowls displayed in every Harvey store from New Mexico to California. This modified Sikyatki ware, often sold by unscrupulous traders as ancient, is the fourth, or present, epoch of Hopi ceramics. These clever imitations, however, are not as fine as the productions of the second epoch. There is danger that in a few years some of Nampeyo's imitations will be regarded as ancient Hopi ware of the second epoch, and more or less confusion introduced by the difficulty in distinguishing her work from that obtained in the ruins.[56]

Another plausible and kinder explanation for Fewkes's claims is offered by Edwin Wade and Lea McChesney in their study of Hopi pottery that went to the Hemenway collection from Keam: "Was it out of personal dislike for Keam; or was it an attempt to cover up the fact that Keam had introduced drastic changes into a traditional Hopi material culture, an act which Fewkes feared would reflect poorly upon himself as the director of the expedition which had in fact instituted innovation in a traditional society."[57]

Was Nampeyo simply copying ancient Hopi ware, or did the old designs open new avenues of creativity as Keam and Stephen had encouraged very early? The few authenticated pieces Nampeyo created before Fewkes arrived on the scene are those of an inspired potter. Prior to her loss of vision, she continually produced pottery motivated by designs from a variety of ruins, including Sikyatki, each having its own character and uniqueness. Confirmation of this is provided by Nampeyo's grandson Dewey Healing, a Hopi-Tewa historian and political leader:

> At one time the people on First Mesa had just about stopped making pottery altogether. One of the few people still making pottery then was my great-grandmother, White Corn. She was making pots when most of the Walpis weren't doing it anymore. Her daughter—that's my grandmother on my mother's side—was Nampeyo.
>
> She and her husband—my grandfather—went to Sikyatki and found some old pottery there. She got the designs and began to make pots in that style. She also went to other ruins. There's a ruin coming out of Keam's Canyon, up on that big point to the right. Down below there's kind of a ridge, and from there you can look down and see other ruins….All those old designs Nampeyo was using were different from what the First Mesa people had been putting on their pots. Some of Nampeyo's designs also came from Awatovi.[58]

Archaeologists Harold and Mary-Russell Colton commented on Nampeyo's innovative abilities in the 1940s.

> Nampeyo, in her early days, may have made replicas of Sikyaki pottery, though this is extremely doubtful as the Indian artist rarely makes an exact copy. However, it is certain that vessels that came on the market were not mere copies but had a living quality of their own. She caught the spirit of the old Sikyatki potters and used her own rare good taste in making compositional arrangement.
>
> Her work was distinguished from that of Hopi potters by a sense of freedom and a fluid flowing quality of design together with an appreciation of space as a background for

her bold rhythmic forms. Nampeyo's interest did not confine itself to design and its application, but also included the basic forms of her pottery. She introduced the beautiful low, wide shouldered jars characteristic of Sikyatki and other fine forms not hitherto in use.[59]

It appears from his actions that Keam planned to limit his commercial activities soon after President Chester A. Arthur issued an executive order that created the Hopi Indian Reservation. This reservation encompassed 3,683 square miles, an area that completely surrounded the Keam homestead. Thus, Keam was prevented from achieving one of his major ambitions, that of investing his land holdings sufficiently to support a large herd of cattle.

Realizing the circumstances, Keam made his own plans. First, he gave one of his buildings to the United States government for use as an office. Then he began the long and costly process of turning over to the U. S. government all of his original holdings in the canyon. By 1889 he had completed the necessary transactions, signed a quit claim deed for most of his land, and moved to the canyon mouth where he built a new home and trading post that still stand today (fig. 1.13).

Fig. 1.13. Keam's home in 1897, located east of the present Keams Canyon Trading Post and Arts and Crafts Enterprises. The photograph is part of an album that Adam C. Vroman made for his friend and expedition host, H. C. Hayt of Chicago. No.25-208, MMSD.

During his tenure in the lower canyon, he became committed to improving the education of both the Hopi and Navajo people—this in addition to running a profitable business, acting as host and part-time guide, providing scientific information to scholars, and working with various educational institutions in the United States and Europe.

With Navajo raids all but a thing of the past, Polacca and Keam cooperated with a government project to move people down from the mesa tops to areas nearer their garden plots where water supplies were more readily available. In 1890 they organized Hopi delegations to go to Washington to request the elimination of boundary ambiguities and to ask for peaceful government intervention that would prevent Navajo encroachment on Hopi lands. Government priorities, however, differed from those of the Indians, and unfortunately neither party made an impression on the other. The plans to move the people down from the mesa tops to land allotments were met with opposition. Petitions to the government to discontinue the program prompted Acting Agent 1st Lt. S. H. Plummer to report the following regarding land allotment:

> [T]he plan of building houses in the valleys for these Indians, with the view of persuading them to abandon their overcrowded pueblo dwellings on the high mesas, does not seem to be as successful as desired. Many of the houses built in the valleys are unoccupied the greater portion of the year. Their habits, customs, and general mode of living are so intimately connected with the conditions of life on the mesas that it is doubtful whether anything else than compulsion will cause them to abandon their pueblo dwellings. It has been the custom for years for these people to cultivate their lands in common. Owing to the shifting nature of their planting grounds, it would be almost impossible to maintain any allotment to individuals. It is believed that the best interests of the tribe would be promoted by granting the petition.[60]

Fig. 1.14. *"Soldiers Surrounding Hopi Prisoners," December 1897. Led by Capt. Constant Williams, soldiers arrested Hopi dissidents who resisted sending their children to the U. S. government schools. Tom Polacca acted as informer and interpreter during this confrontation.* H.R. Voth, photographer. No.53, H.R. Voth Collection, Mennonite Library and Archives,

While some of the Hopis and Tewas were agreeable to the plan to relocate, others resisted bitterly. Land disputes promptly arose between the two factions. Government plans to send Hopi children away to school also engendered disagreements which deeply divided the Hopis. U.S. officials had especially hoped to obtain agreements allowing the Hopi children to attend newly established federal schools. By autumn of 1894 the government moved to crush opposition to their plans by rounding up nineteen Hopi leaders and jailing them in the federal prison at Alcatraz (fig. 1.14). Hopi complaints were ignored, and neither the land disputes with the Navajos nor Hopi and Western Tewa land ambiguities were addressed. Trespass arguments continued.

By 1892 Keam was making preliminary plans to retire to his native land. An old school friend and former mayor of Truro, Nathaniel Bullen, contributed the following letter from "old Truro boy" Keam in the October 10 issue of the *Royal Cornwall Gazette* (also published in the *Western Morning News* of Plymouth previously): "Would like to send something for an upcoming fisheries exhibition, but I am in Indian country, some 2,000 miles inland. Sent some artifacts to Chicago. I wish the exhibition well and promise to bring home curios when I come." Keam did return to Truro with an outstanding collection of Navajo and Hopi jewelry which he donated to the Royal Cornwall Museum. Some pieces were forged from silver dollars minted as early as 1853. At the same time a large collection of minerals, known as the Raleigh Collection, was bequeathed to the museum. With great delight Keam went there on a regular basis to give advice on how the specimens should be cataloged and displayed.

The year 1894 was one of the most frustrating, disappointing, and tragic of Keam's life. On his return to America he realized that he was seriously ill and made out his will.[61] His visions of a vast cattle ranch had long since been scrapped, his appeals to Washington on behalf of the Hopis had fallen on deaf ears, and worse, a confrontation over school attendance had humiliated his Indian friends. The most telling blow was the death of his beloved friend and companion Alexander Stephen, who passed away in April after a prolonged illness which defied treatment by the best of native medicine. Keam reported the circumstances of the death in a letter dated 12 April to Fewkes:

> Alas, poor Steve who kept in harness too long for the good of his health, I have him here now almost at death's door, but with the help of God and proper care we hope to get him strong again. He had not written me of the weak state he was in, but expressed a desire that I call at Mesa for him last Sunday. On my arrival I found him so weak and sick that he could scarcely stand, he had ate nothing for four days, I immediately dispatched a messenger to the Canyon for beef tea and gave that and such as he would eat, stayed with him the night. In the morning I arranged a chair so that he could sit in it comfortably, and then lashed improvised handles to each side, and with two stout Indians carried him safely down the mesa to the wagon, and although

a little tired he felt better on reaching here, he is improving but it will be a slow process as he is nearly worn out. When he is sufficiently strong I suggest a change of climate and rest.

Noted on the top margin of the letter, "Mr. Stephen left the mesa on Sunday and died on the 17th at Keams Canyon.—J. W. F."[62]

Keam buried his friend on high ground at the mouth of the canyon, a few hundred yards south of the new trading post, and supervised the erection of a monument on the site (fig. 1.15). He collected Stephen's papers soon afterwards and refused to release them to Fewkes, as noted in a letter to a friend, Washington Matthews: "I still have all of his letters and manuscripts which Dr. Fewkes has been clamoring for to complete what he calls the Hemenway papers. I have, however, at Steve's request refused to part with them without a proper compensation, a part of which will be sent to his relatives in Scotland."[63] The valued manuscripts remained in Keam's possession until their 1902 purchase by Stewart Culin, then in the employ of the University of Pennsylvania. Stephen's work was organized and published in two volumes in 1936, the result of the herculean work of Elsie Clews Parsons. The original papers now reside in the files of the American Philosophical Society.[64]

Fig. 1.15. Gravestone of Alexander Stephen in Keams Canyon. L. Blair, photographer.

In 1894 a kiln, capable of producing fifty thousand bricks per year, was built at the mouth of the canyon, not far from the present school and hospital complexes for which it provided brick. By 1896 all of the old Keam buildings up-canyon were abandoned as unfit and unsanitary and were replaced by down-canyon structures. Were it not for Kit Carson's name carved in the rock near Bubbling Water, it would be almost impossible to locate Keam's original paradise. Visitors can now find little trace of the spring and no trace of the buildings.

Violent rains and floods are common during late summer and early fall in Keams Canyon. One of these storms in the 1880s was described by John Bourke:

The first evening after our arrival [at Keam's post] as the sun was setting, the mist thickened suddenly, and a fearful cloud-bust broke upon us: in less time than it takes to write these lines it had flooded the creek bed, raised the water level to a depth of three inches on the level ground around the house, carried away the dam, which was built of ponderous sandstone slabs two feet on a side, and then subsided as quickly as it had come.

Inside of a half an hour the whole tempest had come and gone. Eight to ten feet of water had swept like a solid wall down the narrow channel of the creek, and then the stars were again shining.[65]

The magnitude of this flood was dwarfed by the flood of 1902. Water roared down the canyon, cutting a channel forty feet deep in its floor. Thousands of tons of silt were carried from the chasm into the washes below. With the tremendous displacement of soil, the normal water level dropped, causing a drastic change in subterranean fluid pressures. The springs that had gushed from the base of the canyon wall and provided refreshment for Kit Carson's troops—the same springs that long before had been a haven of rest for the Southern Tewas on their long trek to the promised land—had vanished overnight.

Keam's last trading license expired on 24 August 1900. By May 1902 he had sold the remainder of his holdings to the son of his old friend and competitor, John Lorenzo Hubbell.[66] He departed the canyon and on May 21 left the United States for the last time. Between 1900 and 1902 he had negotiated the sale of Stephen's papers to Culin, investigated the climates of Albuquerque and Atlantic City to determine whether they might better agree with his health, and sold what artifacts remained in his possession.

On arriving in England Keam contacted Stephen's relatives to send on the money he had received from the sale of his friend's papers. In June 1904 Keam settled at 21 Lemon Street, Truro, in a comfortable stone home located in a residential neighborhood. He died six months later from heart disease and was buried near his family in the Kenwyn Church burial grounds (fig. 1.16). The *Royal Cornwall Gazette* report read as follows:

> Mr. Thomas Varker Keam, formerly an officer in the United States Army, who died unmarried on November 30th, 1904, left an estate in the United Kingdom valued at [pounds sterling] 11,713.17.6 gross with net personally amounting to 11,495.26.21 pounds sterling. Probate was granted to Mr. Nathaniel Battershill Bullen, Truro accountant, under the date of July 24th 1903, and also to Mr. Thomas R. McElonel, who resides abroad. The testor left 120 shares in the First National Bank of Albuquerque, New Mexico, USA, and 25,000 dollars in trust for his wife in the event of his being married, for life, and subject to her interest, he left shares and dollars, as to two-thirds to the Royal Institution of Cornwall, Truro, and as to one-third to the Central Technical School at Truro. He left 5,000 dollars each to Thomas McElonel and Nathaniel Bullen, Frederick W. Wing and James Stevens, and he left the residue of his estate to his friend, Miss Beatrice Bullen of Truro.

Keam's bequest was used by the officers of the Royal Cornwall Museum to establish an investment trust, the interest to be applied to a general maintenance fund. The trust remains operative today. The other education beneficiary, the Central Technical School, is no longer in existence. In death as in life Keam continued to support the sciences, art, and education.

A majority of the old records of Keam's trading post have been destroyed, with the exception of those kept by the Hubbells at the Ganado post following the purchase of Keam's interests, now in the Special Collections department of the University of Arizona Library.[67] The Ganado records emphasize the importance Keam placed on his trade with Nampeyo, the only potter mentioned by name (fig. 1.17). These records show that her work brought higher prices than were paid to her anonymous competitors.

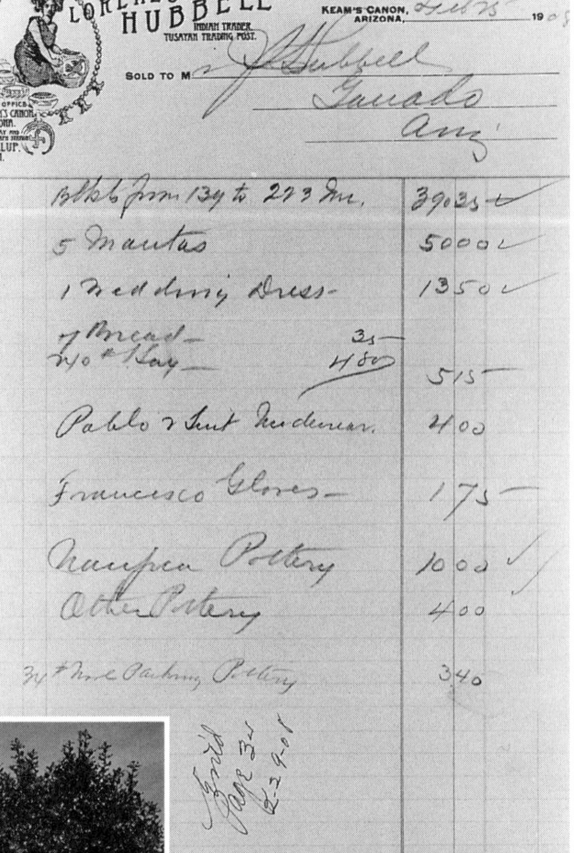

▲ *Fig. 1.17.* A record of sales and transfer from Keams Canyon Trading Post to the post at Ganado, this document distinguishes "Nampea Pottery" from "other Pottery," both in title and price. Note that the last item of thirty-four pounds is wool for packing pottery for shipment.
Courtesy Special Collections, University of Arizona Library.

Following the deaths of Stephen and Keam, Tom Polacca's life changed drastically. Without the backing of his Anglo associates he stood alone. He worked briefly as a truant officer for the school system, periodically cashing paychecks at the Keam trading post. He began to devote more time to raising cattle and less to the education of his people. Were it not for his strong character, Polacca might have been completely destroyed by the "leveling ways" as practiced by Hopis and Tewas alike. When one assumes a position superior to or different from those of the village, all means including gossip, ridicule, shunning, and blaming one for the woes of the group are used to force the errant member back into accepted behavior. Tewa authorities Edward Dozier and Albert Yava confirm that this leveling was practiced on Tom Polacca by his people. Dozier writes:

> Only one case of social ostracism and exile were related to me, but I was told that there were others in the past. This case involved the prominent and prosperous Tom Polacca whose name identifies the budding community at the foot of First Mesa. During the greater part of his life Polacca was highly respected and esteemed, but in later years he lost the good will of his community. Before his death Polacca departed from the traditional pattern of life and was converted to Mormonism. The ire of Hano was aroused, however, when the Tewa learned that Polacca had sold his house and the land below the mesa to the Baptist Mission—land to which he had only use right. Polacca and his family were exiled to Sand Dunes [Wepo Gardens], five miles from First Mesa and he was forever prohibited from participating and viewing Tewa ceremonies.[68]

Yava expands on the reasons for Tom's separation from the community. "Tom Polacca exerted a lot of influence on the side of education. The conservative Hopis were always complaining about him. In later years, after that school business was all settled, he continued to receive a lot of criticism from them, and whenever something went wrong they would say, 'Well, you can thank Tom Polacca for that.'"[69]

Fig. 1.18. This Sand Hills Ranch monument dedicated to Tom Polacca was erected by the Church of Jesus Christ of Latter-day Saints in 1940. The place remains a working ranch and summer residence for the Nampeyo descendants and a hospice for members of the Mormon church.

Brilliant and farsighted, well-versed in the ways of his people, Polacca must have envisioned the probable fate of his family had he remained in the village named after him. Contrary to Dozier's information, those who knew him say that his home was donated to the public school system in exchange for sheep, and he relocated to a remote and beautiful area known as Sand Hills, where he had previously tended cattle. He divided his land among his children, situating the plots to provide protection to the ranch boundaries. His descendants reveal that he placed one troublesome daughter off the mesa top, far removed from the others, to avoid family conflict and that he also relocated a son's plot that he considered to be vulnerable to the few remaining raiding Navajos. The bountiful land amply supported the large family.

Polacca died in 1912 and was buried south of his Sand Hills home where drifting sands now obscure his grave. Nearby a monument has been erected to his memory by the Mormon church (fig. 1.18). The land passed to his children and grandchildren who continue to farm, run cattle, make pottery, and relax, following Tom's example.

Opening the Door: Nampeyo of Hano

CHAPTER 2

Nampeyo was not the first American Indian who knocked at the door of our aesthetic perception, but before her life was over she had left the door ajar for others to enter.

Ronald McCoy, Indian Lives

When Nampeyo sifted through the sands around First Mesa in Arizona during the 1870s and 1880s looking for potshards, she found in them the inspiration for a celebration in clay of a culture older than memory; her success inspired others to search the past in their celebration of cultures vital to the present.

Lester G. Moses and Raymond Wilson, Indian Lives

The social organization of the Hopi is based on matrilineal and matrilocal clans. This system prescribes that all Hopi and Tewa women will own their own homes and clan lands and that all children belong to the clan of the mother. Thus Nampeyo, daughter of Tewa Corn Clan mother Qotca Ka-o (White Corn), was born and reared in the home of her mother and was therefore of the Tewa Corn Clan also. In the Hopi way the female relatives of Nampeyo's father, Ko'icheve of the Hopi Snake Clan, gave Nampeyo a name belonging to that clan. They named her Tcu-anima or Snake Girl (variously translated as Sand Snake—Duwatsu-a, or Snake-that- does-not-bite). In Tewa this name becomes Nampeyo.

Birth to Marriage, ca. 1857–1879

In estimating the year that Nampeyo was born, many have overlooked the writings of W. H. Jackson, who first photographed her in 1875 (figs. 2.1 and 2.2). He referred to her as "Num-pa-yu (Serpent-that-has-no-tooth), sister of Captain Tom [Polacca] of Tewa who served us with bread and corn at our first meal. She was then 17 or 18 and remarkably pretty." The reported birth year has been estimated to have been as early as 1857 and as late as 1870, this despite Jackson's documentation. F. H. Douglas, however, pointed out that the 1875 Jackson photograph was not that of a five-year-old but more like a girl of fifteen. The observations of Jackson and Douglas place the date of her birth between the years of 1857 and 1860.[1]

Nampeyo was born at a time in Hopi history when profound, irreversible changes were occurring. These changes had lasting effects on most facets of the Hopi way of life, including religion, education, territorial restraints, trade practices, diet, and work ethics. Traditional agricultural practices (which are still practiced today) were an important exception.

Prior to 1860, the Hopis lived in a location considered remote by whites. There were no known mineral resources, and the area was thought to have little agricultural or trade value. Considering the travel distances and the fiercely defensive posture of the inhabitants, the clergy were hampered or prohibited from their normal policies of proselytization. Explorers and potential settlers had little

Fig. 2.1. Nampeyo and members of her family, seated on the roof of their Corn Clan house in 1875. The man on Nampeyo's right was identified as Tom Polacca by photographer W. H. Jackson. The unidentified man on her left (barely visible in the photograph) may be her father. *No. 55491, NAA-SI.*

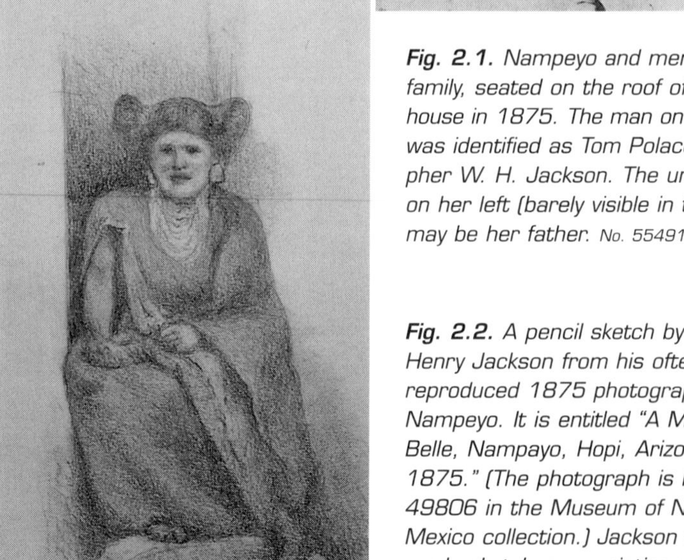

Fig. 2.2. A pencil sketch by William Henry Jackson from his often reproduced 1875 photograph of Nampeyo. It is entitled "A Moqui Belle, Nampayo, Hopi, Arizona 1875." (The photograph is No. 49806 in the Museum of New Mexico collection.) Jackson often made sketches or paintings from photographs. Nampeyo's hairstyle is that of a Hopi, not Tewa, maiden. *R. Blair, photographer. No. SCBL95, Scott's Bluff National Monument.*

incentive to colonize the area. Once a route was established after 1860, profitable trade contact with the Hopis increased, as did the ambitions of clergy and others wishing to Christianize or otherwise profit from this Indian population. The rate and magnitude of the change inflicted on the Indians are difficult to comprehend. Frederick Dockstader wrote: "During the first 310 years of Hopi and White association, contacts of any description, however slight or indirect, averaged only 1.9 per year. Indirect contacts, including such items as maps and written descriptions published by those who had never seen the land were considered in the data. Post 1850 contacts between the two became almost too numerous to tabulate."[2]

During a forty-five-year period ending in 1895, more devastating changes were forced on the native population. This era ended shortly after Hopi male leaders were rounded up by the army and sent to Alcatraz prison for opposing U.S. government educational policies and practices. It is a tribute to the tenacity of the Hopis and their faith that anything of the Hopi way remains. Nampeyo lived the first four decades of her life during this period of upheaval. The entire social fabric of her people came under particularly severe, bigoted, and thoughtless attacks, and often she and her family were part of the turmoil.

In one such instance in 1885, the decision was made to broaden the path leading to the summit of First Mesa, which skirted both Nampeyo's family home and the "Outside Kiva" where wagons were kept. Without permission or discussion, white men destroyed the kiva, forcing the Tewas to blast a new site in the solid rock. This blunder continues to be held against the Bahana, or "white outsiders," to this day.[3]

The need to understand Hopi culture and to preserve it, which was first championed by Thomas Keam and Alexander Stephen, then by Jesse Walter Fewkes and some military leaders, gradually began to weigh upon Washington politicians and bureaucrats.[4] Although the oppression of the Hopis and Tewas eased, deep resentment remained among the native peoples.

Increased contact with the outside world brought the introduction of diseases new to the Indians, which between 1853 and 1861 reduced the Hopi population by sixty percent. Many First Mesa people took refuge with their Zuni neighbors to the southeast, where *many new influences affected Hopi culture that persisted into the twentieth century*. Of course, interchanges among Pueblo peoples were frequent as they visited back and forth for varying periods. Ethnologists point out that this particular interchange involved changes in pottery designs, religious influences, and language. (See fig. 2.3—see p. l.)

The infant Nampeyo survived several epidemics, including the great influenza epidemic and famine of 1866–67. It is not clear whether she or other family members took part in any Zuni migrations, but surviving these disasters may have provided her with immunity to disease and contributed to a long life that lasted into her eighties.

Nampeyo began making pottery at an early age. As all young Hopi and Tewa children, she watched her people produce pottery just as they had for many years. Throughout her life she credited her Hopi grandmother as her teacher; she never mentioned having learned from her mother. Stephen confirmed this fact and commented that the Hopi women of First Mesa, particularly those from the village of Walpi, were the best potters. He conceded, however, that Nampeyo should be included as one of the best potters, probably because she had been taught by the Hopis. At that time, Hano women were making only undecorated, large, narrow-necked canteens and plain cooking vessels. Other researchers, however, have disputed Stephen's conclusions because Nampeyo's work was so untraditional.[5]

With the exception of Thomas Keam and Alexander Stephen, Nampeyo's first known Anglo contact came in 1875 when W. H. Jackson photographed her and her brother, Tom Polacca, at their Corn Clan home. Accompanying Jackson was A. E. Barber, a *New York Times* representative, who described young Nampeyo as "[s]hort and plump, though not unbecoming. Her almond-shaped eyes were coal black, and possessed a voluptuous expression which made them extremely fascinating" (figs. 2.1, 2.2). He described her hair as "characteristically Oriental" and her hair style as whorled, "enhancing her beauty." (It is interesting to note that a Hopi-Tewa girl was photographed at that time with her hair in whorls as an unmarried Hopi maiden's hair would be and not in the double Tewa hair knot or *chango*.) Further, "she was graceful and light complected with exquisitely molded hands and arms and bare little feet."[6]

Nampeyo married twice. The first union, thought to have taken place between 1876 and 1878, was to a young Tewa man named Kwivioya and took place when both people were in their teens. The marriage lasted less than two years and produced one child, a girl named Pela (Cliff Wall), who around the age of twelve was killed by a fall onto the rocks. Legend has it that Kwivioya feared that Nampeyo's beauty would attract other men and that he would lose her, so he left voluntarily to avoid an imagined personal disgrace, a story confirmed by Thomas Polacca in 1982. In 1878 Nampeyo was married to Lesou, variously spelled Leso, Lesso, or Lesu. Lesou's father was one or the other of two brothers: either Mo'ti, a member of the Horn Clan, or his brother Simo, the town chief of Walpi. Lesou's mother, whose name is not recorded, was from the Third Mesa village of Oraibi.

Lesou was an intelligent, extroverted, industrious person who soon became involved in his wife's pottery work. He encouraged her by assisting with household chores and tending to the more menial work of pottery. He located suitable clays and other raw materials for her and also found pottery artifacts from the past whose beauty inspired her. He often worked as a host or guide for Anglo visitors, who were always potential customers for his wife's art (fig. 2.4). When employed by archaeologists, he gathered sherds with outstanding designs and brought them home for Nampeyo to study.

According to custom, the couple lived in the house of her parents at the Tewa village of Hano (fig. 2.5). Her parents shared their space with them and their children from time to time, evidently in harmony. Traditionally, Nampeyo's aged mother and father were the final authority on the interpretation of ancient symbols or cult representation (fig. 2.6). Lesou soon built a home for Nampeyo in Polacca village below the Mesa. The ceiling beams for this home were said to have come from the Awatovi ruins. This house, "topped with

Fig. 2.4. *Standing in the Corn Clan house doorway in 1897, Lesou appears to pose as a concierge welcoming guests. No. 2611, MNM.*

a glowing red iron 'government' roof, [was] Nampeyo's, but she [spent] most of her time in the parental dwelling at Hano."[7]

Nevertheless, the home that Lesou built for Nampeyo was used by many distinguished visitors to the area. Lesou had begun to take Tom Polacca's place as guide and host to the many people of importance now flowing into Hopi.

Climb to Twilight, 1879–1912

Although a time of tumultuous change and hardship for the Hopi-Tewa people, Nampeyo worked most prolifically between 1879 and 1912. It was during this period that she produced her most innovative and artistic ceramic pieces, while also raising her family.

The records of two men indicate that Nampeyo's ceramic talents were first recognized when she was about twenty-seven years old. In 1887, twelve years after he had photographed her, Jackson reported

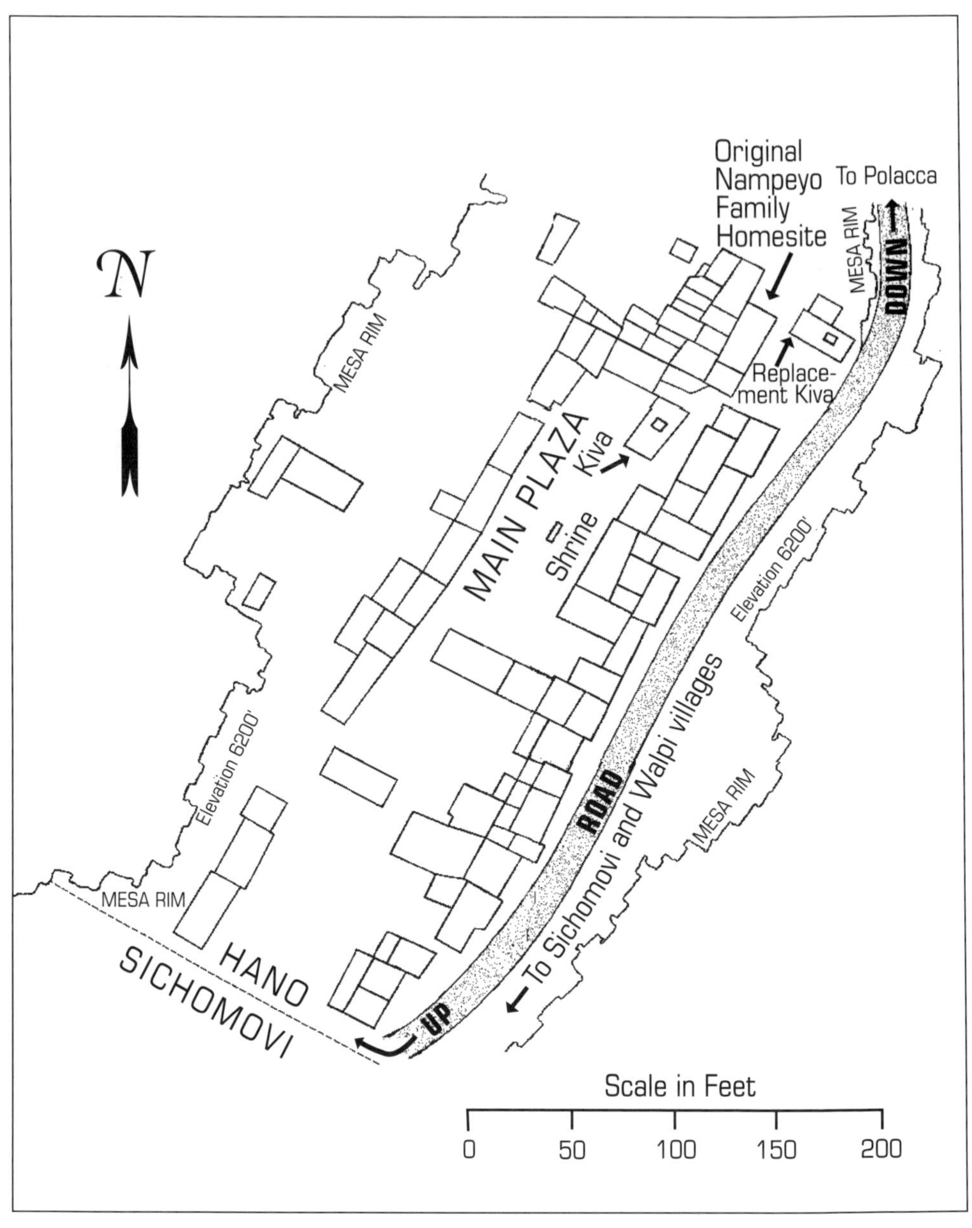

Fig. 2.5. Map of the Tewa village of Hano, located on First Mesa, by L. Blair, based on a map by Stanley A. Stubbs in Bird's Eye View of the Pueblos (University of Oklahoma Press, 1950).

that Nampeyo had become the most famous potter in the Hopi area. He described her skills as having developed markedly between 1875 and 1887. Smithsonian representative William H. Holmes made no mention of Nampeyo in his study of the Keam collection in 1882, but ten years later, he identified early Nampeyo works that Fewkes had acquired from the Hemenway-Keam collection for the Smithsonian.[8] The well-formed vessels and superbly applied unique decorations set her work apart from others in the collection (fig. 2.7). How long Keam had had these works of art before Hemenway purchased them is unknown, but the pieces represent the work of a skilled, mature, and experienced potter.

From early in her career Nampeyo's artistic and technical skills surpassed those of her contemporaries. Besides forming and decorating pottery with distinct talent, Nampeyo and Lesou located clays of varying characteristics for her use. She is known to have used five clays in one creation; the standard seldom exceeded two.

Fig. 2.6. Four generations of Nampeyo's family in 1901. From left to right, they are Annie Healing (holding her daughter Rachel), White Corn, and Nampeyo. Adam C. Vroman, photographer. Neg. No. 33, 909, SWMLA.

Fig. 2.7. This bowl by Nampeyo, decorated with a kachina mask design, was collected by J. W. Fewkes in 1896. The design is a unique Nampeyo creation but resembles designs found at Sikyatki. 3¹/₂ in. by 8¹/₂ in. No. 80-3742, NAA-SI.

Most Pueblo women do not begin to work seriously on pottery until after they are married. The same was most likely true of Nampeyo. The birth of a child about 1883 was undoubtedly an incentive to provide supplementary income through her pottery. Nampeyo's first child by Lesou was named Kwetcawe, alternately Qötsawe (White Dove). She was known as Annie, a name that descendants say was bestowed upon her by Mormon missionaries (fig. 2.8).

The second child was a boy whom they named Kalokun (alternately Kalaokun or Kalaokuno), born sometime during Stephen's period of residence. Little is known about the child except that he accompanied Nampeyo when she demonstrated her art at Grand Canyon and that he died of smallpox shortly thereafter. His presence was briefly mentioned by Fewkes in his contribution to the *19th Annual Report of the Bureau of American Ethnology to the Smithsonian Institution for 1897, 1898* published in 1900, but the elder residents of First Mesa barely remember him. Nampeyo and Lesou's third child was born about 1888. He seldom used his Christian name, William, for he preferred instead his Tewa name, Komalestewa (alternately spelled Komalestiwa). He lived until after World War I and is well remembered by the elders of Tewa village (fig. 2.9).

The fourth child, born in 1896, was a girl, given the Christian name of Nellie and best known to the Tewa as Dahway or Ta-We. Although the most extroverted and fun loving of the family, her pottery was not considered to be among the best (fig. 2.10). She married Douglas Douma, a well-educated man who later played a prominent role in marketing Nampeyo's art. Nellie died in 1979.

A son, Wesley, was born to Nampeyo and Lesou ca. 1900 and lived for eighty-five years (fig. 2.11). He married twice, both times to Pima women whom he met while living in Phoenix during and after his attendance at the Indian School. His first wife was Ida Russell with

▲ **Fig. 2.8.** Annie Healing, and her mother, Nampeyo, whom a label on the original photograph dubs "the boss potters of Tewa," about 1900. Nampeyo already seems to be having trouble with her eyesight, evident from her facial expression. The sculpted serpent designs on the necks of the two vases flanking the potters appeared at approximately the same time that Annie began to work with her mother. Note the two large canteens in the background, which were also made by the Tewas. *S. W. Matteson, photographer. Neg. No. 44743, MPM.*

◀ **Fig. 2.9.** Komalestewa (William) Lesou. This photograph was taken by Barbara Freire-Marreco during her stay at Hano on First Mesa in 1913. *No. BSI10.28A, PRMOx.*

Fig. 2.10. Nellie Lesou [Ta-We], ca. 1913, about the time of her marriage. No. 72251, p. 20, Bentley Album, AZHS.

whom he fathered two children; after Ida's death, he married a woman named Cecilia. The couple moved to the Hopi Reservation, adopted a child named Lynette, and made their home in the house that Lesou had originally built for Nampeyo in Polacca village.

Nampeyo's youngest child, Fannie, was born between 1900 and 1904 and died in 1987. Because she was the only child of Nampeyo still living when research for this book started, much information contained herein was obtained from her (fig. 2.12). During her lifetime, Fannie herself became a recognized pottery maker.

As previously noted, Lesou and Nampeyo raised their family during a time when historical events were profoundly affecting the Hopi people and their way of life. The Santa Fe Railroad had completed tracks linking Chicago to California, and this expanded transportation offered government employees and representatives, scientific expeditions and scholars, and artists and photographers a relatively easy access not only to Keams Canyon and First Mesa but to all portions of the Hopi Reservation. The invasion of outsiders was temporarily curtailed due to another devastating influenza epidemic in 1899, resulting in the imposition of a strict quarantine of the reservation. Although the epidemic lasted only a year, it effectively reduced the population of First and Second Mesas by twenty-one percent.

Fig. 2.11. Nampeyo with son Wesley at home in Hano, Arizona, about 1901. Taken from a hand-tinted photographic reproduction in postcard form sold to tourists. No. 40327, MNM.

Fig. 2.12. Fannie Nampeyo Lesou. *Left, six-year-old Fannie plays the role of a housemaid in a Keams Canyon Boarding School dramatic production. At right, Fannie wears the traditional dress of a Hopi-Tewa maiden, complete with a Hopi manta, belt, moccasins, and jewelry.* Courtesy of Iris Youvella.

Then in the late 1890s a new trading post opened in Polacca village that eliminated the twelve-mile journey to Keams Canyon for First Mesa inhabitants (fig. 2.13). Tom Pavatea, the new proprietor of the trading post, was the first successful Indian trader in the area. He launched his enterprise with money he had earned working as a shepherd for Keam for fifteen years. With this capital he purchased sheep (from Keam) which he corralled in a wash where they were drowned in an overnight flash flood. Temporarily destitute, he returned to sheep herding. With his wages, seventy-five dollars borrowed from his brother Henry, and credit from Holbrook merchant Schuster, he successfully began again in 1896.

As a result of the new trading post, trade relations between First Mesa people and the Keam enterprises fell off. The proximity of the new post to First Mesa allowed residents time to socialize; there sim-

Fig. 2.13. Tom Pavatea Trading Post, Polacca, Arizona, ca. 1929. Pavatea, the first Hopi trader, was Keam's first serious competitor.
H. Sage Goodwin, photographer. No. 119411, MNM.

ply was no financial advantage to doing business at the canyon. Sporadic trade was maintained when Keam or a representative journeyed to First Mesa or when an occasional Hopi, temporarily unhappy with Pavatea, took his business elsewhere. With the exception of Nampeyo's brother Tom, few of Nampeyo's family went to Keams Canyon. Full trade with the owners of the canyon establishment only resumed after Keam's death, when the Pavatea store was purchased by subsequent owners of the Keams Canyon Trading Post.

Ruth Bunzel commented on the dealings of Pavatea and the potters in 1929, indicating the functioning of a remote trading post during the early years of the twentieth century.

> It is impossible to state what a potter receives. The method of marketing operates very unfavorably to the potter. The villages [of First Mesa] are very remote from the market; consequently the whole output is disposed of to Tom Pavatea, the local trader, in return for credit at the store. A woman will bring in her output of two weeks, consisting of some fifty pieces of various sizes. She has an outstanding

debt at the store, and the value of the pottery is used to reduce this debt. The woman has no clear conception of what she receives for her work; and Tom is reticent on this subject. Tom gets for a water jar by Nampeyo two to five dollars, depending on the size—the five dollar size being exceptionally large for any piece. A twelve inch bowl by Nampeyo, seventy-five cents. The work of other potters is cheaper. Small pieces bring from fifteen to fifty cents each. Higher prices prevail on the mesa, potters realizing the extent to which they can fleece the unwary purchaser.[9]

Trade bonds between Nampeyo, her relatives, and Pavatea were close. The store was used as a shipping point for pottery by Nampeyo that was being collected by Herman Schweizer, Fred Harvey's purchasing agent for Indian art. From here as well Pavatea shipped Nampeyo's pottery to the Field Columbian Museum in Chicago (now the Field Museum of Natural History) for a proposed exposition to be held in 1898.[10] Receipts attest to the fact that the store handled special orders for Nampeyo and others often through Douglas Douma (fig. 2.14).

Fig. 2.14. Tom Pavatea, on the left, with Douglas Douma in Pavatea's trading post in 1916. Emry Kopta, sculptor and artist, was the photographer. No. SPC 021 531.50, NAA-SI.

Pavatea could neither read nor write and was able to calculate only by counting on the scales. He had therefore hired Douma (husband of Nampeyo's daughter Nellie) as his manager, corresponding secretary, and chief accountant.

A medical doctor, Joshua Miller, was an important acquaintance of Nampeyo.[11] Not only was he one of the first trained observers who knew Nampeyo for an extended period, kept notes, and amassed well-documented collections that accurately date First Mesa pottery, he also was the first to record Nampeyo's complaints about her eyes. Nampeyo paid his fee with a large, well-decorated bulbous canteen made in 1901 or before (fig. 2.15—see p. l). The record of Dr. Miller's treatment of Nampeyo's eye condition raises a question: Was the treatment of the eyes in 1901 for a temporary ailment only, or did this eye trouble mark the start of the gradual descent of her eyesight that continued over the decades, into total blindness? A photograph of Annie and her mother, Nampeyo, dated 1901, suggests that partial loss of vision was a possibility at that early date (fig. 2.8). Close examination of this remarkably clear photograph seems to reveal an unfocused gaze often characteristic of one phase of blindness. The same gaze can be noted in most later photographs of Nampeyo. As far as is known, Nampeyo was the victim of "normal" glaucoma, a disease that gradually results in total blindness. At that time, the only treatment known for glaucoma was the application of painful drops that gave only temporary relief.

After Miller's reference to it, the earliest mention of Nampeyo's blindness was recorded in Barbara Freire-Marreco's 1913 notes during her expedition to Hopi that was sponsored by Oxford University. She reported: "Nampaju, also a Corn-clan lady, celebrated among American Collectors as 'Nampeyo', used once to do beautiful work, but her sight is now weak and she has grown very careless; much of her work is now so badly fired that the black paint rubs off at once."[12]

Nampeyo's family did not mention Nampeyo's total blindness until late in her life. The fact that she required guidance became apparent about 1940. One afternoon she was following her grandson, Thomas Polacca, down the steep trail from the top of First

Mesa. Thomas ran ahead, leaving her to her own devices but came to an abrupt halt when he heard her scream. Running back, he found that his grandmother had fallen off the trail onto the rocks below. This would be the last time that Nampeyo was left unattended outside her home.

Nampeyo produced pottery from 1876 until 1939. For thirty-nine of these sixty-three years, her eyesight was defective. One can only speculate what the output and quality of her work might have been had she enjoyed full vision all her life. As often happens to those who lose their vision, Nampeyo appears to have gradually acquired a heightened sense of touch, shown in her shift of attention from decoration to form. Although her early work explored variations of form, the main emphasis of her work was on creation and execution of design and its placement on the pottery form. But as her eyesight dimmed, she increasingly paid more attention to the formation of graceful thin-walled shapes with superbly smoothed and polished surfaces than to decoration.

As Nampeyo's fame spread, photographers of the American West were anxious to have her image in their portfolios. Some, working closely with the potter and her family, developed a rapport with them that produced images that reflected accurately both the environment and the way of life of Native Americans.

George Benjamin Wittick, the first photographer to photograph the Snake Dance, succeeded W. H. Jackson in the historical record. Beginning in 1883 and for a period of twenty years, the pioneer photographer was a frequent visitor to the Hopi Reservation. He often stayed either at Keams Canyon or on First Mesa with Polacca or Nampeyo. He took many pictures during these annual pilgrimages to the reservation to witness the Snake ceremonials, including images of Keams Canyon and the Corn Clan home on First Mesa (fig. 2.16). Wittick's rapport with the First Mesa dwellers far exceeded that of most white people. The Hopis placed great trust in him and gradually provided him with access to facets of their lives not granted to most outsiders. Sadly, while preparing to attend the 1903 Snake Dance ceremony, he was bitten by a rattlesnake that he had collected for his

Hopi friends. He died three weeks later at the Fort Wingate Hospital.

A lesser known photographer of the American Indian was the government schoolteacher Jesse H. Bratley. While teaching on Indian reservations, he amassed a collection of images of the Rosebud Sioux and the Hopis. He taught at the Polacca School in 1902 and 1903, living in the house that Tom Polacca had donated to the Hopi school system (fig. 2.17). Although no pictures of Nampeyo were found in his collection at the Denver Museum of Natural History, his photographs of the environs of the Hopis and Tewas of First Mesa provide

a clear portrayal of the surroundings in which the potter lived and of the schools her children attended.

More than others, the images of Adam Clark Vroman accurately portray the Native American in his true surroundings. Vroman built a strong relationship with the Nampeyo family. His pictures provide deep insight into their characters, work habits, and environment, insights that no other photographer had managed to capture (fig. 2.18). Vroman researchers William Webb and Robert A. Weinstein note:

> ...The profound human concerns and exceptional insights displayed in Vroman's Indian photographs establish the special worth of his work. Consider these Indians, too often betrayed and mistreated to give their trust to any white man, cooperating with Vroman to produce photographs of empathy, mutual trust and mutual respect.
>
> This is why one finds in his Indian photographs consistently strong evidence of a remarkable human relationship between the photographer and his Indian subjects, all the more remarkable in that it existed in the early 1900's when the patronizing view of the American Indian was solidly established among White Americans. Vroman's determination to photograph and present the human values of Southwest Indians, to affirm them with grace and strength in his work, was unique.
>
> Study the faces in Vroman's Indian portraits; try to discern even one instance where suspicion of hostility is betrayed in a glance, a posture or a gesture.[13]

Most of Vroman's photographs are distributed throughout the archives of the Bancroft Library, the Henry E. Huntington Library, the Pasadena Library, the Southwest Museum in Los Angeles, the Seaver Center for Western History Research, the Natural History Museum of Los Angeles County, and the San Diego Museum of Man. In addition Vroman accumulated a fine Indian pottery collection, including pieces made by Nampeyo. Unfortunately Vroman's

Fig. 2.18. Nampeyo and her family as photographed by A. C. Vroman. Vroman had the unique ability of capturing the unposed work-a-day world of this family.

A. Lesou fits Vroman for moccasins, 1901. No. V-679, SCWHR.

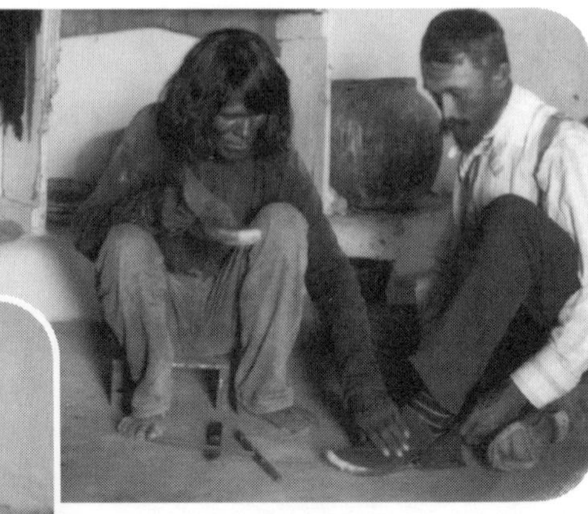

B. Nampeyo builds a pottery jar by coiling. No. 32.357, NAA-SI.

C. Left to right: Nampeyo's mother, Nampeyo, a child (probably Nellie), Annie holding her baby Rachel, Annie's husband Willie Healing (identification tentative), and Lesou about 1902. Neg. No. 33, 909, SWMLA.

D. Lesou cutting up mutton, Hano, 1901. Neg. No. V-678, SCWHR.

pottery pieces, housed in the Southwest Museum, were severely damaged by an earthquake, and some of his photographs appear to have been appropriated by Charles F. Lummis.

A complete photographic record of Nampeyo at work was compiled by S. A. Barrett, who conducted a fieldtrip for the Milwaukee Public Museum in 1911 (fig. 2.19). The collection consists of a series of photographs taken on the roof of the Corn Clan house accompanied by

Fig. 2.19. Three of a series of 1911 photographs taken by Dr. S. A. Barret of the Milwaukee Public Museum that show Nampeyo at work on her pottery. Note the slip grinding and color preparation stones (B and C).

A. Nampeyo kneading clay on a large kneading stone.

B. Polishing a sundried pot with one of the small pebble polishers before applying the paint.

C. Painting a small piece of pottery with a yucca brush.

Neg. Nos. 6636a, 6645b, 6643c, MPM.

notes. The notes were organized, edited, and published by S. H. Schwartz, who remarked: "Nampeyo's pottery techniques are not distinctive, for they follow the traditional Hopi pattern [as well as the patterns of most pueblo Indians]. Only her style of decoration and quality of workmanship are unique."[14] The implements and grinding stones shown in the pictures still exist today. Perhaps these items are inherited by the keeper of the clan home rather than by specific descendants. They have been passed on for two generations, first to Fannie and then to Nampeyo's granddaughter, Tonita Hamilton, both of whom were and are "mothers" of the Corn Clan house.

Two additional photographers whose reproductions of Nampeyo are of minor import are Carl Moon and Edward S. Curtis. Both Moon's and Curtis's photographs are posed shots (figs. 2.20 and 2.21).

The second Hemenway Expedition established a precedent for collecting for museum display large quantities of prehistoric and historic Native American pottery of the Southwest, and much emphasis

Fig. 2.20. *Well composed and artistically executed, this undated Carl Moon photograph does not exhibit the romantic exaggerations found in most of his Native American images.* No. PA38, Special Collections, The Huntington Library.

Fig. 2.21. *This photograph is a classic example of the use of artificial surroundings, static pose, and superb use of light on the subject. Note the pigment grinding stones in the center foreground.* Photograph by Edward S. Curtis. No. 76-5737, NAA-SI.

was placed on obtaining work by Nampeyo. A rash of collectors followed in the wake of the Hemenway Expedition. Both individual and corporate interests were bent on obtaining large collections of pottery from the Hopi. Many of the collectors were from Europe where a strong interest in American Indian art and history rapidly developed. The German Aby M. Warburg, working in April and May of 1896, observed Hopi ways and collected Hopi artifacts for the Hamburg Folk Museum. He was followed by collectors such as Ole Martin Solberg of Norway and Karl von den Steinen of Germany. In addition, Americans such as Fred Harvey, Adam Clark Vroman, Clara Churchill, George Pepper, Stewart Culin, and S. A. Barrett also collected specimens.

The Warburg collection, now housed in the Hamburg Museum, is extensive and well rounded. Although Warburg's expeditions are well documented in the literature, little information is available about the collected artifacts. A study of the pottery collection leaves no doubt that a few of the pieces are the work of Nampeyo.

One of the finest collections of Nampeyo's work was gathered during the height of her career by a member of the staff of the University of Oslo, Professor Ole Martin Solberg. Solberg arrived at Hopi in October 1903 and stayed until February 1904. He apparently kept no field records of his solo investigations, and attempts to trace him through older residents of First and Second Mesas were not successful. The sparse written records of his Hopi visit consist of a minor paper on prayer feathers and meager notes written later on museum catalog cards about the materials that he collected. Attempts to learn more about Solberg and his expedition are best summarized by Dr. Tom G. Svensson, author and curator of the university's Ethnographic Museum: "I can confirm that there are no further notes or diaries of any sort relating to the Solberg collection. And, to our mutual regret, he never published anything from the Nampeyo material either. So to Nampeyo's descendants, as well as the researchers concerned, there is nothing to be obtained but the collection itself with very scanty information noted on the cards."[15]

A description of an attempt to learn more about Solberg may be found in transcripts by Kirsten Aarmo of the Ethnographic Museum, University of Oslo. Aarmo, hoping to track the professor after seventy-seven years, attempted to trace a very cold trail. Arriving in Hopi in November 1980, she learned that two of Nampeyo's children, Wesley and Fannie, were still alive. Although she was unable to contact either, she did manage to locate and interview Dextra Quotskuyva, a granddaughter of Nampeyo who is also an excellent potter. Mrs. Aarmo wished to acquire pottery pieces from the Nampeyo descendants for the museum collection but claimed none were available.

Did Prof. Solberg have any contact with Nampeyo? He was certainly taken by the beauty and quality of her work, but it is still possible that he did not meet her. We know that in at least one instance a bowl in his collection was purchased from a dealer because written in a legible hand on the bottom of the piece are the words, "sold to Dr.

Solberg." The museum card for this same piece states that the maker was Nampeyo of "Walpi." It seems likely that had Solberg visited Nampeyo, he would have known that she lived at Hano, not Walpi.

The pottery collection at Oslo is unique and the exhibit dazzling. Commanding attention as one enters the exhibit hall is a large display of Hopi pottery, primarily the work of Nampeyo, backed by a life-sized Vroman photograph of the artist (fig. 2.22). Her ceramic artwork that is stored in the archives is as impressive as the work on display. All objects are well preserved and maintained. This unusual collection contains many red pieces painted with designs that seem to have been inspired by the decorations of prehistoric Four Mile potters; other pieces appear to be combinations of Four Mile and Sikyatki motifs (fig. 2.23). These works dominate, although there are several examples of classic bowl and canteen shapes decorated with characteristic polychrome designs on light backgrounds.

Another individual who collected Nampeyo's pottery around the same time was Clara Churchill, wife of Frank C. Churchill, superintendent of Indian schools, who accompanied her husband on his

Fig. 2.22. This pottery exhibition is on display at the Ethnographic Museum at the University of Oslo, Norway. In front of the life-sized photograph of Nampeyo by A. C. Vroman is an outstanding display of her pottery. In the upper right corner is a second Vroman photograph of Nampeyo firing. Note the hairstyle. It was her custom to clean her hair with yucca soap and tie it in this fashion to protect it from firing fumes. EMOs.

A. *Bowl, 4¹/₂ in. by 9³/₄ in.*
(No. 13.602)

B. *Bowl, 3¹/₂ in. by 10¹/₂ in.*
(No. 13.611)

C. *Bowl, 3¹/₂ in. by 10¹/₂ in.*
(No. 13.615)

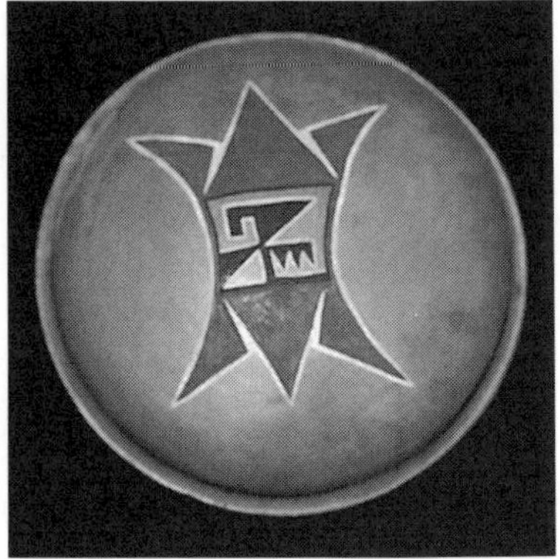

D. *Bowl, 3 in. by 9¹/₂ in.*
(No. 13.604)

Fig. 2.23. *Four bowls attributed to Nampeyo, collected between October 1903 and February 1904 by Professor Ole Solberg of the University of Oslo. The designs contain elements of Sikyatki and Four Mile area potters, with the added Nampeyo touch. EMOs.*

many investigative trips to Indian reservations. Churchill soon became devoted to collecting Indian art with an emphasis on pottery. She kept well-written, informative records about her observations of the people and places they visited, as well as the artifacts she collected. Her journals, at the Hood Museum of Art at Dartmouth College, merit publication since they provide new, firsthand, and accurate information on the history of several Native American cultures.

Several of the pottery pieces attributed to Nampeyo by both Solberg and Clara Churchill can best be described as poorly formed and polished but beautifully decorated (fig. 2.24). One gets the impression that these forms were hurriedly made to allow the artist to move on quickly to the more interesting and pleasant task of painting her newly inspired designs. These pieces are all very small, with the largest being only five inches in diameter. Consequently, the labor of forming and polishing were diminished by the small size, but the decoration would sell the vessel.

Clara Churchill wrote of two meetings with Nampeyo, the first in early 1904 and the second in 1907. She mentions nothing about Nampeyo's poor eyesight except to note that Annie, then twenty-six, was working with her mother. "The handsome pieces made by Nampeyo and her daughter are treasured by all collectors of Indian curios. We made her a visit; several half finished bowls were spread out on the earth floor and a few graceful little vases were drying on the cookstove nearly ready for decorating."

*Fig. **2.24**. Two crudely formed pottery pieces illustrate what appears to be a period when Nampeyo emphasized painted design over pottery structure, although it is possible they were formed by other family members. Both pieces are small and roughly formed with thick, non-uniform walls and obvious surface defects. The defects are obscured by her strategic placement of well-executed, masterful designs. Both were collected between October 1903 and February 1904. **Left,** a pitcher $3^{3}/4$ in. by $3^{1}/2$ in. No. 13.616, EMOs; **right,** two-handled bowl, $3^{1}/2$ in. by $5^{1}/2$ in. wide at handles. No. 13.618, EMOs.*

 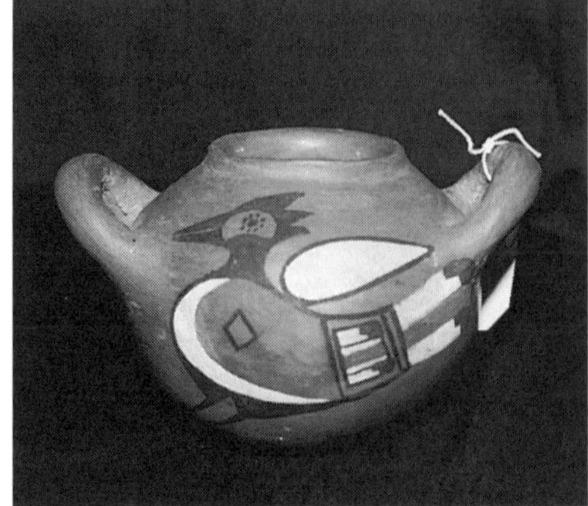

Ole Solberg and Clara Churchill probably met briefly at Hopi. She noted in her 1904 journal: "We found comfortable quarters at the Day School and took our meals at the Teacher's Mess, and at the little table was a young man (clerk in the Trader's store nearby) from New Zealand [and] a young Professor from Norway sent here by one of the Universities of that country."[16]

The collections of Solberg and Churchill represent different tastes in art. Although the Solberg collection is more spectacular, that of Churchill covers a broader spectrum of Nampeyo's work, including one unusual signature piece (fig. 2.25). After her husband's death in 1911, Clara Churchill established a private museum in their home in Lebanon, New Hampshire. At her death in 1945, the collection was willed to the Hood Museum of Art of Dartmouth College.

Another collector of Nampeyo's work was George Pepper, quite a controversial character. Although untrained, he was appointed assistant to Professor F. W. Putnam, curator of the Department of Anthropology of the American Museum of Natural History, and was soon placed in charge of field work to excavate and study the Chaco Canyon ruins in New Mexico. The Heye brothers, founders of the Heye Foundation at the Museum of the American Indian, assumed financial responsibility for the project from 1897 through 1900. From the beginning the expedition was tainted with scandal. The pilfering of artifacts as well as the mixing of personal interests with those scientific and public created immediate problems. Although Pepper was never directly implicated in a

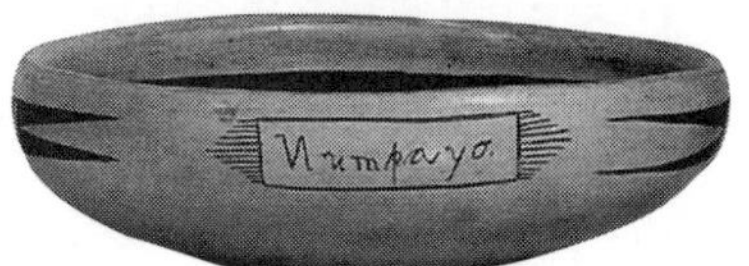

Fig. 2.25. *Two views of an unusual piece, bearing the name Nampeyo, that was painted with brown pigment before firing. It was collected by the Churchills in 1904–1907. The printing on the side of the bowl was probably copied by someone else, as Nampeyo could not write. 2¹/₂ in. by 7¹/₂ in. No.46-17-10111, HMA.*

Fig. 2.26. *George H. Pepper collected a variety of beautifully designed pottery bowls in 1903, many made by Nampeyo.* Photograph from the George H. Pepper Papers, MARI/LAL.

scandal, he was condemned by association, and his career was off to a poor start. After Chaco he became involved with the Heye Foundation and participated in other excavations for brief periods, practicing professional photography, leading tours, and collecting artifacts which he brokered and sold.

As a dealer he bought many pieces of Nampeyo's work, which he sold to several collectors and museums. The collection of the Middle American Research Institute of Tulane University was acquired directly from him, while some pieces in the American Museum of Natural History were acquired from him and one of his customers. Collections at the University of Pennsylvania and the University of California at Berkeley are partially the result of donations of two of Pepper's customers, Mrs. Robert Weeks de Forest and Mrs. Randolph Hearst (fig. 2.26). A portion of the Pennsylvania donations, including a catalog and some photographs, were disposed of through their museum shops. The Hearst collection is now housed in the Phoebe Hearst Museum of Anthropology at the University of California, Berkeley (formerly the Lowie Museum of Anthropology).

Pepper was not known for providing provenence for the materials he collected. Although his notes lack any mention of direct dealing with Nampeyo, they do indicate that he visited the Hopi area intermittently from 1901 through 1904. His photograph of the Corn Clan houses taken in 1903 points to the fact that at least a portion of the Nampeyo material was collected at that time (fig. 2.27). The large amount of Nampeyo pottery that he amassed would indicate that he purchased mainly from wholesalers such as Hubbell and Pavatea.

As her reputation spread, the famous potter was induced to make at least three off-reservation appearances, all arranged by the Fred Harvey Company. Harvey, a transplanted Londoner working in cooperation with the Santa Fe Railroad, first established a series of station restaurants from Chicago to California along the railroad's right-of-way. Driven by his keen interest in promoting tourism in the Southwest, he later established a series of hotels at selected train stops. Each hotel contained an Indian curio shop that often featured, among other items, the craft work of Nampeyo. Automobile tours, called Indian Detours, took tourists from the hotels deep into Indian country and

Fig. 2.27. Nampeyo's house as photographed by George H. Pepper in 1903. This picture gives credence to the 1903 date for the pottery pieces he collected for Tulane University, the American Museum of Natural History, and others. No. 32780, NMAI-SI.

featured stops where Indian arts and crafts could be purchased directly from the makers themselves.

A rail spur to the edge of the Grand Canyon was completed by 1901. By 1903 the Harvey Company announced that it would erect a hotel, to be called El Tovar, near the end of the track. The El Tovar opened with a flourish in 1905, and it designated a part of the village dedicated to tourist entertainment. Within the complex, a pueblolike structure was included and named the Hopi House. This combination of curio shop, museum, storehouse, theater, and living quarters also served as a stage for Indian dances and craft demonstrations. It opened for business a few days before the hotel (fig. 2.28).

In early January 1905 Nampeyo became the first Indian craftsperson to demonstrate her work at Hopi House. She appeared again briefly in 1907. Lesou accompanied her at various times as did her sons, William, Kalokun, and Wesley, and daughters, Nellie, Fannie, and Annie, who was pre-

Fig. 2.28. *Hopi House, 1905.* **Below:** *Exterior view of the structure as it appeared at the time of the Nampeyo family occupancy.* No.94-1447, NAA-SI. **Right:** *Inside Hopi House.* Copyrighted in 1905 by the Detroit Photographic Company. No. 94-1446, NAA-SI.

sent with her husband, Willie Healing, and their children, Rachel and Daisy. The appearances at Grand Canyon were well publicized. Before the arrival of the entourage, Nampeyo was promoted in literature prepared in advance. Photographic images of her were made into postcards and sold at the canyon and at other Harvey establishments. Unable to write, her pottery went unattributed until the Harvey Company supplied labels, glued to the undersides of her pots, that identified her as maker. These labels are now recognized as a possible guarantee of authenticity, and they add to the value of the vessel.

Logistics to support Nampeyo's appearances were complex and arrangements for transportation of the family complicated. To get pottery ready to sell at Hopi House required hours of advance collecting and packing. Often emergency shipments of raw materials were needed, adding to the complication of arranging demonstrations.

As early as 1905 John Huckel, Fred Harvey's son-in-law, complained that Nampeyo put Hopi-Tewa affairs before her pottery making and public appearances.[17] With the passing of her mother, White Corn, Nampeyo inherited the clan duties as the new matriarch of the Corn Clan. Not only were the maintenance of the clan house, the safekeeping of ceremonial paraphernalia, and the supplying of food for those taking part in all rituals among her new responsibilities, but also the role of "mother" for all Corn Clan people. The tasks of all who assume leadership of a clan home are arduous and time consuming, and they take precedence over any other kinds of obligations.

In 1906 Herman Schweizer, Fred Harvey's canny buyer, assumed responsibility for Nampeyo's appearance at the Grand Canyon as well as for the appearance of a raft of other native craftsmen at the Chicago Railway Exposition of 1910. Without license to purchase on the reservations, he arranged with traders such as Hubbell and Pavatea to buy, store, and ship articles for the Harvey locations and for the railway exposition. Porter Timeche, a Second Mesa Hopi who worked for the Harvey Company for fifty years, was also active in organizing the Indian appearances for the Chicago rail fair. He had begun his career making sandwiches for hungry railroad passengers who passed through the Holbrook station; later he demonstrated weaving and organized Hopi dances at Hopi House. From 1910 he assisted Schweizer in purchasing Indian artifacts throughout the Navajo and Hopi Reservations.

Shortly before his death in 1988 Porter reminisced about the 1910 Chicago event. He recalled little about the Nampeyo group, for they were but a few of well over a thousand Indians who brought examples of their arts and crafts for exhibit and sale at the fair. The Navajos had brought their rugs and jewelry, the Zuni their jewelry and pottery, and the Hopi people their pottery, baskets, and weaving, to name a few. The archives of the Field Museum contain more than a thousand unidentified photographs of those who participated in the event. Although the Nampeyo group may have been submerged somewhere in the crowd, Nampeyo is the only Indian mentioned by name in the Chicago press coverage of the event.[18]

During the exhibit much of the food given to the Indians came in cans and jars. Rather than consuming these novel and delectable items, the Indians hoarded them to share with friends and family members upon their return home. Following the close of the show, the Santa Fe Railroad arranged to crate and deliver many precious items to the various reservations.

Lesou assisted Nampeyo more and more as her eyesight deteriorated. As the need to seek out unusually decorated sherds and pottery designs lessened, Lesou spent more time helping her with the chores of clay preparation and pottery decoration, an area where most believe that Lesou had neither Nampeyo's skill nor her creativity. Of the myriads of Nampeyo family pottery specimens we examined, none were documented as pieces by Lesou (fig. 2.29). No well-documented pieces by Lesou have been located, but all pieces that are attributed to him are crudely designed and poorly formed. A difference of opinion arises here, however. At a pottery seminar in Albuquerque in January 1997, researchers discussed the possibility of Lesou's having participated in Nampeyo's work. Perhaps because pottery making was

Fig. 2.29. A. E. Dittert speculated that this crude bowl with two handles and a red and brown geometric design on a cream background was made between 1890 and 1910 by Lesou. 4 in. by 7 in. A-SW-HO-A7-86, HMPx.

not a male occupation at the time, Lesou preferred to remain unrecognized. Whatever the case, Nampeyo came to rely more on the talents of other members of her immediate family rather than on
Lesou. As Lesou aged, he became more involved in helping Nampeyo
with the ceremonial life of their people. When he died in 1930, he
was almost seventy years of age; he was buried in the old Indian
cemetery in Polacca.

Nampeyo outlived her husband by twelve years. As with many
elderly people, she became increasingly senile toward the end of her
life and eventually became almost totally unaware of her family and
surroundings. She began to live in her childhood past and required
almost constant attention. Despite her condition, she relived the
past, often posing for visitors who wished to photograph the aging
celebrity. She died in 1942 and was buried near Lesou in the Tewa
way.

Art is not a handicraft, it is the transmission of feeling the artist has
experienced.—*Leo Tolstoy,* What Is Art?

A study of numerous well-documented Nampeyo works reveals that
the golden age of her exquisitely decorated work was between the
years of 1895 and 1908. Her first pieces were white slipped with
black or brown painted designs. Only a very few
Nampeyo's Art   pieces confirmed to be hers were made prior to
this time, and these do not compare to the works
that were to come later. Although she continued to produce outstanding pieces of art after 1908, her failing eyesight made it necessary to turn over more of her decorative work to family members—a
few possibly by Lesou, others by Annie, and others later by Rachel,
Nellie, Fannie, and Daisy Hooee. Thus, it is even more difficult to
determine whether work done after 1908 is Nampeyo's alone.

The predominant shape of her golden era was a simple shallow
bowl. She became known later for the more complex forms such as
water jars and deep bowls. As previously mentioned, these shallow,

almost platelike bowls were often not well formed, finished, or polished, but they always presented at least one good surface upon which to place her unique and exquisite designs. These pots could be likened to hurriedly stretched canvases of artists anxious to create without regard to the neatness of the bases used for presentation. Commonly, decorations were placed on the interior bottoms of shallow forms, but the slightly deeper bowls were often decorated on both the interior and exterior surfaces. Most bowls were finished with a lip very nearly unique to Nampeyo (fig. 2.30).

Nampeyo's form was not as innovative as her decoration, although there are notable exceptions. Her forms often paralleled those unearthed in nearby ruins such as Sikyatki (fig. 2.31—see pps. II–VIII). Not so her decoration. New methods of design application based on those methods brought to light at Sikyatki included dry brush, splatter, and intaglio; these Nampeyo adopted and improved. In filling space between lines she must have literally scratched into the pigment, probably using sheep's wool. She abandoned the precise geometric patterns in vogue at the time in favor of realistic or stylized designs of animals, reptiles, humans, insects, and most often birds resembling those of the prehistoric potters who once inhabited the nearby ruined villages. Segments commonly depicting bird feathers, tails, or wings were combined into intricate compositions and cleverly placed to blend with the main design.

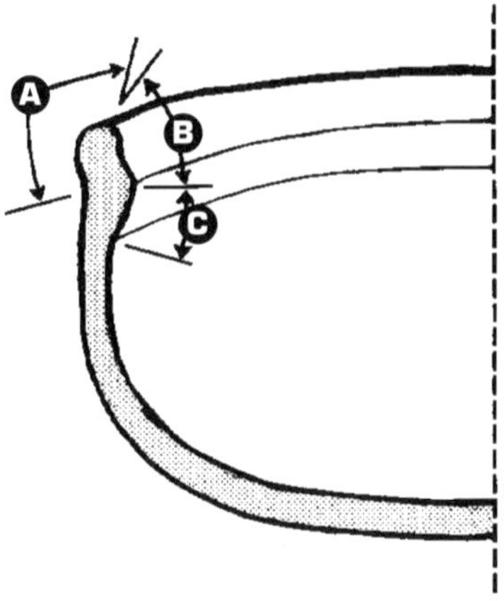

Fig. 2.30. Drawing of a cross-section of a Nampeyo bowl. Exteriors of the rims of Nampeyo's bowls usually show a slight outward flare with a rounded-off rim (section **A**). A slightly concave surface projects on the interior wall (section **B**). The lip is finished with a gentle taper into the interior surface (section **C**). The rim is formed by the addition of an extra coil, which produces a sturdier structure.

Nampeyo's painting at that time followed no set style or pattern but was almost always the product of an unbridled imagination.

Though daughter Fannie declared otherwise, a break in the line band on Nampeyo's bowls sometimes appears. At times she would improvise from the work of the prehistoric Pueblo potters, but primarily she produced original imaginative creations (fig. 2.32). While her free-flowing renditions may have been inspired by prehistoric potters, they were not copies. She seldom made direct copies and only then if she was commissioned to do so. Designs could be complicated or beautifully simple, much like the later renditions of Picasso. Empty spaces or an economy of design indicated that Nampeyo knew exactly when creation was complete.

Unlike the works of most prehistoric potters, Nampeyo's designs were often bold, and at times there was a suitable avoidance of symmetry (figs. 2.32 and 2.33—see pps. IX-XI). Often small, almost unobservable and apparently meaningless design elements appear to have been added as an afterthought or changed with the apparent purpose of altering balance. This observation might appear to contradict the statements of Ruth Bunzel, who interviewed Nampeyo about her art. To quote Nampeyo, the founder and leading spirit of the Hopi school of decoration: "The best arrangement for the water jar is four designs around the top,—two and two, like this [indicating on the floor the arrangement]. The designs opposite each other should be alike." Her own work clearly showed her preference for this type of arrangement.[19] But there is no contradiction. Bunzel referred only to the water jar decorations that Nampeyo created during the period of her peak production. The interview had taken place in the early 1920s, when the artist was teaching her daughters a style much less complicated and easier to reproduce.

Two characteristic designs considered to be "owned" by the Nampeyo family potters are called the "eagle" or "bird tail" and the "migration," also known as the "hatched claw," "bird or bat wing," "bear claw," "badger paw," or "cloud with rain," depending on the configuration (figs. 2.34 and 2.35j and k).

The eagle design is actually a macaw and can be traced unbroken back to the prehistoric times of the Basketmaker III culture. The true eagle design is of tailfeathers that are consistently used in a pattern,

Fig. 2.34. Mercator projection of an eagle design.
A. Shows the open mouth of the jar. B. Classic square placed around the opening with its sides tangential to the opening; the square is usually of a solid color. C. Symmetrical feather designs have been added to each side of the square. The manner in which they are drawn is optional. D. Depending on the designer, the square may be bordered and optional design elements added. Occasionally, the artist may paint a triangle design around the mouth of the vessel, rather than a square, with but three tail appendages.

a design associated with sky beings. The design evolved during the Polacca Polychrome era, an inherited design from the potters of Sikyatki or their contemporaries in the Jeddito area. The older decorations are crude by today's standards, but all are characterized by a square area surrounding a jar opening that is typically painted a shade of red. Attached to the sides are spirals and descending appendages said to represent bird beaks or tailfeathers, such as those of the macaw, parrot, or eagle (fig. 2.34). San Bernardo forms, which followed those of Sikyatki, exhibit many of the same design characteristics. This eagle motif gained sophistication as Nampeyo and her descendants sometimes added new elements, some resembling crosses. Her eagle decorations are commonly in four sections, though occasional specimens are decorated with three. Possibly because of her interest in diversity of design, she did not paint many eagles. The motif has been more popular with her descendants.

An explanation of how the complicated and delicate migration design evolved is fairly straightforward. The term "migration" itself

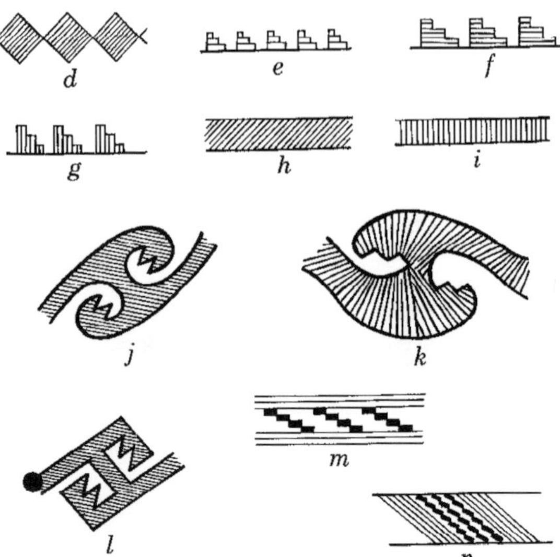

Fig. 2.35. *Copies of early renditions of hatching in the migration design found at Awatovi. Decorations, termed "hatching in claws" by Watson Smith, were found on three pottery types; fifty-five percent of the samples were placed on Tusayan black-on-white (1125–1300), forty-two percent on Jeddito black-on-orange (1250–1350), and three percent on orange polychrome.* Courtesy of the Douglas Library, DAM.

was probably coined by collectors in post–World War II times and is not of native origin. The basic form of the batwing hatched design was uncovered at Awatovi and other prehistoric sites on the western side of the Jeddito Wash (fig. 2.35j, k and 2.25). The batwing hatched designs usually appeared on ceramic pieces classified as Tusayan black-on-white, Tusayan orange, Awatovi black-on-yellow, and occasionally on Jeddito black-on-orange—all types created by potters between the years of 1150 and 1350.[20] This ancient design occurs in the form most closely resembling today's migration pattern in Dogoszhi black-on-white, 875–1150.

The most delicate examples of hatching not associated with the "hatch claw" motif were found on wares produced during the Awatovi black-on-yellow period. The execution on many vessels was meticulous; the lines are said to be painted with a single stroke of the brush, although the same delicate lines have been observed to be painted with multiple strokes. The terminations are so well matched that it is practically impossible to determine where one stroke leaves off and the other begins.

Nampeyo apparently did not favor the migration design during her prime. Only a few crude examples of it have been located, and they cannot compare to the elegant modifications that were developed later by her daughters and their children.

Inspiration: The Immediate Environment

The immediate cultural and natural environment undoubtedly does more to stimulate the American Pueblo Indian potters than any other influence. In addition to the exceptionally fine sherds still found in the area that reveal the art of past masters, there were complete pottery vessels, both old and new, in village homes to serve as textbooks of the past. These forms provide a foundation for new and innovative modifications.

The type of pottery observed by Nampeyo as a child first appeared at Hopi about 1780, some seventy-five years after the arrival of the Tewa at First Mesa. Classified as Polacca Polychrome, according to Wade and McChesney, this ware remained in vogue for a little more than one hundred years, flourishing until 1890. The style incorporated elements of shape, design, paste, and slips that are found in pottery from the nearby abandoned pueblo of Payupki as well as those from Acoma, Zuni, and the Spanish (fig. 2.36—see pps. XI-XII).

The paste or body of Polacca Polychrome generally consists of yellow to red firing clays to which fine quartz sand has been added. Often their decorative pigments can be wiped off, an indication that the potters did not use sufficient hematite to bind the pigment to the body, despite the fact that they were most often fired with coal. Slipped pieces often present a crackled surface (indicating a different coefficient of contraction and expansion in the slip), a prominent characteristic of this ware. Decoration was influenced not only by the Hopi-Tewa religion with its symbols denoting weather control, kachinas, fertility, curing, prayer sticks, birds, and feather use, but also on the preferences of traders. Although some vessels ornamented with Polacca Polychrome designs are still being produced at the villages on First Mesa, a gradual replacement through the elaboration of design, built in large part on Nampeyo's work, has been effected. This fluorescence has come from traders, well-meaning collectors, craft exhibitions with their exposure of other potters' works, all contributing form and decorative suggestions that have produced the Sikyatki Revival pottery.

Pots and Pot Sherds

To a layman like me, it helps a lot

To know that a pot shard is just a piece of broken pot.

To know that behind the talk of color, shape, design

It helped an aborigine to dine—

To see in this bit of broken clay

A brown skinned baby, clumsy at his play

Cuffed by a weary mother, whimpering so

Because he broke a dish a thousand years ago.

Hugh Miller, "The Pot Shard," as inscribed on a trailside monument at Tuzigoot National Monument, Verde Valley, Arizona

Hopi people have within their lands a wealth of abandoned settlements of prehistoric pottery-producing cultures. As a result of the Hopi belief that these sites should be considered sacred and should remain undisturbed, many ancient ruins and their trash heaps remain unexcavated. Each ruin includes at least one trash heap in addition to a few rooms that may contain exquisitely designed or unusually shaped pottery artifacts, artifacts that reveal the production and painting techniques of those who once lived there. Ancient pueblo cemeteries that are relatively undisturbed, or pueblos that for some catastrophic reason had been hastily excavated, are prime sources for the unspoiled artifacts valued so by researchers, pottery artists, and commercially driven pot hunters.

While employed by excavators such as Keam, Lesou found sherds and vessels for Nampeyo, often copying the more interesting designs on paper for her permanent reference.[21] Obscure sites, such as those in Keams Canyon (mentioned by Dewey Healing, Tewa historian and grandson of Nampeyo), also produced some specimens studied by Nampeyo. Her creations went far beyond those inspired by the

Sikyatki specimens to which Fewkes and others often mistakenly limited her.

Payupki (River House, ca. 1680–1780)

Following the 1680 Pueblo Revolt, many groups of Rio Grande Pueblo Indians were forced to abandon their river homes and seek refuge outside the area with other Native American populations. It would appear that the group most affected by the major upheavals were the Tiwas.[22]

The first indication that the Tiwas would be forced to vacate their homes came as the defeated Spanish fled from Santa Fe and took brief refuge in some of the pueblos lying in the path of their hurried evacuation to the south. As the Spanish retreated, they often put temporary shelters to the torch. Other Indian groups mistakenly felt that the Southern Tiwas had given aid and comfort to the enemy during the conflict and therefore deserved punishment. It made no difference that the Tiwas had also fought the Spanish during the great uprising. Any attempts to rebuild pueblos were foiled by hostile tribes bent on false retribution or by Spanish soldiers engaged in punitive attempts to recapture the river province for the Crown.

For protection, some of the remnants of these battered groups joined forces and moved to the land of the Hopis, who were distant from the area of conflict and had a reputation for resisting the Spanish. In comparison to the migration of the Tewa ancestors of Nampeyo, very little is known about their withdrawal. The trek of many of the Tiwas ended on a prong of Second Mesa, a short distance from the present villages of Mishongnovi and Shipaulovi. On this isolated mesa they established their new village of Payupki.

These Rio Grande immigrants quickly became adept in the art of making and decorating pottery, a craft strongly influenced initially by their First Mesa neighbors, although not by their closer neighbors of Shungopovi. The designs and shapes of the Payupki potters soon came to dominate the craft. As noted by Wade and McChesney: "Most Payupki vessels found in the Hopi area come from the actual site of Payupki. Nevertheless, from all indications, Payupki Polychrome becomes the dominant Hopi pottery style during the eighteenth century. Payupki vessels from the Keam Collection were purchased in the 1880's or 1890's from Hopis who had them as heirlooms."[23] This explanation of where the Keam's collection came from seems unusual because Hopis have seldom kept heirlooms; rather, they are more likely to retain articles of interest or economic value. Only recently have some of the younger potters been interested in collecting.

What was it that inspired these refugees to begin producing quantities of fine pottery? When visiting the site, one is impressed with the quantities of sherds left behind by inhabitants of this short-lived, small settlement. The characteristic shape of a Payupki bowl resembles that of the early Zuni (Hawikuh) with their concave bases. Was this resemblance the result of a possible stay at Zuni during their flight from the Rio Grande area? Like some Zuni pieces, their jar shapes often have a distinct division between the upper and lower portions of the body. The vessel surfaces are slipped and polished, usually with a rich orange, or less often, a yellow firing clay. The designs seem cluttered and crowded and resemble early Western Keresan (Acoma) motifs (fig. 2.37).

The refugees' residence at Hopi was temporary, lasting only about sixty-five years. In 1745, according to Robert C. Euler and Henry F. Dobyns,

> A threat that colonial authorities might assign Hopi territory to the Jesuit Order spurred the Franciscans in New Mexico into renewed and evidently frantic efforts to prove their effectiveness either reconverting the natives of Tusayan, or at least reclaiming for Christianity and Spanish colonial rule the 'apostate' New Mexico Pueblo refugee Indians still living with the Hopis. Then it was the Fathers Carlos Delgado and Ignacio de Piño persuaded a reported 441 Indians to leave Hopi country for Sandia, Pajarito, Alameda, and other places in New Mexico which they or their ancestors fled during the 1680 revolt. Three years later the same energetic priests reported leading some

Fig. 2.37. *Payupki pottery shapes and designs, ca. 1680–1745.* **Upper left:** *The sharp mid-body division and busy design is typical of Payupki jars. 8³/4 in. by 12 in.* No. 43-39-10, PMAE. **Upper right:** *This large bowl, decorated with Zuni features such as stylized birds and rainbird elements, may have been made about 1890. During heavy migration of First Mesa people to Zuni during the 1850s and 1860s, there was ample opportunity for this style of decoration to be copied. 8 in. by 18¹/2 in.* No. 428, SAR. **Lower right:** *Modern jar by Kay Charlie and Marcella Kahe of the First Mesa village of Sichomovi. The 1984 adaptation with typical Polacca Polychrome decoration follows the practice of the ancient potters of Payupki whose drawings often covered most of the outside surface. 8¹/2 in. by 13³/4 in.* Private collection.

2,000 Indians out of Tusayan back to Isleta and Jemez. The missionaries, keeping abreast of events in the Hopi towns through native informants, sought reconverts during a period of internecine strife. The original refugees of 1680 may well have been wearing their welcome among the Hopis rather thin by 1745, since their refuge had then lasted for up to 65 years, and they would have established rights to horticultural fields in Hopi territory only with extreme difficulty.

In 1747, Friar Miguel Menchero persuaded another group of refugees to leave Hopi territory to resettle at Sandia.[24]

The group led by Friar Menchero (some 350 refugees) is thought to have been the one departing Payupki. The removal of 2,836 people seems unlikely as Payupki was not that large a settlement.

Again, researchers Wade and McChesney raise tantalizing questions concerning the people of the temporary settlement. "Moreover, if Payupki Polychrome is a Sandian innovation what happened to it once the Sandians returned home in 1740? Did they continue to produce this ware? If so where is it in the ceramic types representative of the eighteenth-century Rio Grande pottery traditions?...Perhaps there was no continuation of the Payupki Polychrome tradition. Why then should the Sandians abandon this ware so suddenly and thoroughly?"[25]

Remarkably, in a relatively short span of time the settlers at Payupki exerted a profound influence on the pottery of their Hopi neighbors. With the exception of minor Keam excavations, Lesou would have had almost exclusive and undisturbed access to Payupki, as well as Sikyatki, to resurrect materials for Nampeyo. This site, like many others, was an easy jaunt from the Nampeyo home and presented no problem for those conditioned to relying on their own leg power or on burros for transportation.

Sikyatki (Yellow House, ca. 1375–1625)

The ruin of Sikyatki is situated on a large flat-topped mound below First Mesa, some two miles northeast of the village of Polacca (fig. 1.11). By crude estimate the area of the mound on which the village was located is 125,000 square feet. The name is probably derived from one of two sources, either the yellow color of the stone from which the pueblo was built or the yellow color of the spring between the ruin and the foot of First Mesa. In the Hopi language *sikya* means "yellow" and *ki* is "house." From the highway a crude dirt road takes one to within easy walking distance of the ruin. Permission to visit all ancient sites is controlled by the Hopis. A permit and the services of a guide are required for each visit, and removing objects of any type is strictly forbidden. These rules are rigorously enforced to prevent artifact pillaging.[26]

J. W. Fewkes described Sikayatki as a rectangular ruin in some respects resembling Awatovi, but having an enclosed plaza. The enclosed plaza also made it unlike Walpi or the ancient and modern pueblos of Middle Mesa and Oraibi. Fewkes wrote: "In fact there is no Tusayan ruin which resembles it in ground plan, except Payupki, a Tanoan town of much later construction....The ground plan of Sikyatki is a type more common in the eastern pueblo region and in those towns of Tusayan which were built by immigrants from the Rio Grande region."[27]

There are many historic versions of what happened to the Sikyatki people. Some of these stories have been confused with the history of Awatovi, to be reviewed shortly. While the mythical versions differ in some detail, they obviously relate to the same series of events. The version by J. W. Fewkes is probably the best available.

> There is current in Walpi a romantic story connected with the overthrow of Sikyatki. It is said that the son of a prominent chief, disguised as a *katcina*, offered a prayer-stick to a maiden, and as she received it he cut her throat with a stone knife....It is also related that the Walpians fell upon the village of Sikyatki to avenge this bloody deed, but it is much more likely that there was ill feeling between the two villages for other reasons, probably disputes about farm limits or the control of the water supply, inflamed by other difficulties. The inhabitants of the two pueblos came into Tusayan from two different directions, and as they may have spoken different languages have failed to understand each other, they may have been mutually regarded as interlopers. Petty quarrels no doubt ripened into altercations, which probably led to bloodshed.... This was apparently the result of a quarrel between two pueblos of East Mesa, or at least there is no intimation that the other pueblos took prominent part in it.
>
> There appears to be good evidence that Sikyatki was destroyed by fire, nor would it seem that it was gradually abandoned.

There is nothing to show that any considerable massacre of the people took place when the village was destroyed.... There is little doubt that many Sikyatki women were appropriated by the Walpians, and in support of this it is stated that the Kokop [Firewood] people of the present Walpi are the descendants of the people of that clan who dwelt at Sikyatki.[28]

A broad path leading to the top of the mound, which marks the ruins, is blanketed with countless pottery sherds exposed by the rains and winds of time. On top there are fewer sherds, probably the result of the land being cultivated in historic times and later picked over by visiting tourists. Traces of more recent low walls that once surrounded garden plots are easily visible. The broken bits of pottery are unlike those found at most sites. The delicate, uniformly walled pieces are rather vitreous, indicating higher firing temperatures than those accorded contemporary Hopi pottery. Their bright, well-oxidized colors cover the spectrum, from reds through light-yellowish tan to near white, and they are well fused to the body, which accounts for their excellent resistance to abrasion. Coal seams outcrop in many places near the ruin, especially from the base of the mesa walls. Easy access to this fuel, which burns at higher temperatures than sheep dung, undoubtedly accounts for the excellent appearance of this ancient ware.

Although a wide variety of delicate ceramic shapes have been recovered from excavations, the shape most associated with Nampeyo's work is a Hopi water jar form. Although this form is not exclusive to Sikyatki, the first water jar to be found came from this location. As a rule the height of this vessel is approximately 60 percent of its diameter. A relatively small opening, centered over a high shoulder, gives the vessel a flat, or nearly horizontal, top that is similar to the tops of some of the ancient pottery formerly produced in the Zuni valley (fig. 2.38).

The surface of this ware is well adapted to the application of decoration. In most instances traditional design placement is limited to

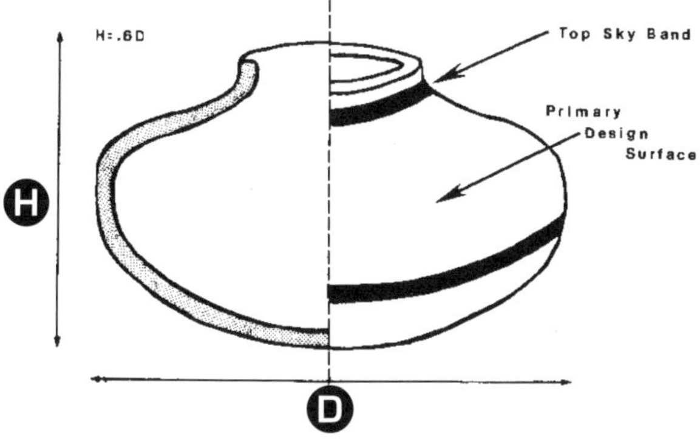

*Fig. **2.38**. Section drawing of the Sikyatki jar shape. The height (**H**) of a classic jar approximates six-tenths of the diameter (**D**). If a bottom band is used, the primary design is usually limited to the upper surface of the vessel. In instances where there is no bottom band, the design often spreads over the shoulder. Geometric designs usually appear on Sikyatki jars, while animal decorations are prominent on bowls.*

the flat upper body, but on occasion it may extend over the shoulder either toward the base or up toward the rim. Viewing the designs is sometimes best done from the top or the bottom of a vessel. Observation of the work of Nampeyo's descendants in progress reveals that their designs are applied from either top or bottom. Exceptions to this come from many of the younger, contemporary innovators, who like most pueblo potters work on the side walls.

Sikyatki patterns showed greater freedom of movement than the geometric motifs of a majority of either older or coexisting cultures. Designs were usually bordered by black bands, now referred to as "sky bands." A typical Sikyatki innovation on jars, however, was to sometimes skip one band, usually at the bottom. Although decorations with varying degrees of symmetry were often applied, again hard and fast rules were not always followed and symmetry was often abandoned. Freedom of expression was a common characteristic of Sikyatki decoration (fig. 2.39).

The designs of Sikyatki may have been as fascinating for Lesou as for Nampeyo. According to noted author Frank Waters:

> [S]ome of the designs...indicated that Sikyatki had been the traditional home of his [Lesou's] own Coyote Clan. Disappointed because Fewkes and Hodge had given up their excavating work after a few weeks, he brooded about

Fig. 2.39. *Two examples of Sikyatki pottery designs, ca. 1375–1625. **Left:** Broken sky bands are not uncommon in Sikyatki decoration, although a sky band broken by a zoomorphic figure, such as this, is. Sikyatki decorators appear to have had few restraints when planning designs. This pot was collected by Thomas Keam or Alexander Stephen and later sold to the Hemenway expedition. No. 43-39-10/25077, PMAE. **Right:** A drawing by William H. Holmes of a Sikyatki water jar for a Fewkes' article on his Arizona excavations in the* Seventeenth Annual Report of the Bureau of Ethnology. DAM.

it for many years. Finally he went to Sivanka (Flower Painting), the oldest member of the Coyote Clan in Oraibi, and obtained permission to dig into a kiva at Sikyatki, thus making sure that no evil effects would result from his digging.

Taking with him to Sikyatki a young man of the Coyote Clan, Lesso located and unearthed a kiva. On the west wall of the kiva was a mural [whose figures substantiated the fact that the kiva was used by his clan].

Lesso carefully drew the figures on a board with charcoal, planted a *páho* at the base of the mural, and sealed up the kiva again. He then returned to Oraibi with the charcoal sketch he had drawn, paying his debt to his religious society and his clan. He had found what he wanted. The kiva mural depicted the Coyote-Swallow race and confirmed tradition that Sikyatki was the legendary home of the Coyote Clan.[29]

Awatovi and the Jeddito Valley–Antelope Mesa (occupied ca. 800–1700)

The extensive Jeddito Valley, or Jeddito Wash, and Antelope Mesa area ruins have supplied Hopi and western Tewa potters and artists with more stimulating design examples than any other locations on the Hopi Reservation. Although Sikyatki is not in the Jeddito area, much Sikyatki-type pottery has been found there, probably as the result of intervillage trade and influence.

The Jeddito Valley and Antelope Mesa region was one of the first areas where Keam and his associates procured both ancient artifacts and pottery for his trading post. In 1893 Keam hired an excavation crew of Navajos to obtain artifacts for him.[30] Here, and at nearby sites, Keam obtained the first artifacts to be merchandised to the outside world, many of which eventually found their way to museums throughout the world (fig. 2.40).

Fig. 2.40. *"Collection of curios belonging to Captain Thomas Keam, Keams Canyon, 1900." A. C. Vroman photographed this variety of crafts that Keam merchandised. Some of the pieces were excavated at surrounding sites and would be illegal if offered for sale nowadays. No. V-1011, SCWHR.*

The Jeddito Valley is located southeast of Keams Canyon, where the road climbs abruptly from the canyon to the summit of Antelope Mesa and then proceeds across its flat top until it drops into Jeddito Wash. At this point, if an imaginary line is drawn at right angles to the road following the lip of the mesa and extending 2.75 miles to the northeast and 8 miles to the southwest, the line would encompass seven of the larger, more important ruins in the district, beginning with Awatovi at the southwest end and finishing at Lululongturque at the northeast. All but two of these Hopi ruins now lie in the land known as the Jeddito Island, which the U.S. government has given to the Navajos.

Access to the area is limited to those who are accompanied by a licensed guide, because the slopes of Antelope Mesa are strewn with ancient pottery fragments exposed to the elements for centuries, sherds that have washed down from these abandoned settlements and become a temptation to pot hunters. Along the terrace are many coal mine dumps, vestiges of locations where fuel was dug by the ancients for warmth, cooking, and pottery firing.

The road crosses Jeddito Wash and disappears over the top of Robert's Mesa as it follows not only the old Anasazi trade and migration trails, established centuries ago, but also a portion of the route of the Southern Tewa movement out of the Rio Grande. These long, partially forgotten routes connected Hopi settlements with those of Zuni, Acoma, and the Rio Grande pueblos. One can also visualize old routes to the north through the Chaco and Mesa Verde areas, or connecting the settlements of Betatakin, Keet Siel, and countless others that are now incorporated in various national monuments such as Navajo, Canyon de Chelly, and Hovenweep.

To the southwest, the path of the old trade route is now a rough dirt road leading to Navajo family camps. Along this route passed a thriving trade in turquoise, exotic birds, skins, and some pottery and copper bells. One trail that led to the Pacific Coast and its sea shells is marked by Jeddito wares as far as California. (Similar evidence has been located in other distant settlements on the Colorado Plateau.)

The women of the Jeddito pueblos were skilled potters. They produced varied types of pottery, from pre-Jeddito styles through Sikyatki, styles that were in vogue after most of the Jeddito pueblos were abandoned.[31] Highly developed Anasazi black-on-white or black-on-gray work resembled some wares made at Jeddito, except that the Hopi clays were fired in an oxidizing atmosphere that brought them to a golden yellow or orange color, making them attractive as trade items.

According to anthropologist Clara Lee Tanner, Jeddito black-on-yellow reflects some of the characteristics of the last examples of black-on-white pottery and the artistic accomplishments of contemporary polychromes. The work changed over time:

> ...Although the variety of design is great, scrolls, frets, and wing motifs are prominent, but much subdued in size and vigor. On jar exteriors, heavy broad bands contain the more discreet and simpler geometric patterns. Some of these earlier black-on-yellow pieces demonstrate fine drawing, or, at least, smaller and well-executed geometrics. In some of the later pieces of this ware shapes changed, that is, bowls may have outcurved rims and there are many poorly or more simply executed geometric designs and quite a few life motifs, such as humans (including masked figures), rabbits, birds, and others. Some of the last of the prehistoric black-on-yellow ware drawing was very degenerate.[32]

Awatovi, the most important archaeological site in the area, is located on top of the southwestern edge of Antelope Mesa not too distant from Keams Canyon. Access to it is by deeply rutted dirt road that has many dead end offshoots. Along the road the vegetation seems to grow more lush than either to the east or the far west end of the mesa. The sagebrush and grasses are greener, and the junipers bushier, with a more pungent odor and larger and more abundant berries. In season the wildflowers appear more colorful and numerous. For the ancient people coming from the arid lands of the south and west, this area would provide almost ideal living conditions.

During prehistoric times, when the migrations occurred, the vegetation was even more lush and the water more plentiful than it is today, making it a desirable place to settle.

It is impossible to miss the site. The ground nearby is quite barren, and protective barbed wire barriers surround it. On entering the ruin, the visitor sets foot on a mosaic of pottery sherds. Sherds, literally thousands of them, extend in every direction and are especially numerous close to the gently sloping mesa edge and extending over it (fig. 2.41). So dramatic is this sight that David Laird, formerly the Director of the University of Arizona Library, described it this way: "Wat Smith once told me that from the archaeologist's point of view, a site such as Awatovi made it look as if all the inhabitants who ever lived there had done nothing but make pots and break them up."[33]

The remains of ancient coal mines are impressive. Most are located southwest of the Western Mound on the terrace below the ruin. The area between the coal seams and the village is dotted with piles of red

Fig. 2.41. A photograph of excavations, probably in the west mound at Awatovi, site of a residential area ruin where most of the pottery was located. No. 94-1440, NAA-SI.

or white ash, white predominating, marking pottery firing locations. This fact was established at the Jeddito ruin to the north where one of the excavated ash mounds contained a nest of fired pottery that had never been removed. (More on this is in John Hack's discussion in the *Papers of the Peabody Museum of American Archaeology and Ethnology*, published by Harvard University.) The Awatovi mines are the largest in the Jeddito Wash group, contributing thirty thousand tons of coal to the total of one hundred thousand tons mined in prehistoric times. Little remains of the pueblo structures. A few excavated walls are still in place, most of which have been at least partially backfilled. If contemporary Hopis had their way, the entire area would have remained covered, leaving only the sherds to view.

Awatovi is the largest ruin in the Jeddito Valley group, occupying a position on a major trade route, which certainly brought it prosperity. The trash heaps and old rooms reveal that prior to European occupation, all the many types of pottery produced in the area, including those of the Jeddito series (fig. 2.42), had been made here. A good summary of Awatovi's history and pottery is given by John Otis Brew in his article for the *Handbook of North American Indians*, Volume 9, published by the Smithsonian Institution, a crucial reference for all those interested in the history of the Southwest.

A small exploration party seeking riches made the first Spanish contact with the Hopi in this area in late July 1540. The explorers passed hurriedly on their way, intent on finding the wealth they imagined existed just over the horizon. Other parties soon followed, but again the Europeans did not tarry.

Not until 20 August 1629 was a permanent white settlement at Awatovi attempted. Two Franciscan fathers, Francisco de Porras and Andres Gutierrez, along with a lay brother and twelve soldiers completed the dry, tiring trek from Zuni and moved in without invitation. The date coincided with the feast day of San Bernardo, and thus the new mission was named San Bernardo de Aguatubi; it remained to the Hopi simply Awatovi. Were it not for a reported miracle performed by Father Porras, he and his entourage might not have enjoyed a long stay. Shortly after their arrival, Father Porras is reported to have

Fig. 2.42. *Jeddito ware, ca. 1250–1700.* **A.** *The shape and color of this bowl are characteristic of crudely painted early Jeddito decoration. The design on the outside is a stylized snake so often found on Pueblo pottery. It is 2³/4 in. by 6 in.* No. 9137, DMNH. **B.** *Corrugating, a method of decorating damp plastic pottery by impressing coils with fingernails or small sticks, was used by prehistoric Indian potters. This method is not common among the Nampeyo potters. The deep vessel was started in a form, which left its mark on the base. 5 in. by 5¹/2 in.* No. 2439, CSFAC. **C.** *A fine example of a necked jar, from the Kayenta (northern) branch of the Jeddito area. 6¹/2 by 7¹/2 in.* No. 4307, CSFAC.

miraculously restored the sight of an Awatovi boy. This so impressed a large number of the Awatovi people that they ceased their hostility and asked for baptism. The Spaniards thus gained a position of trust and respect, one that they were unable to achieve in other Hopi villages or among the pueblos in the New Mexico territory. But unfortunately it did not last long; within four years Father Porras was dead, apparently poisoned. Taking advantage of their acceptance by the natives while it lasted, the Spaniards made drastic changes in the Indian way of life. The changes even extended to the way pottery was made: the Spanish introduced new shapes and additional uses of pottery and changed the style of decoration as well as firing methods.

The early Hopis used local coal mainly for heating, but it was also used in rather large quantities by the potters. Possibly, the padres deemed soft coal too dirty and the high sulfur smoke unpleasant or unhealthy. Dung substitutes allowed the Indians to devote more of their labor to church projects. The use of coal by the Hopi potters continued, but on a gradually diminishing basis, and extended to other Hopi villages through the time of Nampeyo.

Pottery produced during Spanish occupation (ca. 1625–1740) is known as San Bernardo ware and was halfheartedly imitated in limited quantity by outlying Hopi potters (fig. 2.43—see p. XII). As less efficient fuels were substituted for coal, the quality of San Bernardo ceramics deteriorated. Lower firing temperatures impaired the capacity of the painted decoration to adhere to the ceramic material and lowered product strength. It became more difficult to obtain complete oxidation of the transition (coloring) oxides, especially those of iron unless glass was formed to bond the body elements together. Dull and less interesting body and decoration colors resulted, ones that were not well fused and had poor abrasion resistance.

The Awatovi clergy introduced contemporary Spanish decoration, a stilted copy of European designs that lacked imagination. Mass production was encouraged. The use of pottery in burial ceremonies was discouraged, again stifling the creativity of the potter. Ruth Bunzel named this product "Mission" rather than "San Bernardo Polychrome."

> This ware, which is found on or near the surface at Awatobi, associated with articles of Spanish manufacture, is inferior to the preceding product of Sikyatki and Awatobi. The vessels are thick and heavy, the paste soft. The ground color is yellow or buff, with decorations in black and red crudely executed. The beautiful and elaborate designs of the earlier designs have given way to simpler patterns with an increase of geometric forms [similar to those of contemporary Spanish tile and building decorating motifs]. Material of this period is very slight in quantity.[34]

The Peabody Museum of Harvard University has a large, quality collection of prehistoric and historic Hopi pottery, some on display but most of it stored in the converted cyclotron building nearby. The collection includes the unique Hemenway-Keam collection, originally gathered throughout the reservation, as well as what was recovered by the Harvard archaeologists who excavated at Awatovi and its environs from 1935 to 1939.

The variety of shapes of pottery is impressive. Plates, soup bowls, pitchers, lamps, ring-based vessels, candleholders, roof tiles, and other utilitarian items were not known to the Hopis before Spanish occupation. These items were produced for the mission and the presumed enlargement of the Christian Indian population. All have been thoroughly studied and chronicled by Edwin Wade and Lea McChesney in their 1981 publication *Hopi Historic Ceramics* (see References).

The initial occupation of Awatovi took place fifty-one years prior to the Pueblo Revolt. From the start, the miracle of Father Porras posed a threat to the control and way of life of the Hopi religious leaders who were accused of plotting his death. According to Benavides: "It is said that they poisoned him on June 23rd, 1633."[35] This was just two months short of the fourth anniversary of his arrival at the pueblo. No additional records have been found to verify this assertion.

The thirty-seven years of Spanish occupation following the death of Father Porras were difficult for both Indians and clergy. Two outpost missions were established at Shungopovi on Second Mesa and at Oraibi on Third Mesa. These missions were not as effective as those at Awatovi, and their footing was never very firm. In addition, two *visitas* (church facilities having no resident priests) were established, the one on First Mesa at Walpi was served from Awatovi. The other visita on Second Mesa at Mishongnovi was served from Shungopovi.

Rivalries between Spanish civil, military, and church authorities existed in both the Rio Grande area of New Mexico and in Hopi country. The Indians were the ones most hurt by these frictions. Each power vied with the other both to extract tribute from the Indians and to force allegiance to its separate faction. Natives were whipped and coerced by cruel methods to dress like monks and carry large crosses for hours at a time. They were required to cut huge logs from the mountain forests and drag them from 80 to 115 miles across hot, arid land and then haul them up the steep mesa sides for Spanish buildings.

In 1680, at the appointed time, the Hopis joined the Pueblo Revolt. While success came in the Rio Grande area within a short time, it was immediate and more final at Hopi. Priests and other Spaniards were eliminated in short order. The Spanish returned in 1692 to reestablish colonies throughout New Mexico Territory, but not at Hopi. According to Brew, "the struggle, lost by the Christian God in Tusayán in 1680, stayed lost. The *kachinas* won then and [they] hold the field today. From that time on, Spaniards appeared on the Hopi mesas only as unwelcome visitors, except at Awatovi. And Awatovi did not live long enough to enjoy the reunion."[36]

The Hopis of Awatovi continued to live at the pueblo, but in contrast to their neighbors they retained some Christian ways. In addition to Christian burials, the Peabody expeditions uncovered evidence that not all the Spanish structures were razed. It was evident that the Indians used the rectory for everyday living purposes.

Although rebellion, to all intents and purposes, ended in 1692, it was not until 28 May 1700 that the Spanish Catholic church attempted a return to Awatovi and the Hopi mesas to reestablish its missions and visitas. Father Juan de Garacoechea visited Awatovi and decided that the town was ready to accept the return of the Catholic church. At the same time, he endeavored to proceed to other Hopi settlements but was discouraged from doing so by a large group of hostile Indians. He was forced to return to Zuni to gather a party for the resettlement of Awatovi.

Awatovi was destroyed by an internecine clash, precipitated by the Spanish reentry. The sacking of the village occurred eight months after Father Garacoechea's reconnoiter; undoubtedly the hope was to discourage any thought of Spanish return. The version of the demise of Awatovi that we include here is one J. W. Fewkes recorded as related to him by Alexander Stephen.[37]

The chief of Awatovi was a man named Ta-po-lo; he realized that the return of the Spanish meant the loss of his position and hence his control over the people. Equally important to his neighbors in the nearby villages was the fact that Spanish control, once reestablished at Awatovi, would spread to their villages, destroy their religion and their way of life, and return them to hated ways. With encouragement from those pueblos who shared his views, the chief decided to punish the people of Awatovi and remove the threat of the Spanish once again.

Conspiring with friendly pueblos, especially the pueblo of Mishongnovi, he selected a time—the Powamu or Bean Dance when the men of Awatovi would be in their kivas. Ta-po-lo arranged for his accomplices to arrive in the night and enter the village through an east gate that was to be left open. Upon their arrival, they raced to the kivas, where they pulled up the ladders, shot arrows, and dumped burning wood and straw onto the mass of humanity below. They threw dried chile (the people of Awatovi were said to be famous for their chile) on the flames to torture those caught in the fires by blinding them and inflaming their lungs. Following the annihilation of the men, they dragged women and children to a mound, called Mastcomo, and began to slaughter the women. Eventually, by appeals to mercy and reason, they spared the lives of some of the females, particularly those who held ceremonial offices. Today's visitors who know of the demise of the settlement often have eerie sensations of treading on the spirits of murdered victims as they walk about the ruin.

Archaeological investigations, begun by Keam and followed up by Fewkes and the Peabody teams, revealed beyond any doubt that the objective of the Awatovi raiders had not been plunder, but the complete destruction of the pueblo and annihilation of its population. This scenario would account for the survival of the treasure trove of pottery, artifacts, and art which were found at the site of the holocaust.

The kiva mural art uncovered here is second to none in the Southwest. The number and variety of paintings on ceremonial chamber walls never cease to impress viewers. Complex designs were later covered by others, supposedly either to prevent their exposure to the uninitiated or to prepare for the next ceremony. Unfortunately, these murals were not brought to light until after Nampeyo's sight had deteriorated, or else surely the world would have received more inspired designs from her. Some of her descendants, however, have used adaptations of the Awatovi motifs for their paintings, pottery decorations, and carvings.

Unexpected Inspiration

Occasionally, one locates Nampeyo pottery pieces whose inspirational sources are difficult to identify. In most instances it is the decorative design which is unusual or which seems out of place. Designs and shapes sometimes appear to have originated from sources far beyond Nampeyo's reach.

The Ruins of Four Mile Area (ca. 1275–1400)

At the University of Oslo's Ethnographic Museum there are a significant number of Nampeyo designs that are similar to Four Mile motifs. The likenesses raise the question of how ancient pottery designs, far removed from where Nampeyo lived and worked, came to her attention.

The northwest border of the Four Mile area, including the ruins at Pinedale, St. Johns, Springerville, and Snowflake, is located nearly seventy miles due south of Keams Canyon. Ceramics recovered from this area are not particularly noted for uniqueness of shape or quality of fabrication, but the decoration is distinct. A majority of the specimens are decorated with black designs on a red background outlined in white (fig. 2.44) and painted with geometric designs in the interiors with biomorphic forms, such as birds, at times emerging from these backgrounds.

The Oslo examples of Nampeyo's Four Mile designs are documented as having been made between November 1903 and February 1904. A pedestaled bowl decorated in the same style is in the collection of the Philbrook Art Center of Tulsa, Oklahoma. Donated by Clark Field, it is poorly documented (as are many items in his collections),

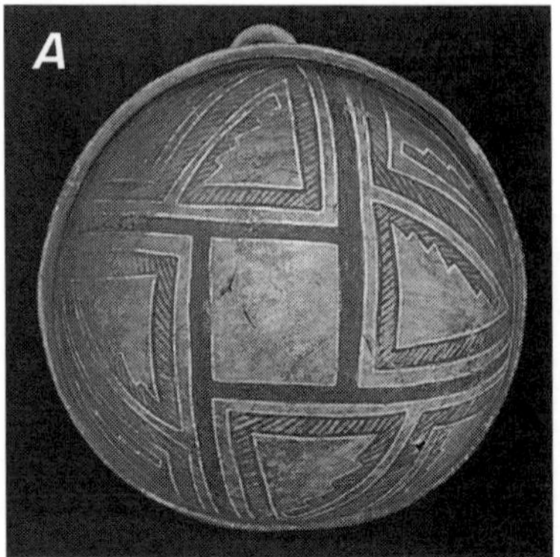

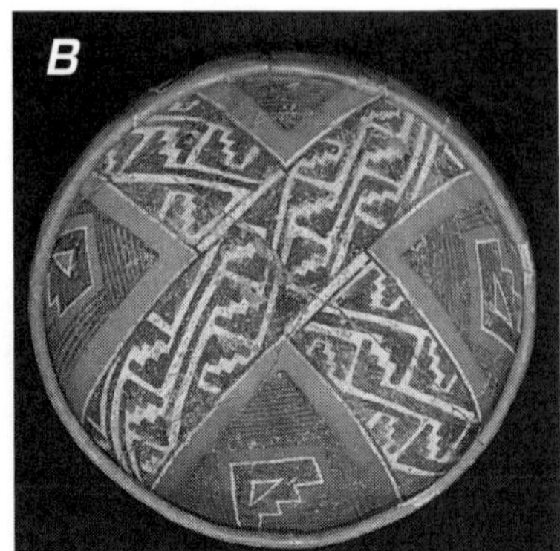

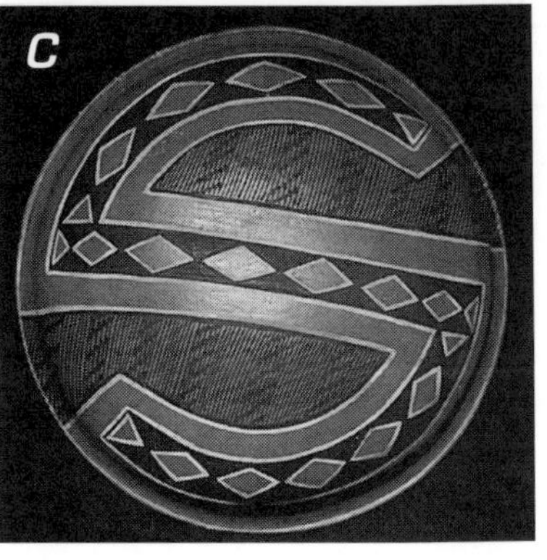

Fig. 2.44. Decoration of Four Mile area ware (ca. 1300–1400) compared to decoration by Nampeyo. **A.** St. John's Polychrome bowl (ca. 1225–1300). Designs such as this one enclosed by parallel lines are often seen in Nampeyo's work. Note the lug for hanging, a feature at times incorporated into modern bowls. 5 in. by 9¹/₂ in. No. 8098R, DMNH. **B.** Pinedale Polychrome (ca. 1275–1350), Cibola Branch. This widely used "step" design is cleverly emphasized to give a negative design impression. 3¹/₂ in. by 8 in. No. 36169, CSFAC. **C.** A Nampeyo bowl, collected by Solberg in 1903–1904. The resemblance of some of Nampeyo's work to the prehistoric Four Mile decorating style is striking. 4¹/₂ in. by 9¹/₂ in. No. 13,607, EMOs.

so we know only that it was made by Nampeyo and purchased in 1938. At this time Nampeyo's vision was fading, so perhaps Annie or another family member was the decorator. Fannie claimed no knowledge of such a design. The bowl may well have been purchased from either a dealer or a collector in 1938 who did not provide Field with proper provenance.

Four Mile Ruin and other ruins in the area were hurriedly sampled by Fewkes in 1897. Fewkes claimed to have first met Nampeyo two years earlier during excavations at Sikyatki and to have had little contact with her after that. It is doubtful that the prototype specimens were provided to Nampeyo by Fewkes, for had they been, he would almost certainly have taken credit. Neither Keam, Stephen, nor Polacca are recorded as ever having dug in the area. No similar specimens were found in the Keam collections, and the likelihood that Lesou would have provided them seems too remote for him to have paid it much attention.

How then did Nampeyo obtain the models from which she worked? Archaeologist Watson Smith provides one plausible answer: The prototypes may have come to Nampeyo from Four Mile via Awatovi. Four Mile pieces were traded by the people of Awatovi before the arrival of the Spanish and remained there until excavated by either Keam, Polacca, Stephen, or the Peabody expeditions.[38] The possibility exists that Nampeyo obtained an infinite number of other design inspirations from pottery imported into Awatovi from a variety of prehistoric native peoples.

Quapaw, The "Downstream Sioux"

Nathaniel Dale, born in 1838 in a cabin near the site of the present Quapaw Baths, located on Bath House Row, Hot Springs, Arkansas, recalled that in his youth he had noticed a large cave extending into Hot Springs Mountain. He said it gushed steaming mineral water and oozed hot mud. Returning to his birthplace later in his life, he noted that the entrance had become covered; he also found it increasingly difficult to convince people that the cave had ever existed.

In addition to the cavern, Dale remembered seeing bands of Indians including Quapaw, Crow, Blackfoot, and Choctaws peacefully sharing baths and mud treatments, despite the possibility that two or more of the groups might have been at war at the time. The spring area was neutral territory, for troublemakers from all tribes were immediately expelled. All shared the healing waters and the invigorating hot mud plasters, and all had unmolested access to the area.[39]

In 1921 a resident of Hot Springs planned a bath house at the posh spa resort on the combined sites of the old, run-down Magnesia and Horse Shoe bath enclosures. He named the new structure the Quapaw Bath House. During the blasting for the foundation, the ground unexpectedly collapsed, exposing a large gaping hole. The cavern mentioned in Dale's stories was exposed. Much of the entrance required back filling to provide a firm foundation for the new structure, but a large chamber at the end of the cave was carefully preserved and its gushing hot (143°F) spring water was channeled with the runoff from other springs to a heat exchanger and then distributed to all the bath houses at a lower, more tolerable temperature.

Placed in various natural stone niches in the walls of Dale's cavern were offerings that previous Indian bathers had left as gifts of appreciation for the wondrous health-giving waters. Outstanding among these were four figurines that came to be known as the "Quapaw Figures." They probably received this name, not from the people who fashioned them, but from the bath house under which they were found. This story is provided in a pamphlet entitled *Legend of the Quapaw Baths*, published for Hot Springs National Park Service in 1984, perhaps as a promotional tool. Barbara Kramer claims that "they were copies of effigies like those made at Tesuque Pueblo in New Mexico."[40]

In any case, the hot springs owner wanted to display the figures in his new structure along with other items of interest. The supposition is that he obtained the names of Nampeyo and Tom Pavatea, who would act as her agent, from the Indian artifact dealer, a Mr. Crossoen, who operated an Indian curio establishment in Hot Springs at that time.

Four figures were ordered from Nampeyo, who completed and shipped them from Polacca, Arizona, in April 1922 (fig. 2.45). They were placed on display in the bath, which was completed in 1922. The hot springs sent word to First Mesa that the pieces were "indeed very interesting, and have caused considerable attention at the Quapaw Baths." The original figurines were said to have been donated either to the Department of the Interior or the National Park Service, but our efforts to locate them were unsuccessful.

Fig. 2.45. *Quapaw figures surround a drawing of the Quapaw Bath House in Hot Springs, Arkansas. They are the only documented large figurines made by Nampeyo. They probably were not decorated by the potter, but perhaps by a daughter. Other figures sold for tourist trade were not as large or as well executed. The Quapaw figures vary in height from 8³/₈ in. to 9⁵/₈ in. and were made in 1922.* Private collection.

✚ We have endeavored to explain how Nampeyo's genius was fed from a multitude of sources. These included the ancient people of the pueblos of the Rio Grande area, Payupki, Awatovi, the Four Mile area, the Navajo, those around her, those who purchased from her, and possibly from such remote sources as the Hohokam culture.

In turn she strongly influenced many others around her. She inspired competition, urging her daughters to become master potters; and working through or with her daughters, she inspired her grandchildren, many of whom are also now recognized as master craftspersons. Great-grandchildren have joined the ranks of the pottery artists whose styles duplicate hers. Moreover, other artists of all backgrounds have been inspired by her work, some of which has even been used as main elements or as background subjects in their own creations (fig. 2.46—see p. XII). Nampeyo was one of the first Native American artists to bring long overdue attention and recognition to Native American pottery and design as a true art form. Her work will undoubtedly continue to inspire artists from a wide range of backgrounds in the future.

Pottery Making, Nampeyo Family Style

C H A P T E R   3

Making a pot has a religious significance for me. When I go to get
my clay, I always leave a little something for the earth when I go
there. A cracker, cheese, even beer. The earth is good to me—it
lets me take the clay. There is a ritual to it—giving something
back as you take something away. If I didn't do this, I don't think
my pots would be any good.

Sharon Reyna, as quoted by Nancy Wood in Taos Pueblo

A Visit to Grandmother

Nampeyo's great-granddaughter Vernida Polacca has left one of the most revealing reports of how the art of making pottery has been transmitted from one generation to another among family members. Vernida's memories of watching her grandmother Fannie at work one afternoon were published in an anthology in 1972 by the Bureau of Indian Affairs. The narrative describes the intense devotion and concentration that these potters brought to their task. It also exemplifies the impact that Nampeyo and her daughters had on their descendants.

One summer afternoon when I went to visit Grandmother, she was busy with her pottery. She was sitting on the floor on her green shawl, with her pottery all around her. In her hand was a small bowl which she was polishing. I sat beside Grandmother to watch her smooth and polish the pottery. To smooth out the rough edges she used a Choregirl. Then, dampening the pottery, she rubbed it with a small, smooth stone until it shown. Her hands at times would move swiftly and then slow down.

While working she sometimes hummed a song to herself. As I was sitting beside Grandmother, she didn't even glance at me for a long time because she was concentrating on her pottery. After polishing the pottery she was then ready to paint her designs. The different kinds of designs mean different things to the Tewa tribe. One of the many she painted represented a bird flying in the rain. The light and dark brown colors of the designs blended harmoniously with the tannish background.

While painting she frequently dipped her small yucca brush into the paint, which was inside of a stone which was broken in half. More concentration was needed in painting than in polishing. Her hands moved very slowly. Grandmother was so quiet that one would not know that she was still working.

After completing the painting, she glanced up at me over her eyeglasses and asked, "When did you come?" I said, "I came a long time ago." Then we both laughed and sat there on the floor chatting for a few minutes. She then arose and put her pottery on her shelf where it would remain until she was ready to bake it.

Soon afterward I left for home. As I was walking down the mesa, I was thinking how great it was to have a grandmother like her. Being around her makes me proud to have such a wonderful person to be with and to talk to.[1]

Traditions of the Hopi hold that the people of different population areas, such as each mesa, were delegated to make different crafts. For example, coiled baskets are made "only" on Second Mesa and wicker baskets "only" on Third Mesa. The domains are often jealously guarded, as revealed by Fred Kabotie. In 1939 Kabotie encountered serious opposition to a course in textile weaving that he had set up as part of an art program for the Oraibi High School. "I began getting a lot of criticism from some of the Hopis, especially at Hotevilla, that we shouldn't be teaching such things....'Weaving should not be taught in high school,' the chief from Hotevilla argued. 'Boys from the other villages will learn our skills; and our weavers will no longer be able to sell ceremonial pieces to other Hopis.'" In this same vein, the residents of First Mesa consider pottery making at Hopi to lie exclusively within their domain.[2]

Today, pottery production on the Hopi Reservation is almost entirely limited to people who either lived on or below First Mesa or their close relatives, who through marriage, employment opportunities, or other pertinent reasons have been obliged to move from that area. (The exceptions are a few potters on Third Mesa.) This limited group has carried on its pottery production for a great many generations. They have defended their domain by the practice of witchcraft and, on occasion, by force.[3] Some potters of First Mesa readily admit to the practice of witchcraft to defend their "rights," and their use of force is on record in the July 1971 minutes of the Hopi Tribal Council. The belief that pottery making on the reservation should be limited to First Mesa people and their descendants is so strong that the inhabitants endeavored to have the Tribal Council issue an edict restricting pottery making to their area.

A few pottery pieces made by the residents of Third Mesa may be found on the market. These are either utilitarian wares or pieces decorated with designs alien to those applied on First Mesa. But pottery from Third Mesa is not common, and on Second Mesa the ceramic tradition has been entirely lost (fig. 3.1).

The Clay

First Mesa people usually do not divulge clay deposit locations to nonresidents. Should a large quantity of clay be removed from what they consider their private property, potters may request part of the excavated material be returned to them.[4]

Fig. 3.1. The Hopi woman on the right coils clay into a large utilitarian vessel in Oraibi, Arizona. This undated photograph was probably taken during the latter part of the nineteenth century. From a stereoscope photo, No. V 23189 Keystone View Co., Meadville, Pennsylvania. Edward I. Comins Jr. Collection.

Fig. 3.2. An abandoned clay mine located on a side face of Antelope Mesa. This outcropping is characteristic of many on the sides of the Hopi mesas. The gray clay bed (A-B) is separated from the lower yellow clay bed (B-C) by a layer of weathered sandstone (D), which reduces its plasticity and complicates the process of clay preparation. As the clay is removed, the area of the unsupported rock (E) expands, increasing the danger of cliff collapse.

Different varieties of high-quality, pottery-forming clay may be found on the Hopi Reservation. The most commonly used clay, and most plentiful, is gray-colored in its natural state and usually requires little or no tempering with sand or ground sherds. Neither does it require soluble salt removal as do the clays found on other Indian lands, such as at Acoma. A clay less abundant but more available to the potter is commonly called yellow clay (*sikyatska*) by the Hopi. It occurs in more restricted and pinched-out strata below the gray clay and contains more impurities. The clays are separated by a thin layer of degraded sandstone (fig. 3.2).

For a very long time, rainwater, an excellent solvent, has been falling on the mesa tops, percolating down through the porous Mesa Verde sandstone until it reaches the impermeable Mancos shales and then seeps slowly outward toward the mesa edge, carrying with it all the dissolved material. The fine silts and iron-containing compounds responsible for the clay colors are the most readily dissolved, and they are redeposited between the shale and the sandstone. Thus the upper gray clay strata is more leached of iron than the bottom yellow strata.

When fired, the yellow clay (in its pure form also called a limonite) changes to an orange or brick-red color. Not only can it be utilized to produce red-bodied ware, but it is commonly diluted and used as a slip or paint over which other colors may be added. Redware forms, made entirely from the yellow clay, are being produced in decreasing quantities as the clay becomes less abundant, contains more impurities, and is harder to work.[5]

Remnants of a gray and yellow clay deposit used by First Mesa potters of the past, possibly including Nampeyo, may be observed as one begins the final ascent to the First Mesa villages from the Gap. On the right, restricting access to tunnels and excavated caves in the cliff, is a stone barrier that seals off a dangerous area where collapses in the walls have resulted in fatalities. Mining clay has always been a hazardous occupation for the potter. The mother of famous potter Garnet Pavatea lost her life as the result of a cave-in, as did Mabel Dashee's mother. Elsie Clews Parsons described a fatal wall collapse that trapped a woman who died shortly before a rescue party reached her.

Harder to find is a bright white clay (kaolin), obtained with some difficulty from First and Badger Mesas. Seldom used to form vessels, the white clay most often finds application as a slip, a decorative paint, or a whitewash material. Barbara Freire-Marreco noted that in the early years of the twentieth century, deposits of pure kaolin were mined approximately one-half mile east of the Gap. Dextra Quotskuyva remembers as a child being shown a deposit of white clay by Nampeyo while she was visiting Wepo Gardens (Sand Hills Ranch). From it she obtained white body and slip materials. Because of its scarcity, few potters use this commodity now, and those who do often obtain it in trade or by purchase.

Four clay materials employed by Nampeyo (who was known to have used as many as five clays in one vessel) were described by Walter Hough in 1915 as "*hisat chuoka,* or ancient clay, white, unctuous and fragrant, to which the ancient Sikyatki potters owed the perfection of their ware; the reddish clay, *siwa chuoka,* also from Sikyatki; the hard, iron-stained clay, *choku chuoka;* and white clay with which vessels are coated and finished for decoration, coming from about twelve miles southeast of Walpi."[6] Hisat chuoka is probably the gray clay used by contemporary potters. Clay-and-temper raw materials were formerly dug at the Gap. Because of the known danger, children were not allowed to participate in digging expeditions there. As families moved from First Mesa, they sought more convenient deposits.

For all of their adult lives, until health fails, the older potters have mined their own clay and become expert judges of deposit quality. Like their ancestors, traditionalists offer prayers of thanks and gifts of cornmeal when they take clay for their work. But ceremonial rites are slowly disappearing. Formerly, they transported clay over the rough terrain in sacks slung over their backs or on pack animals. Now they use four-wheel-drive trucks. Clay digging on the reservation has also undergone change. Many potters now purchase clay from Indian vendors who dig clay for a living, or they occasionally buy it from a crafts shop. The clay purchased from Indian vendors is true reservation clay, which is moistened, bagged in plastic, and sold in a ready-to-use condition. Most of it comes from Antelope Mesa, possibly from the same areas used by the ancients of Jeddito Wash.

Pottery clays from some deposits located on Antelope Mesa are easily carved. Artists who specialize in the carved form of decoration prize these clays for their workability. Although the clays are chemically the same as other deposits, they have weathered differently, have a finer grain, and are remarkably free of harsh, lumpy impurities that interfere with carving.

Seldom does an orthodox potter dig more clay than is needed for immediate purposes. Storing clay for the future in excessive amounts is subject to criticism. Digging is restricted to the Hopi and Tewa people, who may dig where they choose. In 1986 a Bahana (white person), whom the Nampeyo family requested not be identified by name, was legally digging clay because he had had his "hair washed"—a phrase indicating that he had been adopted by a Hopi family and would thus have access to all their resources. His reproductions of old Hopi pottery, usually ancient Sikyatki, are striking. Although resented by many as encroaching on native rights, he has inspired some potters to better efforts through beautifully executed pieces.

All clays are prepared in a similar manner. They must be broken into small pieces and dried well, similar to Rio Grande practices. Further steps of preparation may vary slightly among potters. In former times the clay was crushed and screened while still dry, and small impurities were removed by hand, then moistened and kneaded. Experienced potters say that they can determine clay quality by feeling and tasting it. After the lumps of dried clay are broken into small pieces, they are covered with water, stirred, and squeezed until they disintegrate; they are cleaned of grit at the same time. If required, a fine temper is added and blended before a mass is forced through a sieve. Every meticulous potter follows the more tedious process of straining the "slurry" through cloth. The wet mixture is then spread on canvas or heavy cloth to rid it partially of moisture before it is again kneaded.

Hough described clay being worked on a stone, transferred to a board, and set in the sun to dry to a predetermined consistency, a procedure followed by Nampeyo (fig. 2.19).[7] With the exception of modifications introduced by the use of plastic sheets and containers, today's drying, soaking, straining, kneading, dewatering, and storing processes are basically the same as those of a half century ago. When the clay is a proper consistency, it is stored in plastic bags and sealed to retain the correct moisture content over relatively long periods of time. The availability of thick-walled, flexible plastic containers makes it possible to store larger batches of the clay. Formerly, processed clay was retained in a dry lump condition. Smaller quantities were prepared and kept in pails covered with damp cloths. Nampeyo noted that her work was superior because "of burying the clay in moist sand for a long time, perhaps two moons, which caused something in the clay to rot."[8]

Potters from many pueblos agree that aging clay after mixing keeps it moist and improves quality and plasticity. It has long been recognized that aging moist clays by storing them in damp treatment cellars for periods ranging from a few months to a year appears to improve their workability. H. Ries has suggested that aging is the result of bacterial action.[9]

Tempers

Temper is an inert material that when added to clay modifies its plasticity, makes it more pliable, and—most important—reduces its drying and firing shrinkages to minimize cracking. In Nampeyo's youth, clay was tempered with sand or finely pulverized pottery sherds. Temper made from fired ceramic objects, such as sherds, is known as "grog." In either instance the material was well kneaded into the mass during the mixing process, sometimes by the feet.

Freire-Marreco noted that the temper then employed was "apparently quartz sand with mica" and made no reference to the use of ground sherds. In the early 1920s Edward S. Curtis found "that dried clay was ground on mealing stones and after it has soaked in water, a quantity of pulverized sandstone or pot shards is mixed with it. Ancient decorated shards are preferred for this purpose, fragments of cooking pots not being used. The mass is thoroughly kneaded." Frank Applegate observed in 1922 that potters were adding too much sand to overcome cracking during drying. The traders refused this pottery since 75 percent of it cracked in shipping, despite careful packing. Applegate claimed to have located a deposit for the potters requiring no temper, which produced high-quality ware.[10]

Presently, most Hopi clays used by potters are tempered by nature, and they give the artisans the ability to produce ware up to eight inches in diameter without the use of additives. To form larger-sized pieces, they add temper, increasing the amount with the size piece. The thin sandstone layer that separates the gray from the yellow clay renders a satisfactory temper (fig. 3.2).

Materials for painting Hopi pottery may be either organic or inorganic in nature. Most pottery is decorated with a combination of both, the organics for black and brown and inorganics for other hues such as orange or red.

Organic coloring materials are limited to extracts of sap from closely related plants that grow in abundance in the Southwest—

Decorative Raw Materials specifically, the Rocky Mountain beeweed (*Cleome serrulata*), also known as *guaco,* and tansy mustard (*Descurainia spp* or *Descurainia pinnata*).[11] Most Hopi potters can use either plant interchangeably. Each is prepared in a similar manner, and most agree that it is almost impossible to tell the two apart after the pottery is finished. Mustard is most commonly used at Hopi due to its native abundance. Succulent leaves of the mustard plant are harvested in spring or early summer and boiled until the fluid is reduced to the consistency of a thick sap. This liquid is carefully strained, dried, and broken into small cakes that are individually wrapped in aluminum foil and set aside to age for a year or more. Insufficiently aged cakes produce weak colors. Following suitable aging, the potter prepares a slurry of the extract and finely ground hematite suspended in rain or distilled water for use as paint. Tap water or water that has been treated causes the paint to chip off after the pottery has been fired. The slurry is formed by breaking a small amount of the plant preparation into the hollow of a flat stone palette, adding the correct amount of water, and grinding with a small hematite stone pestle known as a *toho.*

The toho must be softer than the hematite mortar so that it will gradually deteriorate into small, pigmenting hematite particles but hard enough to resist too rapid wear. The potter tests a prospective toho by rubbing it over the surface of a flat sandstone. It must leave a mark of the proper color. A dark brown streak indicates that the toho is too soft, while light or invisible streaks indicate that it is too hard and will not add color to the pigment. Satisfactory hematite is difficult to locate; thus these essential pestles (and the palettes) become prized family possessions (fig. 3.3).

Grinding hastens both the dissolving of the plant extract and the suspension of the small hematite particles abraded from the pestle. As the slurry is mixed, its viscosity is tested by finger, and either more extract or water is added as needed. To ensure color strength on the finished ware, grinding continues until the mixture reaches a dark appearance.

The use of guaco has been noted many times in the literature, as well as the use of similarly prepared beeweed extracts by both pre-historic and historic Tewa of the Rio Grande area; this observation may have led to the false conclusion that the technology was intro-duced to the Hopis by the incoming Tewa about 1700. Hopi pottery made long before the arrival of the Tewa was decorated with the same materials; thus the technology is probably common to all descendants of the Anasazi.[12]

Colors such as white, red, orange, and yellow are produced using different, finely divided clays that have been suspended in water. Raw clays are ground with water on a separate, relatively iron-free stone, a process that minimizes contaminating the suspensions with mate-rials affecting the final color. Slips containing yellow clay will produce a red color when fired. A different red is obtained from a clay bought from the Navajo, which they call *chee*.[13]

A variety of tints can be formed by superimposing slips of differ-ing colors over the pottery or by using different firing conditions. For example, slips of gray clay can be painted over white or red back-grounds to form pleasing shades of yellow or orange. Experimental

Fig. 3.3. Grinding stones used to pre-pare decorative color slips. Termed "painting stones" by the potters, they are particularly treasured. These stones were used by Nampeyo and appear in many old photographs of her. The light-colored stone in the lower left corner is free of iron and is used to make light-colored decorative slips. Dark-colored tansy mustard or beeweed paints are prepared on the blackened slab. Fannie Nampeyo Polacca is testing the viscos-ity of a hematite suspension on the latter stone to determine its readiness for painting.

black pottery has been produced by reduction firing of slips made of different clays, some acquired from the Havasupai of Grand Canyon.

Native Americans, perhaps the artists in particular, utilize and work with the environment more than some other North American cultures. Their vision allows them to convert into efficient tools items normally overlooked or considered trash. Bits of wood, yucca stems, popsicle sticks, and pointed metal can openers can all make efficient forming and decorating tools. Discarded cans, pieces of sheet metal, and grates are ingeniously formed into kiln parts used again and again. The trunk of a discarded car may be used to keep fuel dry and available. Used plastic sheets protect and condition raw materials and fuels. Extracted saps of weeds and scrub trees, not given a second glance by most, are transformed into waterproofing agents and decorative paints. Broken sections of gourd rinds become efficient smoothing tools. Paint brushes capable of forming lines as fine as any commercial brush are fashioned from wild cactus plants. Fine clays and coloring and tempering materials are extracted from the most ordinary looking rocks. Hopi kiln muffles are built of old sherds commonly trampled underfoot. Efficient fuels and kiln construction units are formed from local stone and animal droppings, while polishing agents and other pottery treatment materials can be rendered from animal carcasses and plant saps. This knowledge has been passed on quietly from generation to generation, allowing the ingenious potter to perform miracles by converting unnoticed materials into tools to produce masterpieces of art.

Pottery Forming

The coiling method used by the Hopi and Tewa is common to all Puebloan potters of the Southwest. While the basic principles are the same, each potter applies developed idiosyncratic skills, setting one apart from the other. Master potters work quickly and accurately, producing fragile, thin-walled vessels. For an experienced potter, speed need not result in flawed or distorted finished work. In one session, Fannie Polacca coiled and smoothed a pot six inches in diameter in forty-five minutes and two slightly smaller pieces in less than an hour and a quarter. Vessels ten inches and larger in height or diameter require much more time—one and a half to two days. Potters receive more money for four smaller pots made in one day than for a larger pot requiring two days.

Contradicting Susan Peterson, observations and statements of Fannie's children confirm that she never used a form to start a vessel; she began work on her lap (fig. 3.4). A base form is known as a *tabipi* to the Hopi and a *puki* to the Tewa. One seldom sees a modern Hopi pot with a base marked by the form in which it was made (fig. 3.5). Curtis, however, noted that forms were in use in the early 1920s: "The Hopi potters pushed a clay disc into a concave form called a 'tavipi' which was usually some sort of a bowl formerly either a potshard or basket tray filled with fine wet ashes pressed into the desired shape."[14] In 1985 Rachel (Nampeyo) Sahmie formed a bowl almost nineteen inches in diameter by using a wash tub that had been lined with ashes and covered with a cloth, in the manner that her forebears had done (fig. 3.6).

Speed and mass production methods have been employed by a few potters, either for economic reasons or for lack of skill, and fine handcraftsmanship has thus been compromised. Gary Granzberg noted that some pottery was being mass-produced by the use of molds in which the clay was formed or pressed. To minimize the monotony of the form of mold-cast pottery, these shapes were altered while still plastic.[15]

Like other American Indian potters, the Tewas claim that often a vessel dictates its own form and the clay guides the hands. A pot can unexpectedly change size or shape, for the clay often does not conform to the maker's will. All agree that one must be in a proper frame of mind before beginning work.

Before the abandonment of utilitarian pottery making, the Hopis and Tewas made a greater variety of shapes. There were cooking pots in a range of sizes, ladles, huge water storage ollas, water-carrying bottles or canteens, storage jars for dry commodities such as cornmeal or beans, bowls for food preparation, bowls for serving and eating from, and burial vessels. Alexander Stephen noted that

*Fig. 3.4. (facing page) Fannie Nampeyo Polacca forming pottery. To begin, the artist had flattened a ball of clay into a pancake shape and then formed her base by pinching. **A.** She then began to build the pot by coiling—rolling a large handful of clay between her palms to form a coil that was attached to the base form by pinching, the traditional coiling method. Coils were made as needed. **B.** Adding coil upon coil, the artist's hands were constantly in motion—pinching, crimping, scraping, and smoothing. Fannie shaped and roughly smoothed the bowl as the build-up progressed. As a result of long experience, she was able to sense air pockets in the body and eliminate them without interrupting the process. The wall of the vessel was plastic and flexible at all times, giving the appearance that it might collapse at any moment. When the size and shape was right, Fannie placed the piece in a shallow, cloth-covered bowl that provided support for the plastic walls while preventing the new clay from sticking to the bowl. **C.** Both the outside and, where accessible, the inside of the vessel were smoothed with a gourd scraper. (Sometimes broken pieces of ceremonial rattles are preferred since they become very hard from long exposure to the elements. Soft new gourd shells most be boiled and dried to harden them sufficiently for the task.) If the inside space had been too restricted, Fannie would have used her fingers or tools such as popsicle sticks, shaped pieces of wood, bone, sherds, or a knife. **D.** Fannie formed a perfectly round opening in the top of a jar by either flattening the last coil back on itself or by subtle manipulation of the clay to produce a graceful outcurving lip. Finishing touches with gourd piece and fingers made all surfaces, including the lip, even and smooth. Barbara Freire-Marreco observed in 1913 that a "sharp-edged strip of yucca" was often used to cut and finish edges. Now potters have steel blades. **E.** Fannie set the eight-inch pot on a windowsill to dry, where it dried in approximately two days. Both Freire-Marreco and Edward Curtis (in 1922) noted that pottery was put in a warm place to dry. (Initial rapid drying can result in cracking.) Fannie preferred to dry her pottery in a warm, moist, partially shaded area.*

crenelated bowls were used in kiva ceremonies at the altars, but figurines and effigies were a rarity (fig. 3.7). Stephen also noted that Tewa women made water casks, canteens, and cooking pots, and that the Walpi women knew best how to make decorated vessels, thus reinforcing Freire-Marreco's observation that the women of Hano preferred Walpi bowls.[16]

For the preparation and serving of food, bowls have been important. Utilitarian bowl shapes at Hopi were made for meat stew and piki bread batter. (Piki bread is made from a thin corn batter quickly cooked on a smooth hot stone.) Mush bowls also were made for

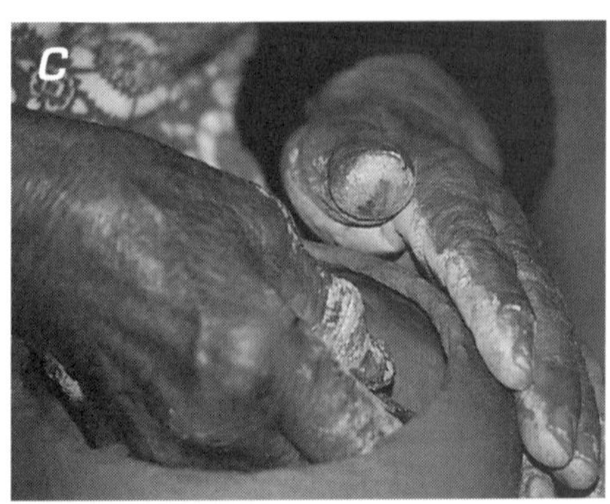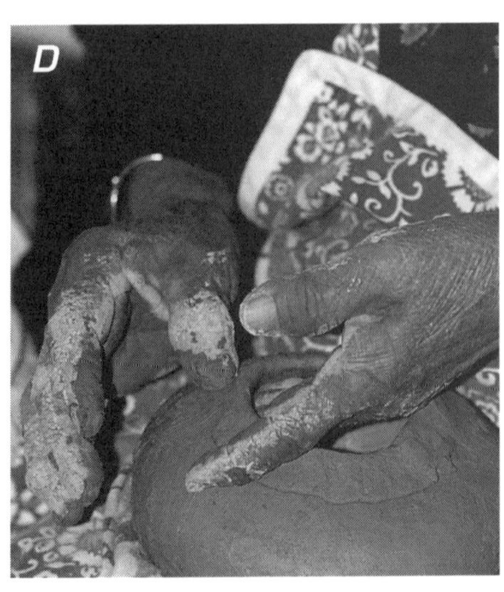

Fig. 3.5. This detail of a Polacca Polychrome jar, ca. 1880, shows a definite impression from a pot-starting form, probably a basket. Impressions are often found on prehistoric Hopi pottery but are more unusual in historic works. *No. PH12, RD.*

mixing cornmeal. Other vessels recognized to be made by the Hopis include *sibvu* (a deep undecorated container for cooking), *talavai cibu* (or morning pot), *nukwif civu* (a stew pot), *nak sibvu* (parching pot), *Kuyi sibvu* (water pot), *eon tan civu* (salt pot), *sakwa pi cibu* (green paint pot), *sivus sivu* (seed jar), and *momo'spala si'vu* (honey pot).[17]

Stew bowls with relatively flat bases and flared rims are considered the result of Spanish influence (possibly by way of Zuni). They appeared at Hopi during the San Bernardo Mission period (1625–1740) (fig. 2.43—see p. XII) and the Payupki settlement period of 1680 to 1780 (fig. 2.37). The people of Payupki were under Spanish influence prior to their flight from the Rio Grande area to take up temporary residence at Second Mesa. Spanish influence persisted through the Polacca Polychrome period from 1780 to 1900 (fig. 2.36).

Fig. 3.6. This spectacular bowl, signed R. Sahmie Nampeyo in 1985, is very large, 6 in. high by 18³/4 in. in diameter, with a 15-in. opening. Ingeniously, the potter made a tavipi form by filling an old metal wash tub with ashes and then covering it with a cloth. The cloth was kept damp as she worked to prevent the new clay from sticking. *Private collection.*

In comparison, bowls for mixing cornmeal are necessarily deeper, with incurved rims to facilitate handling the contents. The walls resemble the straight-sided Payupki bowls.

There are different types of Tewa ceremonial bowls, many of which are plain, that is, with no decoration. Plain bowls that hold charms (*k'agi*, a Rio Grande Tewa word) have been observed in the homes of Tewa families. K'agi come in many forms, such as feathers used during ceremonies, carved stone figures or fetishes, and items such as fragments of stone implements, yellow ocher, copper ore, and so on, found in the ruins, spectacular mineral forms like agates, pyrite, and quartz crystals, as well as sea shells. In every Tewa house there is a receptacle for the sacred cornmeal, which is usually a pottery bowl.

The Hopis do not use a specific bowl in the naming ceremony ritual for a baby, whereas the Tewa use a ceremonial bowl to hold the medicine water (*na-kuyi*) for the ceremony—one of the few differences between Hopi and Tewa versions. The Tewa bowl is shallow and rectangular with a handle on one side. Generally, the rim is cut into three or four terraces at the center of each of the four sides. At Hopi, the Hopi father's female relatives use water from a bowl to wash the baby, but when they confer the name an ear of corn is used to touch various parts of the baby as it is spoken. Among the Tewas, the child is given a sip of medicine water from the ceremonial bowl as the name is pronounced.

Because Nampeyo belonged to the Corn Clan, her children were also of the same clan, but their names were conferred upon them by the clan to which the fathers belonged. The Western Tewas follow the Hopi pattern in naming, while those on the Rio Grande are named by the maternal grandmother after the season or after an object seen on the fourth day after birth.

Most often ceremonial bowls are thought to be those used in kiva rituals. They are frequently of a special shape and unusual decoration. The few studied have designs that consist of symbols related to water, such as rain, clouds, snakes, tadpoles, frogs, and so forth. One such bowl made by Nampeyo, purchased by Stewart Culin in 1905, can be found in the Brooklyn Museum (fig. 3.8).

Fig. 3.7. *These rare Hopi ceramics vary in length and height from four to six inches. The items on the left (catalog nos. 17, 18, 20, 21, 23, and 27) were donated to the Pitt Rivers Museum at Oxford University in 1903. The seated figure holding a jar is in the Hopi collection at the Arizona State Museum in Tucson. It is 6⁷/₈ in. in height and similar to the Nampeyo pieces in fig. 2.45.* L. Blair, photographer.

An interesting use of a small bowl in times past was for an ant trap. As described by Daisy (Nampeyo) Hooee:

> Long ago people wanted to get rid of the Ants. They'd hunt for honey in the bushes to put honey in these little pots, and then they put them on ant hills. All the Ants were coming out and they found it was sweet. The People got an Indian hoe, to cut the weeds with, it was a shoulder bone from a deer. After they removed the pot with all Ants all around it, they walked clear off to somewheres, so they wouldn't come back. That is how they got rid of them and the children were happy as they wouldn't be biting and stinging them. That is why they called them Ant Pots. They were found in the ruins of Sikyatki. That's what they were for. My grandmother told me to make them.

Small bowls or jars were frequently made as honey pots (*momo'spala si'vu*). The contents of these pots were used in the preparation of prayer offerings as well as in most other Hopi ceremonies, and they were often decorated with flowers.[18]

The practice of placing bowls (*mas chakapta*) of water and piki on new graves to feed the deceased on their journey to the Underworld has changed due to theft and vandalism. Inexpensive commercial vessels are now used instead.

Large ollas or canteens (*kuyi sivu*) are no longer required for water transportation or storage. A few of these vessels were still made in the 1970s to hold the snakes for the Snake Dance ceremony. The canteens are stoppered with a corncob cork that has been drilled with a small hole to provide ventilation. The different snakes are usually segregated, with bull snakes and racers kept separate from the rattlesnakes (fig. 3.9). Old, undecorated, piñon-sap treated canteens were large and heavy. Generally bulbous in shape but flat on one side (fig. 3.10), they were carried on the back with a tump line. Hopi men joke that they are now spoiling the women and making them fat and lazy by pumping water to the mesa tops, saving them from hauling the heavy burdens of water six hundred feet up the mesa sides. Nowadays smaller individual canteens are decorated and sold as pottery art.[19]

The shape most admired and associated with the Nampeyo descendants is the Sikyatki water jar, which has been made since the pottery revival period of about 1890 to 1900. The rebirth of the old Sikyatki Polychrome shape has always been credited to Nampeyo, whose family has carried on the tradition (fig. 3.11). Nampeyo's descendants make all sizes of these jars, most with globular midsections and sometimes restricted openings.

Fig. 3.8. *This ceremonial bowl made by Nampeyo represents clouds and tadpoles, with rain clouds painted on both inside and outside. On the bottom is a frog (as a water animal) with corn growing out of his body.* Purchased in 1905 by Stuart Culin. No. 5.217, BMB.

Fig. 3.9. *Huge ollas such as these made in 1906 were used to hold snakes in the corner of a kiva during the Snake Dance ceremonies.* Edward S. Curtis, photographer. No. 94-1441, NAA-SI.

Fig. 3.10. *"Nampeyo, Tewa potter of Hano, carrying an olla in 1901." Adam Clark Vroman took this photograph of Nampeyo posing with an old utilitarian water olla inside her house. The flat side of the canteen rests against the carrier's back, giving it stability.* No. P5890, neg. No. N19, 423, Gates Collection, SWMLA.

Fig. 3.11. Sikyatki-style "water" jars, first produced at Sikyatki and later revived by Nampeyo, had in-sloping upper bodies and small openings which made them practical as water storage vessels because they minimized evaporation. **Upper:** This jar by Fannie Nampeyo Polacca, 1977, is 8³/₄ by 14¹/₂ in. Private collection. **Lower:** This jar was made by Nampeyo and purchased at Tom Pavatea's store in 1921. It is 7¹/₂ by 15 in. Although formed by Nampeyo, the decoration is probably by one of her daughters. No. E770, 1129, MNAZ.

Mary Willard (affiliation unknown) is credited with the introduction of a vase-shape referred to as "Greek," decorated with a bilateral arrangement of bird forms, which she thought would add variety and increase the commercial value of Hopi pottery.[20] Just what this shape was is not clear. Other diverse shapes are made at Hopi but not as frequently as at other pueblos. Wedding vases, not known to have ceremonial use at Hopi, are made sometimes, as are cookie jars, umbrella jars, and bean pots. Occasionally, animal forms appear, but they are unlike the *animalitos* that are popular along the Rio Grande. A few pitchers and miniatures also are produced. Shapes such as ladles, scoops, and spoons made prehistorically are appearing now as a tourist craft rather than utilitarian pottery (fig. 3.12—see p. XIII).

The degree to which a vessel is smoothed and polished depends both on its complexity and on the skill of the potter. When the vessel is dry, it is ready for finishing. Prior to the availability of sandpaper or

Smoothing and Polishing

other substitutes such as plastic or metallic pan scrubbers, sandstone or pumice was used. In 1981 there was only one known Nampeyo descendant who used sandstone. Smoothing is facilitated by the quality of the Hopi clay, which contains few impurities.[21]

Following final smoothing, a slip may be applied. The slip consists of fine clay, often of a different color from the body of the vessel, which is suspended in water and used as a paint (fig. 3.13). Polishing is done on the slipped or unslipped vessel with a smooth stone that is moistened periodically with water. The process of polishing an unslipped vessel is termed floating and is common at Hopi. Floating is difficult if the temper is too obtrusive; unlike many Rio Grande potters, who facilitate polishing by first applying a fine particle slip which they rub with a lubricated stone, the Hopi-Tewa potters traditionally did not use lubricants on slips. In recent years they have begun to use lubricants when producing unpainted pottery. Lubricated surfaces are water repellent and do not accept decorative paints.

Potters most often inherit polishing stones but occasionally may acquire them by other means. Smooth stones, seldom found locally, have a high value. In 1922 Frank Applegate noted that stones came from along the Little Colorado River, some sixty miles distant.[22] Today, rock shops and hobby stores are a good source of tumbled and polished mineral specimens. To fit different contoured surfaces, potters use a variety of stone shapes that have been acquired over the years. Nampeyo's stones were passed on to her daughters, then granddaughters, and now some are used by great-granddaughters.

Some master potters claim to have the ability to recognize another's ceramic piece by touch. By closing her eyes and rubbing her hands over a pot, Fannie claimed she could recognize her mother's polishing. The satiny feel of Nampeyo's work was something Fannie wished she could reproduce.

Brushes used by traditionalists for fine-line work are fashioned from the yucca leaves cut in two- to four-inch lengths and split into shreds of diameters between one-eighth and one-sixteenth of an inch.

Decoration   These are identical to the ones described and illustrated in the 1913 catalog for Freire-Marreco's Pitt Rivers Museum collection at Oxford University, England (fig. 3.14). The fiber of the yucca (*Yucca angustissima Engelm*) is drawn along after the hand, in an Oriental rather than European manner. Fine-line painting differs from the Rio Grande yucca brush techniques described by Kenneth Chapman in his well-known 1977 book, *The Pottery of Santo Domingo Pueblo.*

In recent years many potters have begun penciling in guidelines or drawing a complete design to ensure symmetrical placement of the elements. Experienced designers can study a surface and paint freehand, never requiring a guideline (fig. 3.15). Painted decorative lines are best applied to polished, water absorbent surfaces.

Starting a decoration with a banding arrangement does much to determine the limits and placement of the remainder of the design. Such beginnings have long been a practice at Hopi. Bands were placed on the inside of the bowls or the outside of jars, many dividing the work at either the shoulder or the greatest diameter. The thin, uniform lines incorporated in Nampeyo's decorations demonstrate her complete control over paint viscosity and brushing techniques. Finishing the first stage of a design before starting a second is currently the accepted practice and probably represents a traditional way. Solid color areas,

Fig. 3.13. Nampeyo, photographed here in the 1920s by Charles Loeffell, applies a slip to a vessel, probably using a rag or piece of rabbit fur. No. 57,411, NAA-SI.

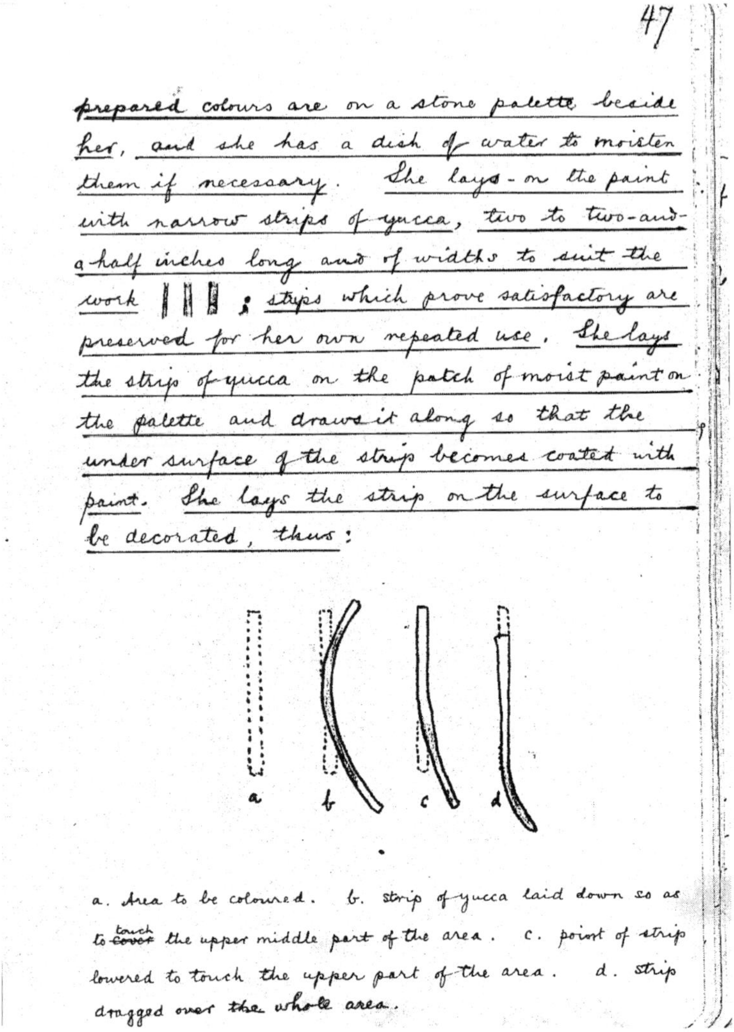

47

prepared colours are on a stone palette beside her, and she has a dish of water to moisten them if necessary. She lays-on the paint with narrow strips of yucca, two to two-and-a-half inches long and of widths to suit the work █ █ █ ; strips which prove satisfactory are preserved for her own repeated use. She lays the strip of yucca on the patch of moist paint on the palette and draws it along so that the under surface of the strip becomes coated with paint. She lays the strip on the surface to be decorated, thus:

a. Area to be coloured.   b. strip of yucca laid down so as to touch the upper middle part of the area.   c. point of strip lowered to touch the upper part of the area.   d. strip dragged over the whole area.

Fig. 3.14. *Barbara Freire-Marreco's Hopi field notes of 1912 (p. 47) describe the application of decorative paints with a yucca brush. The techniques discussed and illustrated are duplicated by today's traditional potters.* PRMOx.

usually bounded by thin black lines, were applied with fashioned pieces of rabbit skin or bits of rag tied to the ends of small sticks. These are now applied with commercially available paint brushes.

Beginning potters are taught all forms of decoration and are assisted with more difficult procedures. It is not uncommon for a pot to be made by an offspring in training and decorated by the instructor. Despite the degree of decorative artistry, the one who forms the vessel usually signs the work. On unfired ware, painting errors are removed by gently rubbing out the flawed portions and then repolishing before reapplying the design. It is also common to repaint weak or damaged areas or lines after the work has been fired and then refire to fuse the repairs to the surface. Repainting fired ware can be detected; but if not too obvious, retouching has little effect on the final value of the piece.

Impressed decoration is ornamentation created by pressing designs or forms into clay bodies while they are still plastic and pliable. Most often they are formed by applying pressure on the outside of a pot, but occasionally they are made by applying pressure from the inside—a difficult process with vessels having small openings. Decoration by impressing is more common with the Rio Grande Tewa than with the Tewa at Hopi, who usually limit impression to the fluted rims on jars and bowls. Nampeyo, working with daughter Annie, did impressed work but only for short periods (fig. 3.16—see p. XIII). Potters impress designs with imaginative and unique tools such as triangular cross-sectioned sticks or stems, pointed beer can openers, or popsicle sticks. Designs of this type are not common among the Nampeyos.

Raised designs, some with detailed finish, may be added by one of two means. The raised portion may either be formed by pressing from the interior of the vessel during formation of the pottery or by adding plastic clay to the damp exterior. In either instance the detail is finished by using a sharp-pointed instrument such as a toothpick or blade point (fig. 3.17).

Incising (cutting a design in the surface of a vessel with a sharp tool) is done on unfired plain or slipped surfaces, or, less often, on fired surfaces.[23] Incised designs on much prehistoric work were sometimes geometric. Modern ones have become more illustrative of plant, animal, or human forms, even though stylized. Incising is

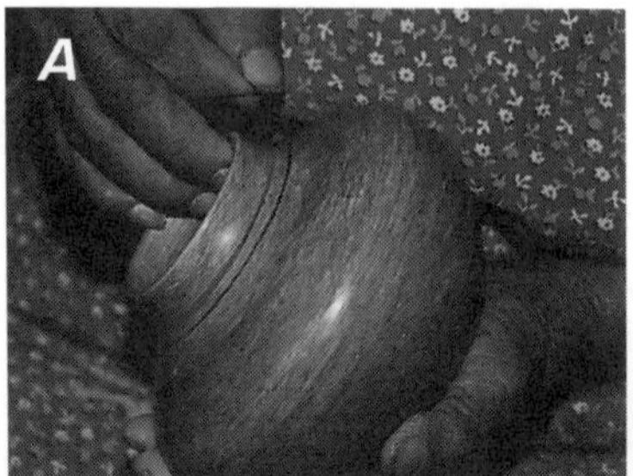

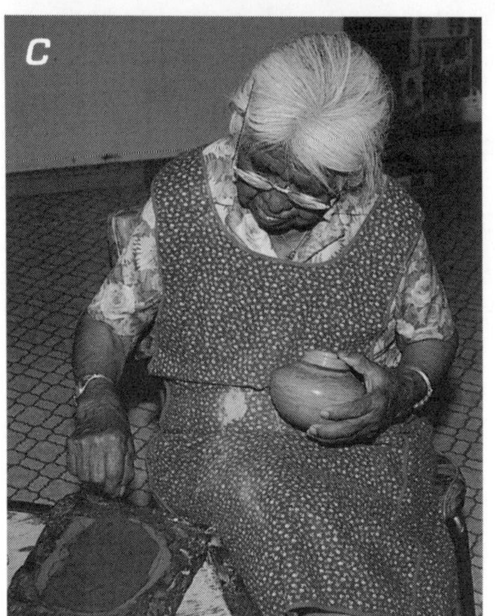

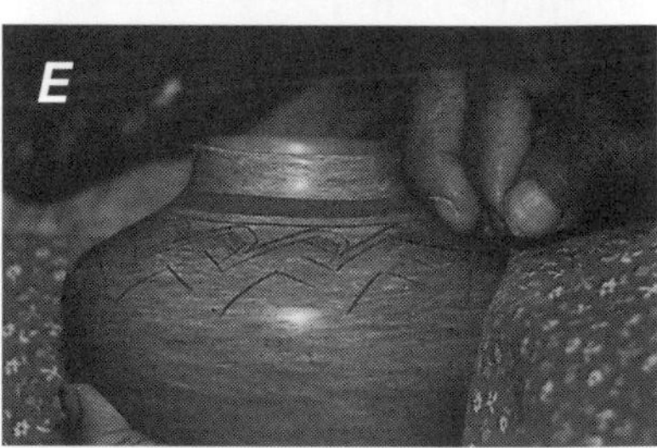

*Fig. 3.15. (facing page) Application of fine-line decoration. **A & B.** After assuring herself that her suspension of hematite in the tansy-mustard solution is the right consistency, Fannie applied two fine lines around the circumference of the jar with a yucca brush, near the base of the neck, establishing the boundaries for what is termed a "cloud band." **C.** Pigments were kept in suspension by frequent dipping and mixing with the yucca brush. **D.** After examining the work at arm's length, Fannie painted equally spaced slashes, beginning at the boundary line and running from the upper right to the lower left. It is remarkable that such pots most often have an odd number of equally spaced divisions (in this instance eleven). Fannie's migration designs usually varied from seven to fifteen. **E.** The same random technique carries the design down the side walls toward the base. Occasionally more detail is added to top sections. **F.** Fannie's finished fine-line migration design.*

first seen on Awatovi ceramics where it is used as an abstract decorative element in larger designs. Nampeyo used this technique, although rarely, in some of her larger vessels. The first contemporary Tewas on record at Hopi to incise were Nampeyo's descendants Dextra Quotskuyva and Thomas Polacca in some of his early work (fig. 3.18). They still use some incising, but Dextra is more interested in other innovative styles. Although designs may be cut into unslipped surfaces, in their most spectacular form they are applied by cutting through polished, slipped surfaces of a different color into the raw clay body beneath.

A stylized, simple form of carving was first developed at Santa Clara by the Tafoya family and at San Ildefonso by Rose Cata in the 1920s. The success in the 1960s of Tewas such as Popovi and Tony Da, Camilio Tafoya and his children Grace Medicine Flower and Joseph Lonewolf of Santa Clara, and Dora Gachupin Gonzales of San Ildefonso transformed incising into a delicate art form. By the 1990s, the pottery produced by Tafoya descendants reached a high degree of sophistication. The financial success of this practice in the Rio Grande region inspired Thomas Polacca to transfer carving of ceramics to the deeper sculptural art of bas-relief. Others such as Wallace Youvella, Thomas's son Gary and daughter Carla Claw, and Tonita Hamilton's son Loren have also pursued this style of decoration, a bold three-dimensional form.

Fig. 3.17. *Incising on raised and appliqued designs.* **Left:** *This embossed vase, 4³/4 by 4 in., was made by Al Qôyawayma in 1977. The raised ears of corn were formed by pressing the pliable clay wall outward from the inside and then incising fine detail on the raised outer portions with a very sharp tool. The work duplicates the style of his famous aunt, Elizabeth White, a Third Mesa Hopi. The vessel was fired in an electric kiln.* **Right:** *This 4¹/2 by 4 in. appliqué was fashioned by Iris Nampeyo Youvella in 1980. The ear of corn was formed by applying formed clay to the outside wall and incising it with a sharp, pointed instrument. Iris has been making sophisticated applied and incised designs since 1980.* Private collection.

Carving may be done on formed but unfired pieces having comparatively thick walls. The sculpture is enhanced by applying colors such as red, brown, black, white, and yellow (fig. 3.19). These often lifelike forms are started by penciling drawings on the smooth, unfired surfaces. Corrections are made to unsatisfactory designs by scraping lightly or sanding and then replacing them with new drawings. Sketches are often obliterated and redrawn several times before the artist is satisfied. Common tools for carving are sharp pocket knives and wood carving sets. Once the potter has completed the design, the flat open surfaces are resmoothed.

Fig. 3.18. *An incised design is formed by making a series of very shallow cuts (carved, bas-relief, or scratched) through a polished slip, usually of a different color, that has been applied to the surface of a vessel. These techniques appear to be of independent origin in the Southwest.* Private collections. **Left:** *This red-slipped bas-relief bowl is signed by Gary Polacca Nampeyo, 1976. 4^1/$_2$ in. by 4^3/$_4$ in.* **Center:** *Jar by Thomas Polacca, 6^1/$_2$ in. by 6^1/$_2$ in. in varied shades of tan and brown. Made in 1974, it is one of Thomas's first innovative pieces. The shallow incising, or sgraffito, technique, combined with dark design elements divides and emphasizes the decoration.* **Right:** *This bowl with a band of pottery sherd designs is signed Dextra [Quotskuyva], 1978. It is lightly incised on some sections to represent sherds from corrugated pottery. 4^1/$_2$ in. by 7^1/$_2$ in.*

Fig. 3.19. *Wood and ceramic kachinas are sophisticated sculptures made by traditional Hopi methods. The ceramic on the right, inscribed "Red Tailed Hawk/Nampeyo '82," was carved by Thomas Polacca. It is 9^1/$_2$ in. high and bears a close resemblance to the tall cottonwood carving on the left by Earl Yowytewa, 1979. Barton Wright identifies the Yowytewa figure as a mountain lion kachina, making the Polacca work a symbolic interpretation of a kachina.*

Skillful use of tansy mustard or guaco slips applied in various layers or thicknesses produces a finished effect, at times similar to stained wood. Sections accidentally stained with slip are scraped clean to ensure sharp color definition.

Potters, including those of Nampeyo's time, are often unaware of the significance or meanings of many designs or symbols they apply.

Designs and Symbols Romantic collectors and sales-conscious dealers may ascribe meaning to decorations where none exists. Freire-Marreco noted:

> The designs painted on modern Hano pottery are copied almost entirely from shards found at Sikyatki and other ruined sites. The women who make and decorate the pottery do not understand the symbolism which they are copying; they can identify a few naturalistic forms, "butterfly," "bird," etc., and also a few symbols still used in other arts, such as *talase*, "corn." For the most part they give merely descriptive names to part of the design—"it is lines"—"it is steps"—"it is holes." A meander pattern was described as holes with reference to the white spaces.
>
> They combine fractions of many ancient designs on purely aesthetic grounds, and if they talk about them and explain them, they generally do so on technical, not symbolical, lines, explaining that such-and-such a space has to be filled or a contrast has to be provided....
>
> This specimen [a dish made by Paelae, #27 in the Pitt Rivers Museum's Freire-Marreco collection at Oxford University], shows the well-known feather symbol discussed by Fewkes and also a design of bear's tracks, but neither symbol was recognized as such by Paelae, who combined them on purely aesthetic grounds.[24]

In a 1983 exhibition catalog Joseph Traugott aptly described the fine-line 'migration' design as a "series of interlocking diagonal hachers which terminate in three prolonged spikes." Ask several of the Nampeyo descendants the meaning of the design and you will hear a variety of answers. Some say it represents the migration of the Tewas from the Rio Grande area (not possible since pottery bearing a similar design has been located in ruins inhabited and abandoned long before the great Tewa migration), while others claim the fine lines represent the relocation of people—the upper scroll symbolizing movement in the northern hemisphere and the lower the southern hemisphere. The design has also been said to represent bear or eagle claws, bird wings, and feathers. Bruce McGee credits the abundance of migration-design pottery to Tran Bowman, a buyer for the Fred Harvey Company, who in the early 1970s requested fine-line work, giving the potters the notion that all they made would be purchased.[25]

Most of Nampeyo's descendants reproduce more fine-line designs than any others. Fine-line is so difficult to execute that a potter will attempt it only after a few years of experimentation and experience working with simple patterns. Since fine-line work appears on only a minority of Nampeyo's work, daughters Annie, Nellie, and Fannie bear the overall responsibility for its continuing popularity (fig. 3.20—see p. XIV). Migration designs are not confined to fine-line work. The striking wave-like or scroll pattern is often painted on in solid colors (fig. 3.21—see p. XV).

A decoration the potters call the "eagle design" is also popular with Nampeyo descendants since the "Old Lady" resurrected it from the ruins. It evolved into today's form during the Polacca Polychrome era, though its origin was a simpler macaw Sikyatki motif.[26] Crude by today's standards, it is characterized by a painted red square area surrounding the jar opening, to which are attached spirals and descending appendages said to represent bird beaks or tail feathers of the macaw, parrot, or eagle (fig. 3.22—see p. XVI). Earlier San Bernardo forms exhibit many of the same characteristics.

The eagle design gained sophistication as Nampeyo incorporated new elements, stylized the tail feathers, and at times added a symbol resembling a cross. Usually, her decorations were in four sections, though at times she used only three sections. She mostly reproduced this design on pieces made between 1890 and 1920. Her descendants added personal variations, which they placed not only on jars but on other shaped vessels.

Skilled decorators arrange their designs to complement the shape of the vessel. Well-executed motifs should flow with the lines of the pottery piece. Traditionally, Hopi and Tewa potters prefer placing multiple designs on one piece, most often using a different form on the sides and bottom or on opposite sides of the same vessel. However, Nampeyo frequently decorated only one side of her work.

Terminology relating to design has been imposed on the language of pottery by those who study, sell, or collect the specimens and need to describe or distinguish one pattern from another. For the sake of clarity and classification, some have proposed the adoption of a uniform terminology. Fewkes classified the designs that he and Stephen had studied. Different nomenclatures have been developed since then, but such classifications have proved meaningless and confusing when describing Hopi and Tewa pottery. It is beyond the scope of this work to either classify or completely explain the meanings of the design elements applied to pottery by the Nampeyo family. To even attempt to do so, one would have to have access to the knowledge of the Hopi elders who have long since passed on. It is doubtful whether most of this lore is still in the hands of the Hopi or Tewa potters, including the Nampeyo family. Stephen did record some explanations, one of the few outsiders who lived with and had the confidence and trust of both Hopi and Hopi-Tewa people more than any other investigator before or since.

Watson Smith and Wade and McChesney, whose studies of ancient pottery pieces have influenced both Hopi and Hopi-Tewa ceramic artists, have described rather than interpreted the designs of the ancients. A few of those, however, that Stephen, Keam, and Fewkes obtained from decorated pottery and sherds they collected from the ruins of the area have been incorporated in Nampeyo family designs and are reproduced in Appendix A.[27]

Nampeyo family pottery is commonly decorated with birds, parts of birds, and often unrecognizable stylized bird designs. At times it is adorned with what Frank Applegate termed "skyline" designs. Realistic renditions comprise many pottery designs, especially those of the younger Nampeyo family potters. In addition to birds, animals, and masked kachina heads, there are human figures, kivas, pueblos and houses, snakes, frogs, tadpoles, ears of corn, corn stalks, and insects.

As Hopi pottery became popular as an art form, its creators not only recognized it as a way to enhance their income but became increasingly aware of the demands of the market. One of these demands was the desire to know who had made a particular piece. Signing their pieces added to the value of their work. Maria Martinez of San Ildefonso is credited with being one of the first native potters to sign her work about 1910. The oldest piece with the Nampeyo name painted on it was collected by Clara Churchill sometime between 1904 and 1907 (fig. 2.25). Since Nampeyo was unable to write, her daughters began to sign her work for her. Annie was the first to sign for her mother, and her printing is different from that of Fannie, who later took over the task. In the beginning Fannie signed her mother's work with a printed name; later, as they began to produce joint work, she used "Nampeyo-Fannie" with an added drawing of a corn symbol.

At first potters resisted signing their work, either because they did not see the need to identify themselves or they were unable to write. In an effort to overcome this resistance, in 1927 the Coltons at the Museum of Northern Arizona began to encourage Hopi potters to use identification marks on their work.[28] One of the first potters to adopt the practice of using a symbol or hallmark was Paqua (Frog) who used a frog as her sign. Her descendants have continued the use of her mark, changing the shape and adding their initials to it. In many instances an artist will change her or his mark with the passage of time, feeling that the change better expresses his or her current status. An illustration of this is found in the hallmarks of Tom Polacca. At first Tom used the Nampeyo name "as a tribute to the old lady" but later dropped it since he felt that he should rely on his own name alone to identify his distinctive work.[29]

Most pottery is now decorated on the bottom with a clan symbol or names and a clan mark. Many of the pottery-making families use one of these symbols as a hallmark for their groups' distinctive work (fig. 3.23). In addition to the claims to certain designs by Nampeyo

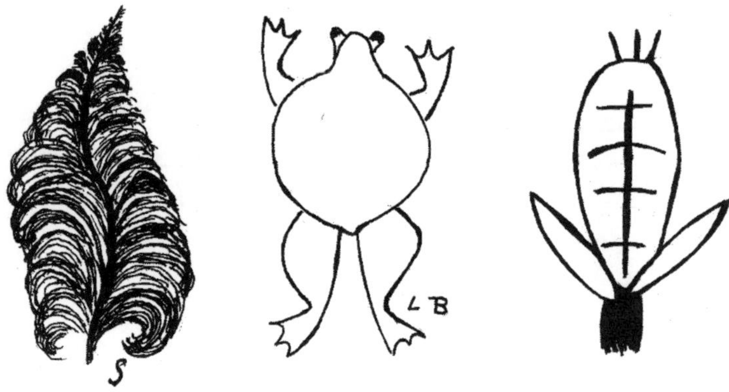

Fig. 3.23. *Formerly, symbols such as these took the place of a signature by those who could not write. Later, their descendants continued to use the symbols along with their initials, sometimes changing the symbol slightly. As a potter's reputation grew, his or her symbol became a mark of recognized excellence.* **Left:** *The feather is the symbol for Helen Naha's Hopi name and has become a family hallmark. This example contains the initial, S, which is the distinguishing mark of Helen's daughter, Sylvia.* **Center:** *This frog is the symbol used by Paqua, without her name. Appearing about 1920, it may be the first symbol to be added to pottery. Paqua's daughter, Joy Navasie, continued its use with an added initial "J" and a slight change in the rendition of the frog. Following Paqua's death, Joy became the family matriarch and used her mother's mark without the initial. The illustration has the added initials "L. B.," signifying that it is the work of Joy Navasie's daughter, Leona Benn.* **Right:** *A version of the symbol that can be used by any member of the Corn Clan; as such, it is not a family mark but a clan symbol. The name of the maker of the vessel nearly always accompanies this symbol. It is thought that Nampeyo's daughter Fannie was the one who began this tradition.*

descendants, the family also asserts that the Nampeyo name and the corn symbol are their exclusive hallmarks. These claims do not take into consideration that there are other members of the Corn Clan who have an equal right to the corn symbol and that all potters have access to the designs that Nampeyo used. They feel nonetheless that the corn symbol is theirs and that it increases the value of their work, forcing at least one legitimate descendant to use the standard American copyright symbol © to prevent misrepresentation. The Nampeyo name belongs to her clan descendants and in keeping with Hopi custom would not be given again as long as she is remembered, since it is unique to her.

Drying and Firing

Pottery drying done by experienced potters is not rushed. Vessels are dried first at ambient temperatures, the time depending on the size and thickness of the piece. Attempts to shorten the initial drying period by elevating the temperature result in strains that may cause cracking. Immediately prior to firing, after the pot has been well dried, the ware may be heated in or near a kitchen stove to eliminate the last vestiges of absorbed water and minimize the effects of thermal shock encountered during the first stage of firing. Prior to the advent of stoves, Nampeyo achieved the same result by carefully placing her dry but unfired pieces around a firing of earlier completed vessels (fig. 3.24).

High-quality Hopi clay fires well, allowing the potter to form thin-walled items which are more resistant to cracking during drying or firing than the thick-walled pieces formed from inferior clay such as those available to the Rio Grande craftsmen. Nevertheless, it is all but impossible to repair drying cracks in unfired pieces by applying moist clay unless the dry body is thoroughly moistened and brought back to its original pliable state—a difficult procedure. Slow and uniform moisture additions must be applied to the entire volume rather than just to the damaged area. In addition to plastic repairs, rim cracks and surface spalls in unfired work may sometimes be masked by carving, incising, or painting the damaged portions.

Fig. 3.24. *Nampeyo pottery receives a final high-temperature drying around a pottery fire, 1900. Edward S. Curtis, photographer. No. 7605722, NAA-SI.*

One well-recognized Hopi-Tewa artist spent days forming and incising the interior of a large exquisite bowl, considered his finest to date. During drying, rim cracks developed. To salvage as much as possible, the side was cut down, converting the object from a bowl to a deep dish. During firing further rim cracking developed. All was not lost—the cracks were ground off to form a plate decorated with a fine, intricate, internal pattern. The item was subsequently sold at the Santa Fe Indian Market for a handsome price.

Traditional Pueblo potters fired their work in specific locations that belonged only to them and which provided protection from the wind. A rear barrier such as a niche in the cliff edge that shielded the flames from the prevailing winds was of great advantage. Nampeyo fired her pottery in an open area. Many potters now devise elaborate barriers to protect their firing locations from unwanted draft. Contemporary firing sheds represent a recent innovation on the Hopi

Reservation. They consist of a back barrier, a roof that slants upward to the leeward side with no opening to vent the smoke, which simply follows the rise of the roof to an open front. At least one side, in addition to the front, can be opened to give easy access to the firing area near the back wall. Portable partitions, such as plywood sheets, wallboard sections, corrugated iron, and so forth, are strategically placed to protect the fire from changing winds and at the same time allow adequate ventilation. The firing area at Sand Hills was not enclosed and is similar to firing areas used by some potters who continue to fire in the open (fig. 3.25). In Polacca the well-constructed firing shed in back of Fannie Polacca's home was torn down following her death and has been replaced by a modern electric kiln in an undisclosed location.

In Nampeyo's later years the fuel of choice was compacted sheep manure. Family members recall Nampeyo and Lesou taking green pottery out to sheep camps and firing at the source. Today the manure is usually purchased from neighboring Navajos and may be delivered

Fig. 3.25. Pottery firing site at Sand Hills Ranch. The location on the leeward side of the house gave the kiln some protection from the wind. It was used by Nampeyo family members some years ago, mostly during the summer months. Judging from the number of sherds, many firings took place here.

in the back of a pickup truck or sold on a "come and get it" basis. It is usually stored near the firing areas under a convenient covering to keep it dry.

In the past, dried corncobs were used as fuel because they burn at a much higher temperature than does wood. (Wood burns at 900°F, sheep dung at 1700°F, corncobs supposedly at 1900°F, and coal at over 2000°F.) Stephen observed that toward the end of the nineteenth century "about a peck of corncobs" were consumed in a fire to which sheep dung was also added. The firing spot was "about two feet in diameter." Sand was built up around it, and stones were placed at the base to protect the pots from touching the fire. Other fuels, such as burro and horse manure, have found use in the past, but Hopi informants doubt that these would generate sufficient heat.

Coal remained an important fuel until recently. Nampeyo informed Curtis that the pottery at Hano was of superior quality since the use of lignite enabled potters to fire their vessels slowly for several days. Freire-Marreco noted the use of a combination of coal and manure whereby a base of shaley coal was laid on the ground and ignited at a preliminary fire and that Corn Clan women often stayed at their Sand Hills country homes to fire since coal was readily available there. In 1922 Applegate observed that potters at Hopi were mixing coal with sheep dung, a practice that was continued in 1930.[30]

Outcroppings of coal are visible in many cliff faces on the Hopi Reservation, particularly at Awatovi. A firing experiment performed at that location in the 1950s by Anna Shepard compared juniper wood and coal as fuels. As expected, the coal was slower to ignite but reached a higher temperature and burned for a longer period of time under oxidizing conditions, thus explaining why pre-Spanish sherds at Awatovi are more brightly colored and vitreous than those that were fired under Spanish domination.[31]

Firing by Hopi-Tewa potters is a complicated procedure, best understood by following the illustrations of a modern potter at work in figure 3.26. Nampeyo's great-granddaughter Melda Garcia Navasie, who learned from her grandmother Fannie Nampeyo, conducted the demonstration for us using Fannie's familiar tools and firing shed. Rather than firing several pieces at once, as did most of her predecessors, she fired only one item.

With the exception of a few odd or experimental pieces, Hopi potters fire under oxidizing conditions. Localized rosy or tan areas on the surface are the result of hot spots. Unless too dark and numerous, the warmth and depth of color adds value to the work, both pleasing collectors and indicating that the piece was fired by traditional means. Sooty black smudges resulting from fuel touching the pottery, however, may render the piece unsalable. Pottery with an overall dull gray appearance is the result of underfiring (fig. 3.27—see p. XVII). This error can be corrected by refiring the piece. To ensure the best firing results, Nampeyo often placed miniature pots on the bottom of the vessels to be fired as a gift to the fire. Vessel explosions during firing are less common with the Hopis than with the Rio Grande potters. This is partially explained by the fact that the Hopi clays contain fewer organic materials that release gas suddenly when heated.

In recent years pieces fired in electric kilns have begun to appear at First Mesa, a practice that was already common with potters from Third Mesa. Modern kiln-fired pottery, as produced in pueblos such as Jemez, Zuni, and Acoma, has been accompanied by a decline in the quality of hand-crafted work. Firing in electric kilns produces pieces that lack the warm glow and artistry of traditionally fired pottery. With a little study, one can distinguish the too perfect and cold appearance of kiln-fired pottery and as such is often rejected by the informed collector. Astute and knowledgeable traders also often refuse to buy kiln-fired work unless it is properly labeled by the maker and is sold at a lower price.

In 1975 a group of well-intentioned university people visited Hopi with the express purpose of easing the potters' year-round firing problems by introducing commercial kilns. Due to the fine reputation of Nampeyo's daughter Fannie, the delegation asked to discuss the

Fig. 3.26. *Pottery firing by Melda Garcia Navasie, Fannie Polacca's grand-daughter.* **A.** *A small warming fire of manure kindled with cedar bark or other small wood chips rid the ground of any moisture that might damage the pottery during firing.*

B. *Melda's husband, Elroy, worked constantly in the background erecting wind barriers, shaping manure briquettes, and helping with the fire.*

C. *The unfired work was carefully placed on a thin layer of sherds spread in the bottom of a suitably sized metal pan. The open structure of the sherds allowed free circulation of air around the interior of the pot, assuring proper oxidation during firing. Sherd muffles were placed around the sides and top of the pot.*

D. *A layer of fuel, completely dry and free of impurities, was added to the warming fire, and three pieces of stone were strategically arranged to help air circulation and to act as leveling bases for the pan containing the unfired ware. The fuel ignited from the warming fire.*

E. A metal cover on top of
the sherd muffles pre-
vented ash or fuel from
falling through to the vessel.
A layered wall of dung briquettes was built around
and over the muffle structure. The fire underneath
soon ignited the dung walls.
Cinder blocks and rocks
held the manure in place.

F. Once the restraining
blocks were in place and
ignition was well underway,
the potter was free to
leave the area. Nothing
more could be done until
the fuel was exhausted
and the fire had died out.

G. When the spent fire was cool enough to disassemble, the perfectly fired pot was
dusted, lightly greased, and delivered to a local trader.

Fig. 3.28. Nampeyo stands in a posture typical of the potter as she bends over her work, stacking pieces of dung, in 1901. The insert on the right is a posed picture of Fannie doing the same task. Those who knew both potters remember how their left elbows rested against the left knee as they stacked pottery for firing. Both prepared for work by washing and tying their hair in a bun, just above the forehead. Today's potters marvel at the number of pieces fired at the same time by their elders and how casually they seem to be stacked. A. C. Vroman, photographer. No.V-675, SCWHR. Photo insert of Fannie courtesy of Thomas Polacca.

idea with her. They found her in her usual stiff-legged stance at her firing site, tending to her work (fig. 3.28). Snow was falling, but Fannie proceeded undaunted with her firing tasks, not at all impressed with what the learned people had to offer; she responded little to their questions or suggestions. The academics retreated.

Unfortunately, within the past few years, and much to the chagrin of most family members, a few of Nampeyo's descendants have begun kiln firing their work. Most attribute this switch to laziness, although those following the practice state that it increases their output, decreases their firing losses, and thus gives them additional income. They have now adopted techniques that they formerly shunned and tried to suppress. It is regrettable that a few of some of the younger members of the family who use the Nampeyo name on their work have never fired traditionally and probably are unable to do so.

Finishing

Common practice at Hopi is to allow a fire to burn out, often until the ashes are cold. Vessels may be removed from the site as soon as they can be handled. Pieces with serious firing defects are broken, to be used as muffle sherds for future firings. Those with barely visible but not repairable imperfections are either sold at discounted prices or given away. Some firing faults can be corrected. When designs have been marred by scraping or scratching, the pottery can be redecorated and refired. Skillful decoration makes the defects practically invisible. Rio Grande potters are not so fortunate, since refiring their highly polished ware usually results in a lusterless surface than cannot be restored.

Well-fired perfect pieces are dusted and given further treatment with an animal fat or petroleum gel to enhance the sheen. Occasionally, other products like Pam, hair spray, and Krylon have been tried as well. In the past, a waterproof utilitarian finish had been applied to canteens immediately after removing them from the fire, by coating them with piñon gum mixed with fat. Formerly, sheep fat was used for a final polish, but difficulty of application and a disagreeable odor forced the substitution of commercial products as they became available. The fat or gel is applied to the vessel and gently rubbed with a soft cloth, always in one direction. A back and forth or circular motion may cause a design to chip or flake. One potter, after instructing a dealer client in the procedure, thereafter delivered her ware to him on a "finish it yourself" basis.

More recently, some potters are replacing the fat and gel finish with a coat of spray lacquer. Initially, this provides the work with a very attractive finish. Unfortunately, many of these sprays tend to dull and peel with age and can only be removed by a skilled pottery restorer.

Marketing

Potters may sell to a collector or dealer directly from their homes or bring their work to a trading post or gallery. In most instances the sales are made on a face-to-face basis in private. Potters are well aware of the dealer markup and may mark up the selling price to a private party so as not to undercut the dealer, who is an ongoing customer. Bargains are seldom available to private collectors, even if their timing is perfect—they must arrive at the artist's home during the short interval between the finishing of a piece and the arrival of a dealer or another buyer. Instances have occurred where the potter will remove a piece "hot from the fire" and rush off to a nearby dealer to obtain instant, much-needed cash. In addition, the works of outstanding artists may also be booked years in advance.

Presently, selling is done much as it was in the days of Thomas Keam and often at the same locations, with one major difference. Bartering has been almost entirely eliminated at trading posts, and transactions are now in cash. Competition among dealers is fierce and is often carried to comic extremes. Should a dealer hear that a well-known potter has completed something, he or she may rush to the potter's home to buy the piece before another dealer arrives. It has indeed happened that a second dealer literally knocks at a potter's front door while the first arrival is exiting from the back with all the available treasures.

Special orders from collectors are seldom accepted. Potters have had unfortunate experiences with seemingly sincere order placers who never come back. Often, when they do show up, they may reject an ordered work and request that it be redone. Conversely, collectors who leave a deposit may return only to find their order unfilled, the work probably sold to an earlier arrival for ready cash.

The unemployment rate for Native Americans is the highest of any group in the United States, the average income the lowest. Most Hopi families, including those of the average potters, always need money. This accounts for Hopis seldom keeping an inventory of deposits and their reluctance to sell on consignment; they need cash to satisfy basic and immediate family needs.

Specialized galleries frequently hold exhibitions featuring the work of one or several artists. The invited participants usually prepare well in advance, often taking several works to exhibit and sell. Galleries obtain commissions ranging from 20 to 50 percent of their selling price. Potters set their prices and the galleries add their markups. All exhibitors want the potters present during the shows and may pay transportation and per diem expenses. Some buy all the pieces that the artist brings, while others may request that the unsold work be left behind on consignment, the potter to be paid only after the work is sold. Few artists agree to consignment sales but instead will take the unsold pieces for sale elsewhere, possibly at reduced rates, all depending on the need for cash.

Negotiations for gallery appearances may be quite sophisticated. Often contracts spell out specifics such as appearance fees, travel, and accommodation costs. Many galleries will request total or geographic exclusives, usually not acceptable to a potter with an outstanding reputation. Recognized artists can become very demanding with contract terms. On the other hand, some potters simply dislike travel away from home.

A majority of Hopi artists, however, take great pleasure in attending the three largest competitive shows in the Southwest, held annually in summer: the Heritage Marketplace at the Museum of Northern Arizona in Flagstaff, the Southwest Association for Indian Arts, Indian Market at Santa Fe where sales are made directly to collectors, and the Gallup Inter-Tribal Indian Ceremonial where sales may be made through dealers. Each event gives artists the opportunity to meet serious collectors from around the world and receive high prices for their work. Also important is visiting with friends and exchanging ideas on the latest in pottery innovation at these events. Perhaps the most important of these to the Hopi and Hopi-Tewa artists and craftsmen is the annual July show at the Museum of Northern Arizona. It is geographically close by and has a history of encouraging Hopis to upgrade their arts.

Continuing the Legacy: The Nampeyo-Lesou Progeny

It is too late—and perhaps not even desirable—to reverse the momentum of modernization. Both technological societies and developing nations want change even at the expense of their ancient traditions. Yet the specter of a world devoid of tribal cultures and of their rich aesthetic expression is desolate. Posterity deserves at least an accurate record of the brilliance of native traditions, for we, the "civilized," have yet to surpass them in either conviction or vision.

Edwin L. Wade, The Arts of the North American Indian

About 1904, as Nampeyo reached the apex of her career, potters of the Southwest pueblos began to be recognized as artists rather than curio makers. Following World War II they gained the recognition due them, and the objects they made became respected as beautiful and distinct art forms. Outstanding Pueblo potters strove to improve their living standards by simultaneously increasing their output and upgrading their craftsmanship. It was not until the 1940s that Indian men, as well as women, began to emerge as recognized artists.

The Recognition of Indian Pottery as Art

Europeans were generally more receptive than people in the United States to the concept of the work of the American Indians as art. Americans began to accept the true beauty and significance first through the efforts of a few early traders such as Thomas Keam, John Lorenzo Hubbell, J. B. Moore, and the Spiegelbergs, and then through contact with the Indians themselves, who sold their wares on trains and railroad station platforms, on the roadside, or to tour groups who visited their reservations.

Others who understood the significance of the ceramic creations soon furthered this development. Academic institutions, as exemplified by the Museum of Northern Arizona in Flagstaff under the direction of Harold S. and Mary-Russell Colton and the School of American Archaeology (now the School of American Research) in Santa Fe, New Mexico, under the direction of Edgar L. Hewett and Kenneth Chapman, encouraged potters to improve their work, showing them that better pieces brought higher prices. They hired Indians who chanced to be good potters as part-time maintenance workers and so forth, to provide them with sustenance income that gave them more freedom to pursue artistic work.[1]

The Museum of Northern Arizona at Flagstaff and the School of American Archaeology in Santa Fe would both sponsor exhibitions and sales of Native American work later. They also encouraged artists to sign their work or attached stickers bearing their names to facilitate individual recognition and engender pride in their work. The concept was entirely alien to the natives.

Almost simultaneously to the work of these philanthropic institutions, the managers of trading posts began to realize the financial benefits of retail versus wholesale selling. Tourists began to invade the Southwest in increasing numbers. Indian curio stores such as Selegman's and Candelario's in Santa Fe, the various Fred Harvey stores and hotel shops associated with the Santa Fe Railroad, and Ralph Meyers' pioneer Indian Store in Taos increasingly offered artistic works rather than the usual run of curios. The merchants who operated these emporiums preceded the contemporary Indian art dealers and galleries, which are now located across America and throughout the world.

Railroads transported affluent pottery customers drawn from the tourists and other travelers and often unwittingly accommodated selling wares on station platforms and in the aisles of passenger trains during prolonged railway stops. This became the accepted practice, particularly at Zuni. Often the items sold were odd forms thought to be attractive to tourists.[2] Many platform merchants set up outlets at various stops along the railroad that carried passengers from Chicago to California. The well-known potter Lucy Lewis of Acoma recalled that in about 1910 she got the jump on her competition in Grants, New Mexico, by going "to the front of the train, where you got a head start with your basket of potteries. I always went where I would have first chance at the passengers. I charged seventy-five cents for the big jar, a tall one, and if I sold that I knew I had done really well."[3]

As the automobile became a popular means of transportation, Pueblo potters, including Lucy and her children, set up portable roadside stands along the now abandoned U.S. Highway 66. There the children were "allowed to do their own trading, rather than selling, for magazines or ice cream." One customer used to come by with sweet potatoes, trading them to the children for small pots. "That was the first time we ate sweet potatoes!"[4]

The role of roadside and railway potters in introducing the public to their artistic products cannot be overemphasized. Many travelers who purchased from them would later donate their acquisitions to museums throughout the country for observation and study.

In the early twentieth century, little pottery was traded among different Indian peoples, much less than was exchanged during prehistoric times. According to Barbara Freire-Marreco: "In New Mexico and Arizona, pottery doesn't travel far unless there is a famine. . . . [W]hen women got desperate to save their children, they would make pottery and travel in search of a market, or send their young boys."[5]

Presently, with minor exceptions, pottery outlets for craftsmen are limited to selling to or bartering with store or gallery buyers and collectors. Not only has intertribal trade been restricted, but utilitarian pottery pieces, either for trade or home use, have been rapidly replaced by factory-produced ceramics, metal, and plastic utensils. With many Indian potters even the sacred *puki* has been displaced by mass-produced containers.

The Nampeyo family had no easy access to either road or railway outlets. To sell pottery would have required several days of packing animals and loading wagons to travel to a destination where they would have to spend an extended period of time with no assurance that the items they had brought would sell. If they did sell, then there was the return trip home to negotiate.

Nampeyo lived and bore all of her offspring in the traditional Corn Clan home located atop First Mesa near the spectacular gap in the mesa known as Walpi (fig. 4.1). (The house is now surrounded by other structures.) Yet the forces of modernization reached the family even there, and Nampeyo and Lesou adapted to make the best of inevitable change. Their home offered more advantages to their children than most Native American families knew, especially so when Nampeyo reached the zenith of her career and attained worldwide recognition. The home had become a mecca for collectors who were anxious to obtain her art and for visiting scientists, photographers, and other artists. The contacts of the Nampeyo family with many distinguished people from the world outside of Hopi certainly must have had stimulating effects. Some people also came to interview, study, paint, or photograph Nampeyo and her surroundings. Early in the twentieth century wealthy philanthropists and organizations sponsored research trips to the Southwest, partly to collect artifacts

Fig. 4.1. *Watercolor of Corn Clan House, Hano, Arizona, 1905, by H. B. Judy. The home, with subsequent restorations, remains standing on the original site. BMB.*

and art objects for themselves as well as for educational institutions. The scientific expeditions that were conducted early in the lives of the Lesou children also must have had the effect of motivating them to produce their own art and of engendering an appreciation of their heritage. (Unfortunately, a few collections were made indiscriminately by uninformed individuals who failed to record pertinent data and sometimes collected either inferior specimens or sacred artifacts that Indians now are fighting to have returned.)

Stewart Culin began investigations with sponsorship by John Wanamaker in 1900 and brought expeditions to the Hopi area under his leadership from 1901 to 1905. Expedition members made notes, sketches, and paintings that shed light on the surroundings in which the Nampeyo children lived and on the rapid changes the Hopis were experiencing at that time. They also revealed brief informative details of Nampeyo's associates, such as Tom Polacca and Tom Pavatea. In his report on his 1901 expedition, Culin recorded borrowing a horse from James Allen, manager for Keam, and riding to First Mesa where he "secured an Indian interpreter, Tom Polacca, and at once climbed the trail to the Hopi [First Mesa] towns. The trail winds up the rocks and skirts the precipitous edge of the cliff. We turned to the east and entered the little village of Hano [Tewa Village]. The houses built of stone and cemented with clay are in part four stories in height [not so at present]. I was well provided with tobacco, cigarette paper, and candy for the children, and went about buying freely of the things that were offered to me." Later during the same expedition he noted that "pottery making occurs only at Hano, at the First Mesa, where a famous woman potter named Nampeyo, whom I saw at work, makes finely decorated bowls and jars both for local use and for the traders. This is the best modern Hopi pottery, does not compare, however, with the prehistoric ware."

On a similar expedition in 1905, accompanied by the artists and photographers Albert L. Groll and H. B. Judy, Culin spent considerable time with the Hopi-Tewa people. "[I] had the Indians carry everything over to a house belonging to Nampeyo, which I hired for a month from her. This house, at the foot of the Mesa, had been occupied by the artist Burbank until recently....It is a substantial one story, one room adobe with a smaller house in the rear." Culin was impressed with the modern comforts that had been introduced since his visit in 1901. Material items such as windows, iron wheelbarrows, and beds were becoming common. Culin wrote that Nampeyo was selling items other than pottery. "On my way back alone I stopped at Nampeyo's and she sold me a pair of mano [sic] earrings for one dollar, the same pair that boys had brought down to me to try to sell for five dollars." It might well be that the boys were Nampeyo's seldom-mentioned sons, Kalokun and William Komalestewa.[6]

While Culin worked, Judy and Groll photographed, sketched, and painted. Groll sketched the Polacca village home of Nampeyo (fig. 1.8) and photographed the landscape while Judy painted superb watercolor paintings, including one of the Corn Clan home (fig. 4.1). The efforts at photography were wasted. "The camera had been out of focus, the pictures were no good, and there was really nothing doing

The Legacy of a Master Potter

A Color Portfolio

Fig. 2.15. (Below) This polychrome canteen, made by Nampeyo ca. 1901, was given to Dr. Joshua Miller in return for eye treatment. 14^1/$_2$ in. by 11^5/$_8$ in. by 11^1/$_2$ in. *L. Blair, photographer. Pot No. 4099, AZSM.*

Fig. 2.3. (Above) This Polacca Polychrome jar (4^1/$_2$ in. high by 6^3/$_8$ in. in diameter) was collected in the 1880s by Fred Voltz, a trader at Canyon Diablo, Arizona, and purchased later from the Fred Harvey Company in Albuquerque. The design shows a strong Zuni influence, typical of mid-nineteenth-century output. *No. XH212P, DAM.*

Fig. 2.31. (Next 7 pages) Eighteen sample bowls and jars, representing the scope of Nampeyo's output during the height of her career.

BOWLS: *Nampeyo's bowls often emphasized design with the use of an unsophisticated open shape as the base. The diversity of painting style, color, and balance with many unusual touches is impressive. All have the distinctive Nampeyo lip formation.*

The Sikyatki-type bird-feather design on this bowl enhanced jars as well as bowls. It is often found on pieces Nampeyo made jointly with her children and grandchildren.
3¹/₂ in. by 10¹/₂ in. No. 11299/12, MMA.

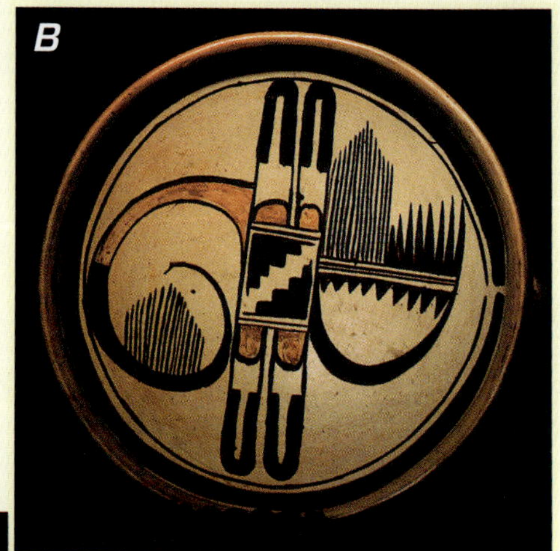

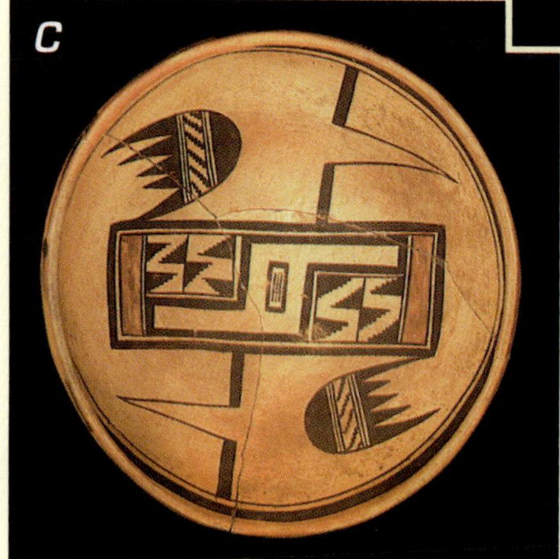

Attributed to Nampeyo, the lug, lip, and banding line are characteristic of much of her work. Variations of this design, which contain many Sikyatki elements, are found scattered throughout her work. 1 in. by 5⁵/₈ in. No. 25123, MMSD.

This design might be interpreted as the termination element (claw or feathers) of her later migration designs. 4 in. by 10¹/₂ in. No. US.2.7, 41-146, MARI.

The small ghostly figure and ticks on the rim of this bowl are a mystery. Perhaps they were included to upset the symmetry of the piece. 3$^1/_2$ in. by 9 in. Collected by George Pepper ca. 1901–1903. No. US.2.5, 41-55, MARI.

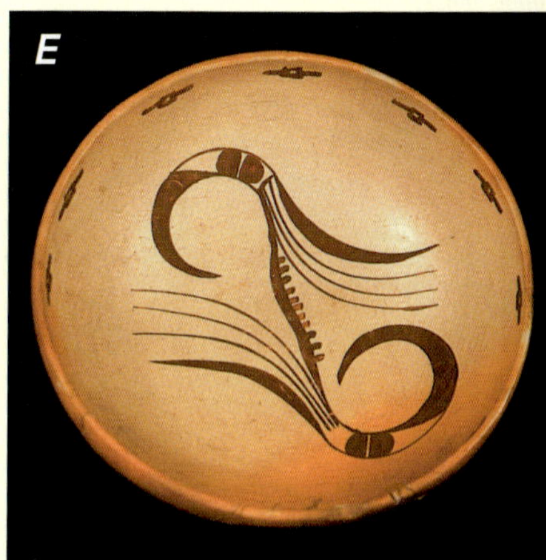

This simple, flowing design is a product of Nampeyo's imagination. Note the paint lines on the upper portion of the stem that connect the two outside elements. This small touch seems to upset the balance deliberately. 2$^7/_8$ in. by 9 in. Collected by George Pepper ca. 1901–1903. No. US.2.6, 41-116, MARI.

This classic Sikyatki-motif bowl was collected by George Pepper in 1903. 2 in. by 9$^3/_8$ in. L. Blair, photographer. No. 29.0/ 348, AMNH.

Fig. 2.31. BOWLS (cont.)

G

The bird design demonstrates a strong resemblance to those designs produced by potters of Acoma or Zuni. 3¹/₈ in. by 8⁷/₈ in. Collected by George Pepper ca. 1901–1903. No. US.2.8, 41-58, MARI.

H

This bowl is decorated with a blend of Payupki and Sikyatki or Awatovi elements that represent ears of corn, an appropriate design for a Corn Clan potter. 3³/₈ in. by 9 in. Collected by George Pepper ca. 1901–1903. US.2.6, 41-154, MARI.

I

This is probably a Sikyatki feather rattle design, which Nampeyo has surrounded with a broken band painted on the interior. Although her daughter Fannie claimed Nampeyo never painted a broken banding line, this, like B, page II, is one of a few pieces which does have one. 2 in. by 9⁷/₈ in. Collected by George Pepper ca. 1901–1903. No. US.2.3, 41-159, MARI.

Fig. 2.31. *BOWLS (cont.)*

J. W. Fewkes claimed that the upper decorative element in this bowl represented a nakwakwoci, or prayer offering. In the simplest form it consists of a straight line terminating in a knot (ball) from which spring multiple parallel lines that represent feathers. Below the nakwakwoci, Nampeyo placed "conventionalized" insect representations, adapted from the potters of Sikyatki. 3 in. by 8⁷/₈ in. Collected by George Pepper ca. 1901–1903. No. US.2.8,41-150, MARI.

JARS AND OTHER VESSELS: Although famous for her Hopi water jars, Nampeyo also produced other jar shapes, each painted with a different design. Although many such specimens are found in her earlier work, she concentrated almost exclusively on jars as blindness overtook her; she allowed others to do the decoration.

Few square-necked vessels made by Nampeyo have been located and none as large as this. The design is a combination of Sikyatki and Awatovi elements. Note the meticulous repair work on neck and sides, joining both halves of the broken jar. 14³/₈ in. by 18¹/₂ in. No. 52543, AZSM.

*The white slip indicates that this may be an early work by
Nampeyo. The design is reminiscent of the Payupki potters who
used straight-line elements. 3⁵/₈ in. by 7³/₈ in.* No. 1905.9, donated
by W. Crewdson, F.S.S.,in 1905 to the Museum of Mankind, British Museum.

*Possible Nampeyo
rendition, this is a
pleasing, light
design of mixed
elements. 3 in. by
9¹/₂ in.* No. 75.104,
donated in 1935 by
Mrs. B. V. Schauffler of
Downington, Pennsylva-
nia, to the American
Museum in Bath.

This jar was originally collected by the artist Jo Mora (1876–1947) who frequently visited the Hopi Reservation. The left portion of the jar is cream-slipped while the right portion is red. Two other Nampeyo pots have been located that are slipped in this fashion. All decoration was done on the upper half of the vessel. Cream portions of the pot are decorated with Payupki-like designs, while the red area has a simple storm cloud illustration, similar to that applied by prehistoric Hopi and Rio Grande people. The body is crudely formed. 2$^{1}/_{2}$ in. by 6 in. Private collection.

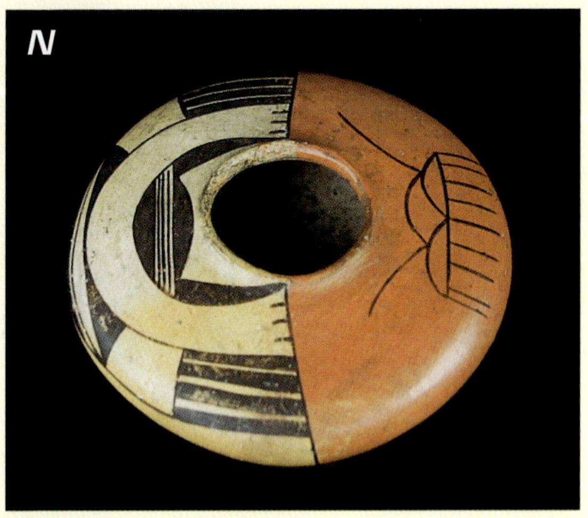

Cream-slipped vessel with sparsely applied Sikyatki-like designs, topped by a black "sky" band. Made in 1912, 10 in. by 7 in. "Collection Nampeyo" is written on the bottom. No. E.156,774, donated by Mrs. H. S. Colton, MNAZ.

Finely formed seed jar attributed to Nampeyo, similar to those made ca. 1910. Identified by Daisy Hooee as the work of her grandmother. The walls of the jar are extremely thin and well executed. 4 in. by 10$^{1}/_{2}$ in. Private collection.

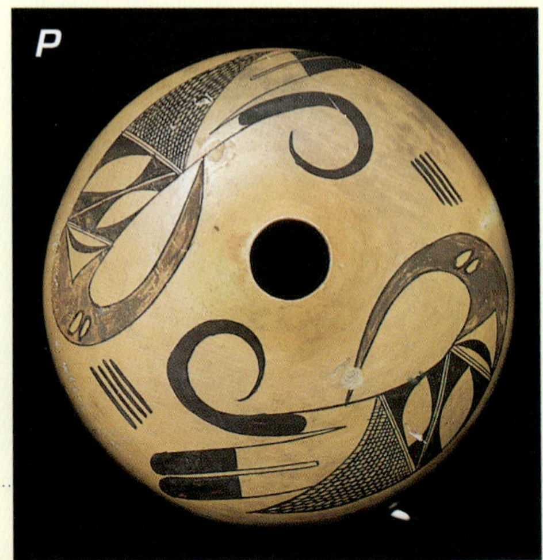

A letter of authenticity accompanies this very large jar as well as an attached card that reads, "Pottery by Nampeyo, First Mesa by Tom Pavatea." Because of its date, listed as 1920s, it was probably decorated by another family member, perhaps Fannie, who painted decorations of this type. 5$^{1}/_{2}$ in. by 14 in. Photographed in 1987. Collection of Tom Woodard.

The shape of this large water jar is most often associated with Nampeyo's later work. The Sikyatki-like designs are enclosed by upper and lower bands that resemble the later placement of Fannie's bands. Dated 1915, 7 in. by 15 in. No. 410, SAR.

Fig. *2.32.* UNUSUAL NAMPEYO POTTERY SHAPES (Next 2 pages)

A. *"Man with painted vest sitting on a cylindrical object; man's body hollowed. A tourist piece."* *An effigy figure, it has "Nampeyoh" penciled on the bottom. Pre-1933, 3¹/₂ in. high.* Eugene Prince, photographer. No. 2-47043, Phoebe Hearst Museum of Anthropology.

B. *This ceremonial bowl basket was a gift to Maurine Grammer from Nampeyo, ca. 1928. It is 6 in. high at the strap handle and 5 in. in diameter.* MG

Fig. 2.32. UNUSUAL NAMPEYO POTTERY SHAPES (cont.)

C. This vase with extended neck and side lugs was identified as Nampeyo's work by C. W. Douglas, who donated his collection to the Denver Art Museum. Undated, 7^1/$_2$ in. by 5^3/$_8$ in. at widest part of the bowl. No. H291-G, DAM.

D. Tall vase with typical Sikyatki design. Written on bottom, "1929 trip with...Edna, Sarah L. Davey. Given to me by Nampeyo." 7^3/$_4$ in. by 4 in. MG.

E. Dipper, made by Nampeyo during the winter of 1899–1900 and collected from her at Keams Canyon by C. M. Thompson, then an employee of Thomas Keam. Displaying simple Payupki-type decoration with a broken band around the rim. 9^3/$_4$ in. in length. No. XH209P, DAM.

Fig. 2.33. Nampeyo's avoidance of symmetry is evident in this piece. Note that the birds' eyes and the diamonds on the birds' necks appear the same but are negatives. Nampeyo often used optical illusion of this type to give the impression of balance. Made before 1915, 9 in. by 11¹/₈ in. No. E7573, 3174, MNAZ.

Fig. 2.36. POLACCA POLYCHROME VESSELS, CA. 1780–1890.

A. Utilitarian salt box in use in 1885 by a Hopi family at Polacca. Collected by J. Stevenson for John Wesley Powell and the Smithsonian and later transferred as part of a large collection to Oxford University. Pitmarks on the surface are the result of disruptive pressures from the gradual build-up of salt deposits in the pores of the vessel. Continued use of salt, especially when combined with high humidity, will eventually destroy a piece. 6¹/₂ in. wide by 5⁷/₈ in. deep. No. A9-F18-33, PRMOx.

B. Flared-lip bowl. This typical geometric design was applied by the Hopi potters of the Polacca Polychrome period; scholars think the motifs were borrowed from the Payupkis, who abandoned the area in 1748. 4³/₄ in. by 11¹/₂ in. L. Blair, photographer. No. 50.1/6699, AMNH.

Fig. 2.36. POLACCA POLYCHROME VESSELS (cont.)

C. *Jar, ca. 1880. The vessel has a typical shape, although the decoration shows both Spanish influence in the floral line painting and Zuni-Acoma influence on the remainder of the decoration. 4^1/$_2$ in. by 6^1/$_2$ in.* Photographed in 1989. No. PH16, RD.

D. *Bowl collected by Dr. Washington Matthews in 1885. The penciled number 1422 on the lower center right is similar to pencil notations 14510 (43-39-10/25615), 1441 (44-8-10/23736), and others in the Thomas V. Keam Collection of the Peabody Museum of Archaeology and Ethnology, Harvard University. The notations on the pottery appear to be in the handwriting of Alexander Stephen. 2^1/$_2$ in. by 6^5/$_8$ in.* No. E2335, AZSM.

Fig. 2.43. *San Bernardo pottery, ca. 1625–1740. The design on this jar is what Hopi potters now designate as a variation of an eagle design. This rendition has been copied by generations of Nampeyo potters. 14^1/$_2$ in. diameter, height unknown because of a broken base.* No. 43-39-10/25132, PMAE.

Fig. 2.46. *Navajo artist Jimmy Yellowhair's 1972 oil painting of a stylized migration-design Hopi pottery piece with an Apache Gan dancer in background.* Private collection.

Fig. 3.12. Soup tureen with handles, made by Marcella Kahe, Hopi potter from Sichomovi, First Mesa, in 1983. Few potters today make pieces such as this. $6^3/4$ in. by 8 in. with a 9-in. ladle. *Private collection.*

Fig. 3.16. Impressed designs. The Nampeyo family usually restricted impressed decoration to the necks of vessels, as in these examples. Such decoration is now something of a rarity.

Left: Signed "Nampuyo," this jar was probably painted by a daughter. $5^1/2$ in. by $9^7/8$ in. *Is. No. E2273, acquired by AZSM in 1946.*

Right: Attributed to Annie Healing, this large, unusual jar is 14 in. by 17 in. and combines a beautifully painted migration design with impressed areas both around the neck and on the snakelike applications at the shoulder. It provides a unique example of impression on the added fillets of clay. *Ronald Read, photographer. No. 86-11, Museum of Church History and Art, Church of Jesus Christ of Latter-day Saints.*

Fig. 3.20. *The fine-lined migration design requires a high degree of skill. Pictured are similar but distinctive renditions of the same design by Nampeyo and her three daughters.*

A. *Jar by Nampeyo, 1912, 5³/4 in. by 12 in.* W. Bruce McGee Collection.

B. *Bowl signed "Nellie Nampeyo," 3¹/2 in. by 7 in. Though Nellie's linework is often criticized, this work is very well done.* No. H50, RD.

C. *Bottom view of an "Annie Nampeyo" jar, 3¹/2 in. by 7 in. Although this example barely shows it, Annie is known for having used dots and squares to fill spaces between lines.* No. PH41, RD.

Fig. 3.21. Migration designs without fine-line painting, by Fannie Polacca. This striking decoration was adapted to fit many shapes.

A. Produced between 1930 and 1940, this large bowl has different interior and exterior versions of the migration design. 4$^1/_2$ in. by 12$^3/_8$ in. No E615, 1026 MNAZ.

B. Formed in January of 1987 by Fannie's daughter Tonita, this is one of the last pots Fannie decorated. The outstanding designer retained her ability to paint a fifteen-segment rendition to the end of her life. The signature on the bottom is accompanied by a drawing of an ear of corn. 4$^1/_2$ in. by 11 in. KCAC.

C. Made ca. 1971, this design does not contain a bottom boundary band. 5$^1/_2$ in. by 7 in. Hank Gans, photographer. KCAC.

Fig. 3.22. Eagle design. This style has its origin in Hopi history, but it evolved during the Sikyatki Revival, with each subsequent potter adding a distinctive touch.

A. Polacca Polychrome jar, ca. 1850–1900. Simple by today's standards, the basic elements (divided in thirds) are easily distinguishable. 8 in. by 12⁵/8 in. No. 12080/12, UNM.

B. A documented jar by Nampeyo, ca. 1920, this work lacks the red painted square that usually surrounds the opening. And as in the Polacca Polychrome jar, it is divided into three segments rather than the usual four. 2³/4 in. by 17 in. No. ASWHO-737P, HMPx.

D. **Below** Jar by Fannie Nampeyo Polacca, 1963. The slightly outcurved lip enhances the grace of the design. 8¹/2 in. by 10⁵/8 in. No. 63.32.1, UNM.

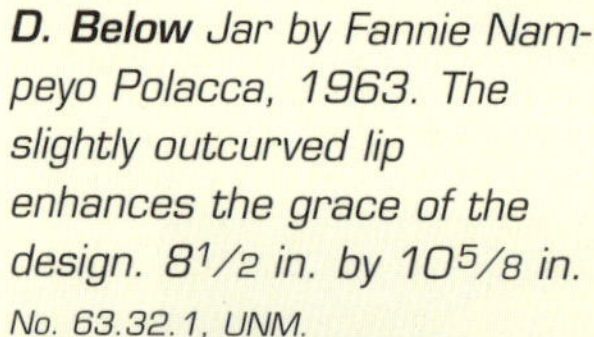

C. **Above** Jar attributed to Nampeyo, 1910–1915. This vessel was fashioned from yellow clay, which is more difficult to manipulate than others. When fired, the clay provides a red background for the black and white decorative elements. The design is perfectly adapted to the shape. No. 1207, SAR.

Fig. 3.27. Underfired jar. The gray areas and dull colors of this otherwise beautifully executed piece indicate that it was not completely fired. It could have been refired to correct this flaw, but the potter preferred to use it as a gift.

Fig. 4.6. Pottery by Annie Healing, Nellie Douma, and Cecelia Lesou, daughters and daughter-in-law of Nampeyo.

A. Below: This bowl is signed "Annie Nampeyo," a rarity. The narrow fine-line decoration and row of dots are characteristic of Annie's work. 3 in. by 7 in. No. PH41, RD.

B. Above: This bowl with the head of a Hopi maiden was made by Nellie Douma and given to Maurine Grammer in about 1928. 3³/4 in. by 3¹/2 in.

C. Left: A polychrome jar attributed to Cecelia Lesou. Although a Pima Indian, Cecelia applied Sikyatki and Awatovi designs to her pottery. 4 in. by 8¹/2 in. No. 1984-41, SAR.

Fig. 4.13. Rachel Namingha decorated this jar with a classic fine-line migration design in 1976. Rachel lost her eyesight in 1978. Beginning about 1976 and continuing until her death, she was assisted in her pottery decoration by her daughter Priscilla Sahmie and her sister Daisy Hooee. $7^1/2$ in. by $6^3/4$ in. Private collection.

Fig. 4.14. A modern adaptation of the old water storage jar with an applied decoration of two ears of corn made by Les Namingha in 1989. The slender-walled vessel was covered with a thin, white, polished slip, which allows portions of the natural-colored body to show through. $3^1/2$ in. by $7^3/4$ in. Private collection.

Fig. 4.15. Polychrome vase made in 1973 and signed "Priscilla Namingha Nampeyo." The thin-walled vessel is decorated with a precisely painted, fine-line migration design. $6^1/2$ in. by $7^1/2$ in. Private collection.

Fig. 4.17. Ceramic plaque made ca. 1987 by Ida Sahmie, a Navajo married to Andrew Sahmie, a great-great-grandson of Nampeyo. Although Ida has mastered Hopi potters' techniques, she has avoided all the restrictions placed upon her regarding Hopi and Hopi-Tewa designs. Here she reproduced a version of the Great Seal of the Navajo Nation. $7^{7}/_{8}$ in. in diameter by $^{3}/_{16}$ in. thick. Private collection.

Fig. 4.18. Flat-shouldered and curve-necked pot made by Darlene James Vigil in 1987, a shape considerably difficult to form. Darlene inscribes her pieces "Darlene Nampeyo," accompanied by an ear of corn. 6 in. by $10^{3}/_{4}$ in. Private collection.

Fig. 4.19. Although this jar by Steve Lucas, son of Eleanor Namingha Lucas, bears a shoulder decoration that appears similar to that of Darlene James Vigil (above), the work on the overall surface is more complicated. The base contains four geometric designs, highlighted by surrounding incised surfaces. Signed "Steve Lucas Koyemsi" and made in 1992. $4^{1}/_{2}$ in. by $6^{1}/_{2}$ in. Private collection.

Fig. 4.21. *A classic rendition of a "sherd bowl" by Dextra Namingha Quotskuyva. This 1973 bowl shows her artistry at its best, adapting an exact reproduction of prehistoric designs in the creative work of the present. The individual renditions are miniature replicas of sherds from surrounding prehistoric Hopi ruins. Very thin-walled and smooth, this masterpiece is signed simply "Dextra" with an accompanying drawing of an ear of corn. 4¹/₂ in. by 7 in.* Private collection.

Fig. 4.23. *Pottery of mother and daughter, Daisy Hooee and Shirley Benn.* **Left:** *In this joint work by Daisy and Shirley, decoration is a unique combination of Zuni and Hopi-Tewa design. The interior is decorated with typical Zuni frogs and tadpoles, while the exterior has a band of elements bordered by unbroken cloud bands. The bowl was made in 1988, late in Daisy's professional life, and signed "Daisy H. Nampeyo and Shirley Benn." 2¹/₂ in. by 5 in.* **Right:** *Early bowl by Shirley Benn, made in 1977 and decorated with Sikyatki design elements. 3³/₄ in. by 4 in.* Private collections. L. Blair, photographer.

Fig. 4.24. *Art of Cheryl Naha and Marlin Pinto, grandchildren of Daisy Healing Hooee.* **Top center:** *Sikyatki-style, flared-rim jar made by Cheryl Naha in 1991 while she was helping to care for her grandmother, Daisy. The work is signed "C. Naha Nampeyo." 3^1/$_2$ in. by 4 in.* **Front:** *Entitled "Hunting Mountain Sheep," this 1981 sculpture by Marlin Pinto consists of two finely carved [and painted?] wooden figures mounted on*

a branch. The hunter with bow and arrow at the left is 1^3/$_4$ in. high, and the mountain sheep on the right is 2 in. high. Private collection.

Fig. 4.27. Left: *A jar by Alton Komalestewa made in 1996. The jar is 8^1/$_2$ in. by 11^1/$_2$ in. and is signed "Alton Komalestewa," accompanied by his symbol.* Bahti Indian Arts. **Right:** *A pot by Helen Baca Shupla, master potter of Santa Clara Pueblo, who taught her Hopi-Tewa son-in-law Alton Komalestewa the art of ceramics when he lived at Santa Clara. Helen made this tan, float-polished melon bowl in 1983, a difficult shape*

to construct because the grooves are formed in the pliable clay simultaneously from both the inside and the outside. The opening at the top is so small that it is hard to envision how Helen made the ribs. Signed "Helen Shupla Santa Clara Pueblo." 8^3/$_4$ in. by 9 in. Private collection.

Fig. 4.36. (next two pages) Cooperatively created pottery pieces which appeared shortly after 1920. Presumably, they were decorated by Fannie and formed by Nampeyo. As time passed, Fannie gradually assumed more tasks but always maintained that her mother's smoothing and polishing techniques were superior to hers. L. Blair, photographer.

A. Polychrome bowl made between 1934 and 1940. The curved arrow motif (pointing to the left) is a characteristic found on many of the Nampeyo family's pottery. 3³/4 in. by 6³/4 in. No. PH53, RD.

B. Triangular pitcher, signed "Nampeyo/Fannie," with a rather unusual heart-shaped opening and a lug for hanging. Made for the collector trade about 1930. 3³/4 in. by 7³/4 in. No. A-SW-HO-A 7-98, HMPx.

C. *Bowl decorated with a classic fine-line migration pattern, typical of Fannie's work. It was made in 1935 and signed as shown. The detail that terminates the fine-line area, particularly the four wavy lines, is characteristic of Fannie and has often been duplicated by her descendants. 9$^1/8$ in. by 14$^3/8$ in. No. E2630,774, MNAZ.*

D. *This 1936 bowl is decorated with a combination of stylized Sikyatki birds and Polacca Polychrome elements. Signed "Nampeyo Fannie." 7$^7/8$ in. by 14$^1/2$ in. No. E245,774, MNAZ.*

Fig. 4.38. *(next three pages) Miscellaneous pottery produced by Fannie Polacca from 1970 to 1980. Fannie became famous for her fine-line migration patterns and eagle motifs. A few of her individual design variations are pictured here. The simplest of these were primers for teaching her children and grandchildren, but most appear to be made with no objective other than for sale to the general market. Two exceptions, E and F, are of a more intricate design, indicating that they were perhaps made for competitions or for select purchasers. Note that with the exception of C, each design is topped with a solid black cloud band, the starting element on most of Fannie's work.*

A. These decorations contain termination elements of the migration design, combined with random curved-line geometric forms of no particular significance.

B. This simple decoration, except for the heavy lines, resembles the early uncomplicated and flowing decorations of Nampeyo. According to Fewkes, the design elements represent prayer feathers tied together to the ends of strings; the black circles represent knots. This motif is peculiar to prehistoric Hopi pottery.

Fig. 4.38. *(cont.)*

C. *A crudely formed and decorated piece, probably made for quick sale.*

D. *Design elements which Fannie taught her descendants. They were either developed or transmitted by Nampeyo.* Pieces A through D from the collection of William Bruce McGee, photographed by H. Ganz.

Fig. 4.38. (cont.)

E. *This often reproduced design of Fannie's, a modified eagle motif, was made in 1922 during the time that she worked closely with her mother. Designs of this period are said to represent the last phase of Nampeyo's experimentation, when Fannie was beginning to exert much influence on her mother's work.* 4^1/$_2$ in. by 9^7/$_8$ in.
No. E.433,918, MNAZ. Obtained by Harold S. Colton.

F. *Dated ca. 1940, this large bowl is decorated with designs resembling those of Meso-American Indian artists. The head in the center is strikingly similar to the representations of the Mayan gods so often applied to prehistoric Mexican architecture, pottery, and sculpture, especially the creator god, Ixhel, and the god of corn, Yum Kax (Chan 1970: 76, 77). The designs in the band surrounding the interior are composed of six red, gray, and black geometric elements similar to the silhouettes of Mayan temple structures.* 4^3/$_4$ in. by 13^3/$_8$ in.
No. E.947, MNAZ.

Fig. 4.41. *The Elva Polacca Tewaguna family and their work.* ***A.*** *A bowl by Elva Polacca Tewaguna with the classic eagle decoration so characteristic of Nampeyo family members. This well-formed, thin-walled piece was made in 1979 and signed "Elva Nampeyo" with an accompanying drawing of an ear of corn. 5 in. by 10³/4 in.* Private collection.

B. *An innovative vase made by Neva Tewaguna in 1978. The deep brown decoration is applied over a sanded, unslipped portion on the bottom, while the top section is red-slipped and polished using a technique familiar to the potters of the Rio Grande area. Signed "Neva Nampeyo." 4¹/2 in. by 3³/4 in.* Private collection.

C. *Adelle Tewaguna Lalo made this in 1975, breaking with tradition from the standpoint of surface finish. She applied the Awatovi design to a finely sanded, unpolished surface. Signed "Adelle Nampeyo." 3³/8 in. by 4¹/8 in.* Private collection.

D. *A beautiful Sikyatki-shaped jar by Miriam Tewaguna Ami. 4³/4 in. by 10¹/2 in.* KCAC.

Fig. 4.43. The moth or butterfly design is thought to have been developed first by the potters of Sikyatki ca. 1600. Pottery so decorated was buried with the dead and lost until recognized by Thomas Keam ca. 1880 and J. W. Fewkes in 1895. Since then, the butterfly design and other Sikyatki elements have been copied by many Hopi-Tewa potters, including Grace Chapella, Nampeyo, and their family members. **Left:** Jar excavated by Fewkes during his brief 1895 expedition. Color plate CXXV, Fewkes 1895. Douglas Library, DAM.

Right: This thin-walled, deep jar was made by Leah Polacca Garcia's son James Garcia in 1988. Although uncomplicated, his modified decoration includes all the design elements found on the old Sikyatki piece discovered by Fewkes. It is signed "James Nampeyo" with an accompanying drawing of an ear of corn. 11 by 15 1/2 in. Private collection.

*Fig. 4.45. Innovative artist Thomas Polacca was one of the first to produce art pieces that departed radically from the ancient Hopi designs yet retained the essence of Hopi culture and design. **A.** Thomas made this spectacular jar in 1978 with delicately incised designs of kachina faces and bear paws. Occasionally he put turquoise insets such as these on his work. Signed "Thomas Polacca." 8 in. by 10 in. KCAC.*

B. Two views of a carved and painted seed bowl commemorating the tricentennial anniversary of the 1680 Pueblo Revolt. The boldly executed upper surface depicts a priest about to be killed by the kachina. The lower section is covered by classic Payupki design elements. The coloring agent, from an extract of the tansy mustard plant, both emphasizes the design and gives the appearance of carved wood. It is signed "Nampayo." 7 in. by 7³/₄ in. Private collection.

Fig. 4.46. Left: *Salako Mana figurine or effigy, ca. 1869–1890. It was probably made for the tourist trade under the direction of Thomas Keam. 7³/8 in. by 3¹/2 in.* No. PM44-14-10/27118, KM83917 *from* America's Great Lost Expedition: The Thomas Keam Hopi Pottery from the Second Hemenway Expedition, 1890–1894, *p.90.*

Right: *Salako Mana figurine made in 1982 by Gary Polacca. This version has a removable upper body that acts as a stopper for the lower feather-draped section. 4 in. by 1³/4 in.* Private collection.

Fig. 4.48. The work of the Tonita Polacca Hamilton family.

A. *The beautiful execution of the fine-line painting on this pot provides but one example of Tonita's skills, illustrating innovative decoration with classic design elements. The work is signed "Tonita Nampeyo" with a drawing of an ear of corn. Made in 1985. 7 1/2 in. by 11 3/4 in.* Adobe Art Gallery.

B. *Eugene Hamilton assists his wife with her ceramic art. He occasionally produces work on his own, such as this small seed bowl, made in 1981. This unique piece is carved and partially white-slipped. Signed with a symbol of a deer's hoofprint. 4 1/2 in. by 4 3/8 in.* Private collection.

C. *Following the teaching and encouragement of his mother, Tonita, and his uncle Thomas, Loren Hamilton was recognized for his outstanding pottery work at an early age. The 1986 piece shown here illustrates his flare for unusual designs that incorporate classic Hopi ceremonial symbols. The shallow carving, delicate and finely detailed, differs from that of Thomas Polacca but resembles that of his cousin Gary. Loren signed the work by incising "Loren H. Nampeyo" and a symbol of a stalk of corn bearing ears. 3 1/2 in. by 5 3/8 in.* KCAC.

Fig. 4.50. *Iris Polacca Youvella family and their work.*

A. *This jar by Iris Youvella illustrates her outstanding ability to produce firing tones of a delicate pink hue, which add much to the value and beauty of her work. Incised with the signature "Iris Youvella" and a drawing of an ear of corn. 6 in. by 7 in.* L. Blair, photographer, KCAC.

B. *Wallace Youvella learned pottery making from his well-known mother, Susie Youvella, and his brother-in-law Thomas Polacca. The brilliantly colored portions of this contemporary artpiece, such as the bright cobalt blue area beneath the arrow, result from commercial ceramic stains. Most of Wally's work is traditionally decorated with natural pigments. Made ca. 1990. 2$^1/_2$ in. by 9 in.* KCAC.

C. *An Iris Youvella polychrome bowl with the prehistoric motif of tied prayer feathers. It was made in 1974 and signed "Iris Nampeyo." 2 in. by 2$^3/_4$ in.* Private collection.

D. *A bowl by Charlene Youvella, one of Iris and Wallace's four children. Charlene made the simply decorated bowl and then polished it with the assistance of her mother. Made in 1983. $^7/_8$ in. by 1$^3/_4$ in.* Youvella collection.

in the way of good in the photographic development of the Indian this trip."[7]

Artist William R. Leigh made numerous trips to the area to capture Southwest scenes and people on canvas. In the summer of 1905 he was introduced to the countryside and shown around by his former Munich classmate, Albert Groll. This was the year after Groll photographed and sketched at First Mesa. Over the next several years Leigh sketched and painted the area while he endeavored to establish his own reputation as a gallery artist. While a guest of Lorenzo Hubbell, he worked at First Mesa and also did an oil painting of Keam's second trading post. Although there is no mention of his ever contacting Nampeyo or members of her family, he admired the Nampeyos' pottery and acquired a few of their pieces to decorate his studio. They are housed in the Nampeyo collection of the Thomas Gilcrease Institute of American History and Art, Tulsa.

Amateur and professional photographers along with anthropologists and the curious continually interrupted Nampeyo family life for pictures. In 1920, for example, the photographer Charles Loefell took 35mm motion pictures of Nampeyo and other Hopi artisans at work.[8] A cursory study of images taken of Nampeyo between 1904 and 1935 clearly reveals the development of her blindness with age. A photo taken by Tad Nichols shows Nampeyo after she was totally blind (fig. 4.2).[9]

Fig. 4.2. One of only a few photographs of Nampeyo dressed in her everyday clothes, taken by Tad Nichols in the late 1930s. No. MS264-3-6, Gretchen Swinnerton Collection, MNAZ.

As early as 1913 the notes of Barbara Freire-Marreco shed some light on other outstanding potters who were beginning to vie with the Nampeyo family for a place in the Indian art market. These include Paqua (the original Frog Lady), Paelae (a Corn Clan potter), and Grace Chapella, all of whom Freire-Marreco met during her stay at Hopi (fig. 4.3). They had all begun making pottery before the turn of the century. These and other First Mesa potters had good technical skills, but Nampeyo stood out for her artistic flair. She also had the advantage of good publicity because of her willingness to travel and to demonstrate her craft for photographers.

In 1922 Fred Kabotie, one of the founders of the Hopi Indian Arts and Crafts Cooperative Guild and himself an outstanding Hopi painter, made arrangements for members of the Heye Foundation, the Smithsonian, and Dr. E. L. Hewett of the School of American Archaeology to visit the Hopi Reservation. Kabotie recalled:

> We borrowed cars and bed rolls for going up there. It took four or five days [the distance between First Mesa, Arizona, and Santa Fe, New Mexico, is close to 305 miles]. I remember we spent a night at Grants, barely made it, so rainy. We went through Gallup, then the third night at Steamboat, over the hill between Window Rock and Ganado. No road but end up in a Navajo hogan. Most of the time Hewett was walking. The Model T had no power. We would go up a hill backwards with the car. We found Nampeyo. She had some pottery with wonderful painting on it sitting on a stack of corn, some broken. Dr. Hewett had men from Washington (Smithsonian Institution) and New York (Heye Foundation). These men bought all the potteries, even broken. My, my, Hewett thought they were so good he even bought the broken ones.[10]

Mary-Russell Colton, wife of the director of the Museum of Northern Arizona, was also an outstanding contributor to the preservation and improvement of Hopi art. She conceived and launched the Hopi Craftsman Exhibition, which, with the exception of World War II

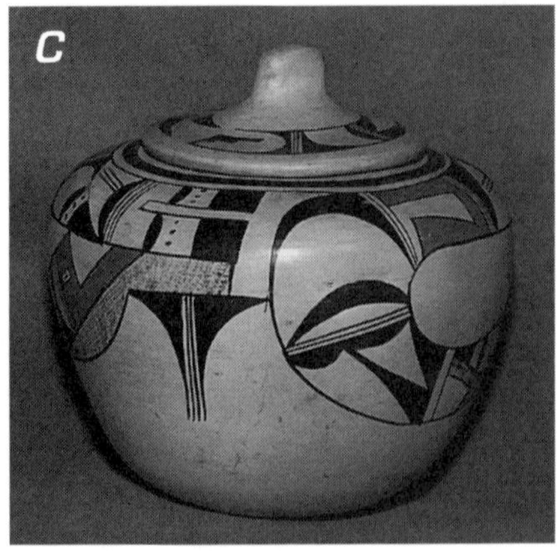

Fig. 4.3. Pottery by Nampeyo's contemporaries. As Nampeyo's fame and income increased, other potters were inspired to improve their own work. As increasing blindness slowed Nampeyo's output and diminished the quality of her work, the work of others began to attract buyers. **A.** This canteen with lugs was made by Paelae, also Hopi-Tewa of the Corn Clan. Approximately 4$^1/_2$ in. in diameter. L. Blair, photographer. PRMOx. **B.** A polychrome jar made by Grace Chapella, a Hopi-Tewa, in about 1968 when she was ninety-four. The butterfly or moth design, often applied by Grace and her great-grandson, Mark Tahbo, is an old Sikyatki design favored by Hopi-Tewa potters, including Nampeyo and her family. 7$^1/_8$ in. by 8$^1/_2$ in. Private collection. **C.** A polychrome jar with lid, made by Paqua, the original Hopi-Tewa Frog Lady, in about 1940. Paqua lived near the Awatovi ruins and was known to have used designs from there for inspiration. 5$^3/_4$ in. by 8 in. with a lid 2 in. by 3$^3/_4$ in. Private collection.

years, has been held annually at the museum since 1930. The Nampeyo potters have participated since its inception and contributed toward raising the quality of ceramic work to the high level it now enjoys.

In the 1930s, however, the quality of Hopi pottery deteriorated while the output increased, a result of several factors. Early traders such as Keam and Hubbell, inadvertently or otherwise, had encouraged potters to make large artistic vessels after the fashion of prehistoric pottery, but for more than thirty years after the turn of the century, the emphasis shifted to a knickknack type of souvenir. The traders at that time wanted small curio type pottery that could be easily shipped without breakage. The Great Depression that affected all of the United States was especially difficult for Native Americans. Tourists who did get as far as the Hopi Reservation wanted to purchase small, easily transported items, and there was no demand for larger, more expensive pottery. Potters sold small, poorly decorated, and carelessly formed and fired pieces to those offering quick cash, whether licensed traders or those who came to the reservation. Cheap souvenirs had replaced the beautiful Hopi artwork of earlier times (fig. 4.4).

The depression was also responsible for a decrease in the number of visitors to the mesa villages. Sales dwindled and what was sold

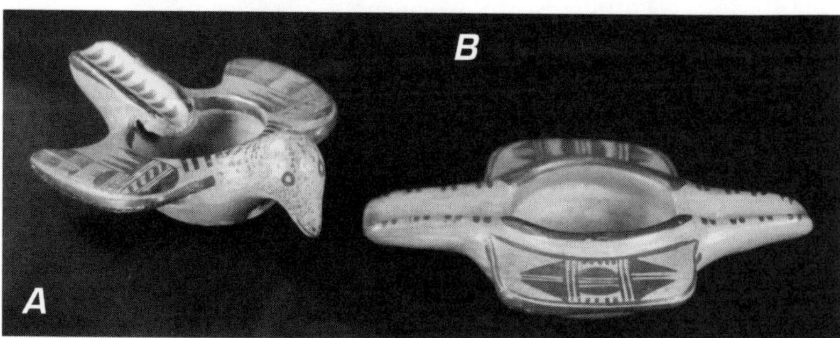

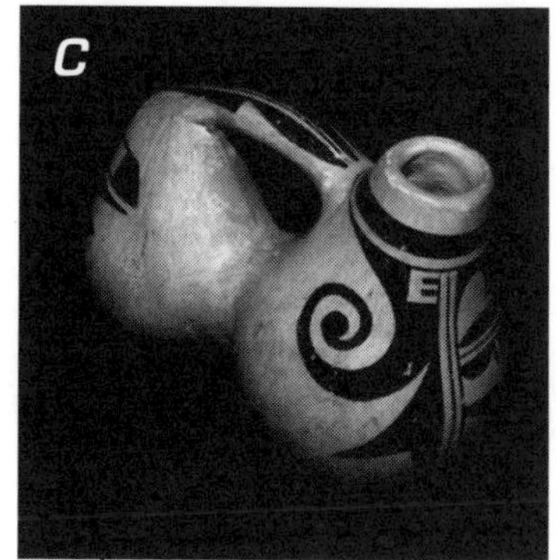

*Fig. 4.4. Examples of souvenir pottery made by members of the Nampeyo family. All pieces are signed, indicating that they were made or decorated by her daughters. **A** and **B**. Two ashtrays signed "Nampeyo." Each is 5⁷/₈ in. by 4³/₈ in. Fannie Nampeyo Polacca was known to have made ceramic objects similar to these. Nos. 72.10.61 and 72.10.62., UNM. **C**. A very crude copy of a prehistoric shape, decorated with Sikyatki elements. It has a combination signature, "Nampeyo-Fannie" and measures 5 in. by 7 in. L. Blair, photographer. Hanging Tree Gallery.*

brought depressed prices. Admirers of Hopi art became concerned and took steps to help the situation. Fine Hopi pottery was featured in the 1931 exposition of Indian Tribal Arts held in New York and at the 1939 San Francisco Exposition. The U. S. Department of the Interior, in an attempt to remedy a bad situation, established the American Indian Arts and Crafts Board.

The Nampeyo-Lesou descendants and others like them survived the 1930s by working the land. They raised crops, much of which they dried. Sheep and a few cattle provided animal products that were traded for clothes, coffee, butter, and other subsistence items. One descendant recalled: "A lot of people were exchanging things. I don't think that it [the depression] really hit them that much. I can remember some of the things that went on that we were exchanging.... People were good at exchanging things." Dozier commented on the complex system.

> The most characteristic aspect of Hano and Hopi economics is the exchange system [reciprocity]—the method by which food, services, and certain types of goods are exchanged. These practices link all of the people on First Mesa, at times involve Hopi from more distant villages as well. The system operates within the household, clan, linked clans, kiva groups, and between the three communities on First Mesa. Exchanges occur on specific occasions in an individual's life cycle [puberty, entrance into a ceremonial association, and at marriage] and are an integral part of every ceremonial rite. These practices have prevented economic stratification; the Hopi and Tewa population is essentially on an equal economic footing. In addition to this economic leveling effect, these activities have contributed to the increasing trend toward social and cultural integration on First Mesa.[11]

Sharing included water conservation and the maintenance of communal springs and wells also. Prior to the installation atop the mesa of large storage tanks that were fed by pressurized wells, water had to be hauled from Coyote Spring several hundred feet below. Springs were critical for survival, and water from them continues to be used for ceremonial purposes. In the past, rainwater and melted snow flowed into rock holes that acted as reservoirs. Water preservation and distribution work was shared.

Preparation for a wedding still requires a sharing of responsibilities. The groom's male relatives must provide the bride's traditional wedding apparel, an expensive wardrobe consisting of a large cape and a smaller robe, a *manta* (dress), a broad braided belt, a narrow woman's belt, and thigh-length moccasins. In addition, the male's relatives must find a particular kind of reed and make a "suitcase" to hold parts of this costume. Nowadays, few Hopi households have male members with the skills to fabricate these items; they are most often purchased for cash or exchange from individuals outside the family. Recently, the cost of the manta alone was set at six hundred dollars. Quite often, the marrying couples, including Nampeyo descendants, must wait years beyond their civil marriage before they can afford the essential traditional Hopi wedding, the only legitimate marriage in their view.

Hunting of large game is a family activity and is not governed by traditional patterns of clan behavior. The kill is shared equally among family members and does not depend on past contributions of any individual. Prior to dividing the fruits of the hunt, the family and invited guests hold a large gala, a tradition observed almost every year during deer hunting season in November.

Cooperation within the same family or clan can also extend to pottery making. Occasionally, they share clay digging responsibilities as well as fuel for firing. They also exchange new pottery designs and forming techniques; however, they will often resent direct copying without consultation. Cooperation within Hopi-Tewa families seems more prevalent than that observed in the Rio Grande Tewa. Seldom does a potter make derogatory remarks about the work of another family member as do some Rio Grande families. A Hopi-Tewa is less apt to claim "secret" procedures, a term often used to attempt to cover up commercial kiln firing or the substitution of commercial ceramic colors for those made from the plants and soil of their environments.

Overall, life in the past was no easier for the children of Nampeyo's household than for those of other Hopi families. In spite of outside influences, their standard of living was no higher than others nor were their household tasks any lighter than the neighbors' children. They worked as hard as other Hopis; the quality and quantity of their worldly goods and food supplies equaled that of others—no better, no worse. What they did receive, however, was a unique example of artistic achievement in their mother's pottery and in the world's response to it. All but two of the known offspring of Nampeyo would develop artistic statements of their own, continuing the legacy in their own ways. Nampeyo's children Pela and Kalokun died before they could contribute much to life.

Annie Healing

The oldest child belonging to Nampeyo and Lesou was Annie, known through most of her early life as "Quachewa" (phonetic spelling Kwe-tea-we), or Blue Corn Piki Bread. Born in 1883, when the intrusion of Euro-Americans into the Hopi-Tewa culture was in its infancy, Annie lived through the U. S. government-imposed rules on the political, social, and educational conduct of her people. However, many of this family cleverly used a few of the imposed edicts to their advantage.

The earliest located photograph of Annie was taken by Ben Wittick in 1897 (fig. 4.5). The picture shows a lanky, barefooted, tall (for a Hopi-Tewa) young woman, whose hair style is that of a Hopi maiden; she carries a burden to the roof of the Corn Clan house. Shortly after this photo was taken, she married Willie Healing. Although Willie had a strong interest in farming and ranching, the first years of his marriage to Annie were spent in close association with Nampeyo and Lesou. The couple lived with Nampeyo and Lesou at the Corn Clan house and accompanied them when they demonstrated their craft at the Grand Canyon.

In about 1900 Annie was working with Nampeyo on pottery, adding innovative touches of her own. She was pressed into service for two reasons: Nampeyo, deluged with requests for her work, was under pressure to increase her output; also she was beginning to lose her

Fig. 4.5. *Annie climbs to the roof of the Corn Clan house.* Ben Wittick photographer. Neg. No. 2614, MNM.

eyesight and hence her dexterity at decorating pottery. She did not hide her daughter's contributions but promoted Annie's work on all occasions, posing with her for photographs (fig. 2.8). In 1907 Clara Churchill noted that Annie was assisting her mother in her work.[12]

An innovation, possibly by Annie, was serpentlike, impressed design or applied fillets of clay added to the necks and rims of pottery (fig. 3.16). Although many of these pieces are designated as being Nampeyo's, they all appear to have been formed during the period when Annie worked closely with her mother. Only a few works signed "Annie" have been located, and it is not known if Annie could write; so it is possible that the signature had been applied by someone other than Annie. The particular pots in question are often decorated with migration designs, which are characterized by elongated crosshatched patterns that are separated from the feather terminations by rows of small dots (fig. 4.6—see p. XVII).

Following her marriage, Annie had less time to work with her mother on pottery. Chores now included caring for children and the preparation and preservation of food supplied by her husband's farming and ranching efforts. A portion of the land on which the Healings raised crops was allotted to the Tewas by the Hopis when they first migrated to the area from the Rio Grande valley following the Second Pueblo Revolt of 1692.

Livestock was kept at the Sand Hills Ranch. With a generous supply of water from Tom Polacca's well, Willie's animals thrived. The only practice with which Willie disagreed was Tom's planting of many cottonwood trees, which Healing felt demanded too much water and would eventually seriously deplete the water supply. The family kept horses, sheep, goats, and cattle at the ranch. These provided meat, milk products, and animal skins in amounts generous enough to share with relatives and to trade to Tom Pavatea for food staples and hardware. Contrary to some opinions, the Healings considered Tom to be a fair trader. The families were friends. Their grazing areas were in close proximity, for Pavatea's were located just below the Polacca holdings. Willie was able to provide his family with one of the finest homes in Polacca. It was located northeast of Nampeyo's house (figs. 4.7 and 4.8), and the grounds were landscaped and partially surrounded with a large peach orchard. The house stands to this day, while other houses have crowded in at the expense of the orchard.

Fig. 4.7. *This 1926 or 1927 photograph of the Healing home was taken by Beatrice Blackwood. No. BB3N, Courtesy of the Beatrice Blackwood Collection, PRMOx.*

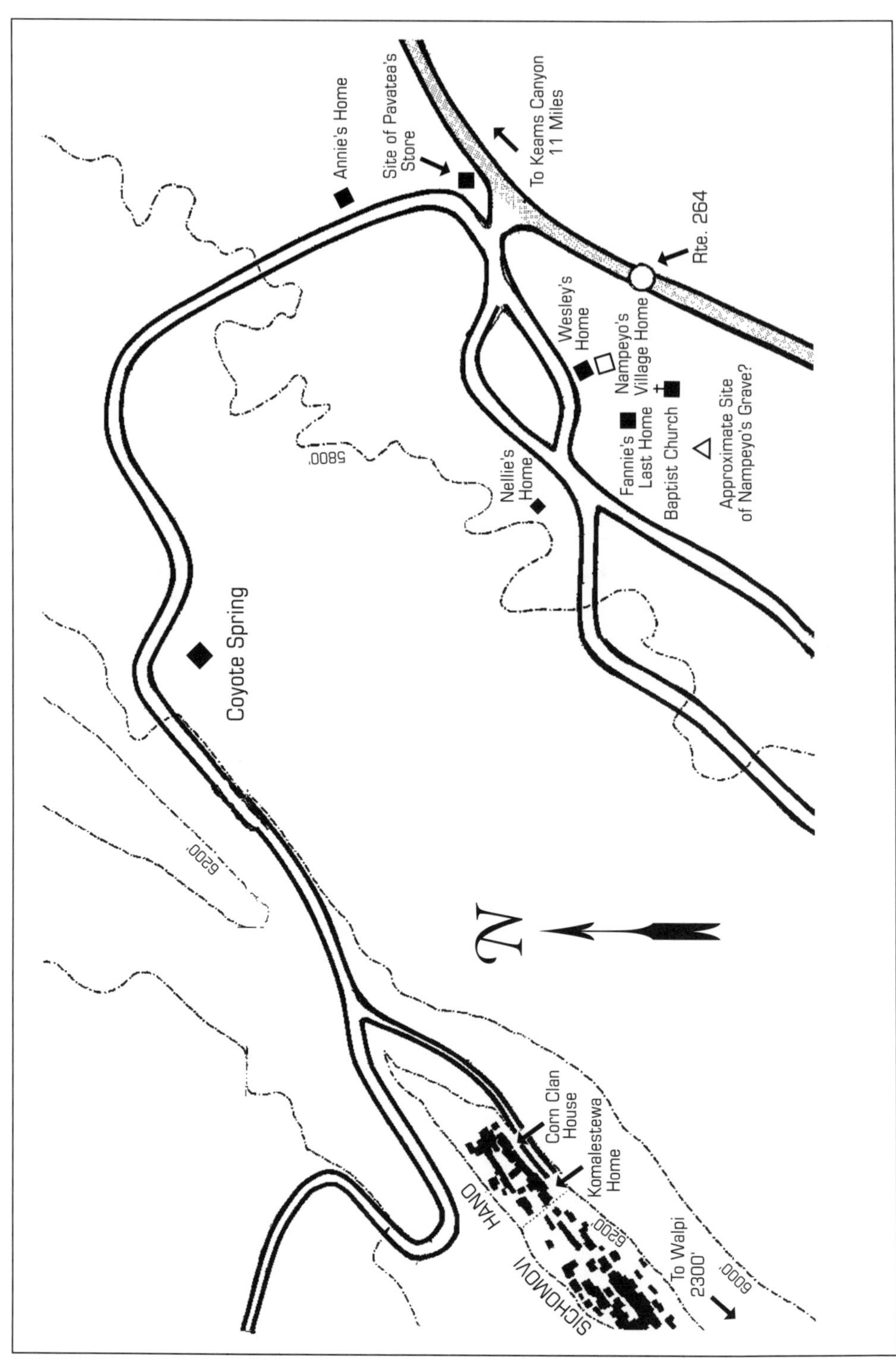

Fig. 4.8. *This historic map of Polacca shows points of importance to Nampeyo family members. (Map not to scale.)*

Annie's life and the lives of her children were influenced by Anita Baldwin, the philanthropist and founder of California's Santa Anita Race Track. In 1924, pursuing a strong interest in studying American Indian ways, she came to Winslow via a private railroad car and from there by wagon to Polacca to study the Hopi people, their customs, and their music. With a group of friends, she camped near the Healing peach orchard and took an immediate interest in the family. She encouraged them to pursue their art and provided much needed medical help for one of the children.

The word "camp" does not do justice to the temporary home erected on the flat land below First Mesa (fig. 4.9). The camp consisted of a group of large, decorated, imposing tents that might make the homes of any bedouin prince pale in comparison. Most tents were connected to one another to resemble the rooms of a well-appointed home, and they included sleeping quarters, a dining room, a living

Fig. 4.9. *The Healing family poses for a photograph that was presumably taken by Anita Baldwin. The spectacular Baldwin tents almost surround the family.* **Left to right** *are Rachel Healing Namingha, Annie Lesou Healing holding Priscilla Namingha Sahmie, and Lydia (Lucia?) holding the hand of Willie Healing. First Mesa stands in the background.* Photograph courtesy of Dextra Quotskuyva.

room, and a library. Portable wooden sidewalks were built on the site, leading to the entrance of the main structure and to adjoining service tents. All was supported by a staff of Chinese workers and cooks who formed part of the entourage. In this setting, Mrs. Baldwin hosted Annie and members of her family.[13]

Authentic pieces of Annie's pottery are difficult to locate. Her time for making pottery was limited by her responsibilities in raising a large family. Her early work may be attributed to her mother, for signing Nampeyo's name to vessels on which she had done work brought higher prices. She probably did more decorating than forming. Later in life, Annie was plagued by poor health and failing eyesight, as had been her mother's fate. The children noted that she was subjected increasingly to severe coughing spells as well as arthritis, and she required more rest than normal. Dust generated as the result of working with pottery clay did not improve the situation. As her eyesight dimmed, Annie's children began to help her with pottery decoration. Rachel most often assisted her and was repaid with cotton stockings.

Despite her weakened condition, Annie lived a long life. She passed away in 1968, well into her eighties.

The Healing Children

Annie and Willie Healing parented a close-knit family of five children, the first and last separated in age by twelve years. Rachel the first, was born in 1900, Beatrice, the last, in 1912. The parents insisted that their children receive the best education available at the time.

During that era the education of a Hopi child was in no way comparable to that provided today. The descendants of Nampeyo, with few exceptions, followed a set educational pattern. They first attended either the Polacca Day School, opened in 1894 in a building made available by Nampeyo's brother Tom (fig. 4.10), or other schools close by such as the ones at Keams Canyon and Oraibi. Their education was usually completed at the Phoenix Indian School (fig. 4.11). The educational objective of all government institutions was based

Fig. 4.10. *Children line the wall of the Polacca Day School. Wesley Lesou, Nellie Douma, and Fannie Polacca attended this school approximately two decades before the photograph was taken in 1926.* No. BB2N, Beatrice Blackwood Collection, PRMOx.

Fig. 4.11. *Phoenix Indian School. The photograph was taken shortly after 1900 and shows the campus as it appeared to Nampeyo's children, who attended the institution. The large structure in the center housed the girls' dormitory on the second floor.* Photograph courtesy of the Arizona Historical Foundation, Hayden Library, Arizona State University.

on the philosophy of the Commissioner of Indian Affairs. The commissioner at the time of the Phoenix Indian School, Thomas J. Morgan, wrote, "The Indian must conform to the white man's ways, peaceably if they will, forcibly if they must." Morgan viewed the establishment of all nonreservation Indian schools as a means of obtaining his goals.[14] The early objectives of government education did not accommodate the study of Native American crafts until 1935, when the school first employed Indian craftsmen to supposedly teach skills such as pottery and basket making. These arts were far better taught at home by parents and grandparents. Many regret that forced attendance at these institutions retarded the development of ceramic art amongst many of Nampeyo's descendants. One of them offered the opinion about the education of Hopi and Hopi-Tewa girls in general: "If she had not wasted the time in the schools she might have learned to shape the pottery and draw on it the symbols of an old faith with the brush of the yucca fiber,—and some day she might have made it fine as the work of Nampeyo, but all the years were lost in the schools."[15] The Healing boys received vocational training, while the girls were taught domestic skills. Such an education was all that was available to most Indians.

The Rachel Healing Namingha Family

Rachel Healing, born in 1900, was of preschool age when she accompanied her parents and grandmother Nampeyo to the Grand Canyon in 1905 (fig. 4.12). She was undoubtedly one of the family's children that the Harvey people complained were spoiled, ran around uncontrolled, and did nothing unless they were paid.[16]

Rachel's children are of the opinion that their mother learned more about pottery making from Nampeyo than from her mother Annie. Nampeyo, Annie, and Rachel worked together, assisting one another with various aspects of pottery making, even triple firings. Rachel Healing Namingha was a strictly traditional potter whose classic decorative styles resembled those of her mother and grandmother (fig. 4.13—see p. XVIII). She did not approve of broad adaptations of ancient designs but instead chided her children when she considered their

Fig. 4.12. Annie Healing and daughter Rachel posed for this photo taken about 1901 by Adam Vroman. No.V-682, SCWHR.

work too innovative. Among those who occasionally departed from her norms were daughters Priscilla, Dextra, and their offspring.

As a young woman, Rachel worked as a cook at the Hubbell Trading Post in Ganado. Several other Hopi-Tewa girls who later gained reputations as fine potters worked at the post at the same time, including Fannie (Rachel's aunt who was near her age), Laura Lomakema, and Sadie Adams. The three conspired to play a prank on Rachel by shutting her in a dark closet which so frightened her that she left for home.

The marriage of Rachel to Emerson Namingha took place about 1923; the couple had seven children whose births, beginning with Priscilla, covered a time span of more than a decade. The number of potters, artists, and carvers included in the ranks of Rachel's descendants is impressive. Rough count indicates that they include at least eighteen potters, four artists, and three carvers related by blood, and two potters, two artists, and two carvers related by marriage.

Emerson Namingha Jr. married a Zuni woman. Their son, Les, grew up at Zuni but also recognizes his Hopi-Tewa heritage, especially admiring the work of his aunt, Dextra Quotskuyva (who also inspired his cousin Steve Lucas and Dextra's daughter, Camille, at about the same time). Les studied design at Brigham Young University and earned a bachelor's degree. He is now producing high-quality, original pottery, work which he finds consuming and demanding great patience (fig. 4.14—see p. XVIII). He obtains clay from Melda Navasie and uses the traditional beeweed paint. His designs are often geometric and are always uniquely his own. His Zuni wife, Jocelyn Quam, who started making small owl figures in the Zuni tradition in 1996, also claims Dextra as an inspiration. They both hope to pass on to others the knowledge and motivation Dextra has given them.

Priscilla Namingha Sahmie, wife of Donnelly Sahmie, an excellent potter, had eight children, five of whom are known potters (figs. 4.15—see p. XVIII, and 4.16). These include Randall, Jean, Rachel, Nyla, and Bonnie. Bonnie's son Doyle is both a potter and a carver. Priscilla's son Andrew married a Navajo woman, Ida, who learned pottery making from her mother-in-law. About 1984 she began a career of her own, signing her work "Ida Sahmie." Her work has drawn criticism from both Navajos and Hopi-Tewas, however. Her painted designs follow Navajo themes rather than the themes and patterns typical of the Nampeyo family (fig. 4.17—see p. XIX). Some say that her pottery making was not appreciated while she was living at Polacca and that some of her work was destroyed. She and her husband, Andrew, moved to the Pine Springs area of the Navajo Reservation where she again encountered problems. To assuage tribal criticism for using *Yé'ii* (Navajo holy people or deities) designs on her pottery, her Navajo family had a "sing" conducted for her to ward off any possible harm that might come to her or the Navajo community. The Hopi-Tewas objected to her pottery making because she was Navajo; the Navajo objected to her subject matter.[17]

The daughters of Rachel Healing—Ruth, Eleanor, Lillian, and Dextra—are all potters themselves, and some of their children show promise as well. Ruth, born in 1926, married Dalton James. Two of their children, Daryl and Darlene, became potters.

Contrary to the usual development, Darlene James did not learn pottery making from mother Ruth but instead from grandmother Rachel and her aunts, Dextra and Priscilla. In a reversal of roles, she taught her mother the art of pottery making around 1977. Darlene makes both conventional pottery and unique ceramic pieces. Her works strongly reflect a Hopi-Tewa design influence and are formed from Hopi clay. Her output consists of a variety of forms, ranging in size from one-and-one-half-inch-wide dolls to uniquely decorated eleven-inch-wide jars (fig. 4.18—see p. XIX). While living at Jemez, she was one of the few potters who did not use an electric kiln. Darlene usually inscribes her work "Darlene Nampeyo," and her name is accompanied by a corn symbol.

Eleanor Healing, who was born in 1930, is both a potter and an artist. She and her husband, Leslie Lucas, have three children, two of whom, Karen and Steven, also became potters. Steven has developed into an outstanding ceramic artist whose work is becoming widely recognized (fig. 4.19—see p. XIX). He works closely with Dextra Quotskuyva and is considered one of several of her protégés. Although he lives in Gallup, New Mexico, he prefers to work at his mother's home in Polacca, where there are no distractions and he can produce quality work, under the tutelage of Dextra, while he is firing. He signs his work "Steve Lucas Koyemsi."

Several potters who are descendants of Rachel Healing created works that have been difficult to locate in either museum collections or in dealer inventories. A few of these are in private collections and are shown in figure 4.20. In most instances, the pieces illustrated here are not the best examples of the work done by these students but are presented nonetheless for lack of better ones.

Beyond question, daughter Dextra has become the outstanding potter among Rachel's descendants. Her intense approach to pottery making contrasts with her relaxed approach to life. She is gifted with a fine sense of humor, an infectious laugh, and a love of and respect for the land and its bounty. She also has a deep sense of pride in the artistic work of her extended family.

She enjoys reminiscing about her great-grandmother Nampeyo and her extensive contributions to Dextra's pottery career. She was impressed by Nampeyo's fair complexion, her vast knowledge of clay locations (sources upon which Dextra still relies), and the blind matriarch's uncanny ability to identify people by sound and touch. (Nampeyo could identify Dextra by the sturdy calves of her legs.) Although Dextra learned many of her pottery-making skills from her great-grandmother, she credits her mother, Rachel, with most of

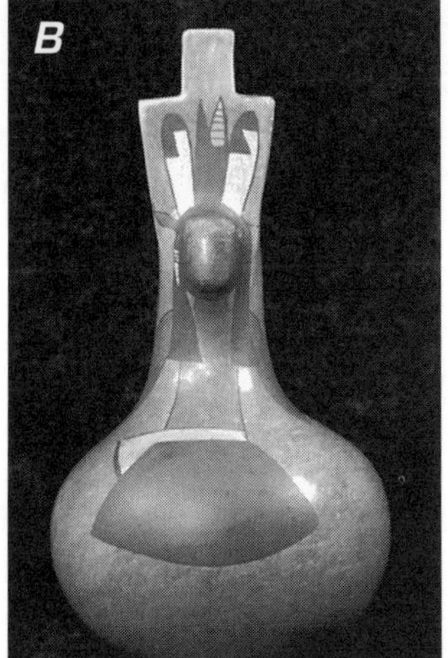

Fig. 4.16. Pottery of the children and grandchildren of Priscilla Sahmie. **A.** Jar with a traditional migration design topped with a classic red slip made by Bonnie Sahmie Chapella in 1978. The signature is "Bonnie Sahme," an old spelling of the name noted in the 1919 census records. 3 in. by 2³/₄ in. **B.** Red ceramic kachina figure made in 1987 by R. Sahmie. Rachel and her brother Randall (see C below) both sign their pottery "R. Sahmie," making it difficult to distinguish the work of one from the other. 8¹/₂ in by 3³/₄ in. **C.** Cream bowl made in 1982 by R. Sahmie. The float-polished bowl is decorated with a mild stipple finish and a superimposed painted spider. 3 in. by 3¹/₂ in. **D.** Small red bowl signed "Maude Sahmi Nampeyo" and decorated with a crude, stylized migration design. Maude sometimes alternates with the name "Nyla" when signing her pottery. Made in 1978. 2¹/₂ in. by 3¹/₂ in.

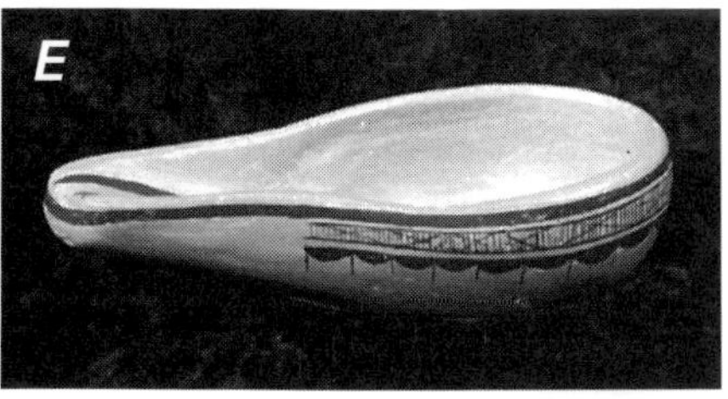

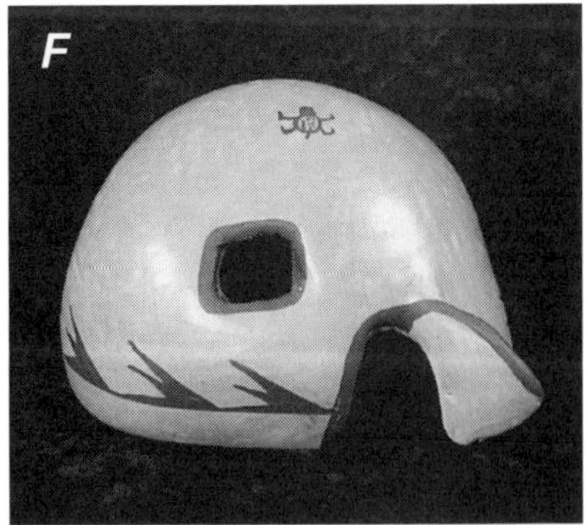

E. Ceramic ladle with a fine-line motif partially banded on the bottom by a fluted brown trim and a complete solid band on top. The interior of the handle is painted with three parallel lines. It was made by Jean Tom and signed "J. Tom Nampeyo." $4^5/8$ in. long. F. Doyle Chapella, son of Bonnie Chapella, completed this stylized Indian home in 1974. Bird tracks surround the base of the structure, which has an open, brown-framed window. Two turtles and two hunchbacked flute players face each other on the upper portion. $2^1/2$ in. by $3^3/4$ in. G. Small polychrome bowl by Kenneth Lynch, son of Nyla (Maude) Collateta. He made it in about 1992 and signed it "Ken Lynch." $1^3/4$ in. by $2^1/8$ in. Private collections.

her instruction. Among her prized possessions are two of her mother's polishing stones and the family piki bread cooking stone.

Dextra followed the educational pattern of many of her contemporaries, attending the Oraibi Day School and then the Phoenix Indian School. She worked with her mother but took only perfunctory interest in making pottery until 1972 when she developed an intense academic and creative interest in the craft. Although she has become well recognized for her art, she has other interests and responsibilities, including the traditional practice of preserving food and providing baby-sitting services for grandchildren. She also enjoys passing on the knowledge of her craft to an ever-expanding extended family.

Fig. 4.20. The work of two great-granddaughters of Nampeyo. **Left:** Small black-on-red bowl made by Ruth Namingha James in 1977, her first pot. The elements are reminiscent of the migration design. **Right:** Black and white kachina figure on a bulbous jar with a distinct lip, made by Camille Quotskuyva Joy in 1987 and signed "Hi Si." 8¹/4 in. by 7¹/4 in. Private collections.

Although Dextra's pottery forms and firing methods are traditional, her designs are contemporary, even innovative at times. Her execution is flawless. Her extraordinary interest in design leads her to search continually for new ways to present ancient patterns. She enthusiastically exclaims, "I can't wait to paint!" A creator of all shapes and sizes, from miniatures to larger vessels, she prefers the bigger ones since they offer a greater area on which she can create designs.

Like other devoted potters, Dextra searches nearby ruins and old sherd locations that might yield inspiration. She attributes much of her creative drive to pottery fragments from Awatovi (fig. 4.21—see p. XX), particularly those of pre-Spanish origin. In her efforts to resurrect the past, she has experimented with the ancient techniques of coal and dried-corncob firing, both ancient techniques used before the Spanish occupation. She found that even though both fuels produced hotter fires, the firing cycle took more time, a phenomenon that she cannot explain. As she experiments, she paces herself. Each piece must satisfy her self-imposed and exacting demands. Both her vegetable and mineral paints are prepared a year in advance. Dextra envisions her designs to be a map, first laid out by following crude paths revealed by old patterns and later detailed by her feelings of the moment and the inspirations provided by the world around her.

She disdains the use of commercial kilns and chooses rather to fire in the traditional way in the open outdoors, using dried sheep manure as fuel. She does not use the metal sheets or portable wooden barriers as windbreaks that are commonly employed by her contemporaries, but instead protects her work from the elements by very careful stacking of stones about the kiln.

Seldom flustered, Dextra has an even disposition that allows her either to block out or to accommodate distracting influences while working. An illustration of her ability to "roll with the punches" provides Bruce McGee with one of his favorite anecdotes. Dextra had accepted a commission to make an expensive pottery piece for a client who had set a deadline that was thought to have been dictated by a wedding anniversary. A short time before the delivery date, McGee phoned to see if the work would be completed on time. Dextra did not reply directly but insisted that he come to her home to learn for himself. He was greeted at the door by a laughing Dextra who ushered him in to show him a smashed masterpiece. She had fallen asleep while applying finishing touches—her work had fallen to the floor and shattered into countless fragments.

Dextra worries about many of the younger Hopi potters who she feels lack patience and are too money-oriented or easily discouraged when not rewarded by immediate success. She is not inclined to enter competitions such as the Santa Fe Indian Market of the Southwest American Indian Association, the Gallup Inter-Tribal Indian Ceremonial, or the Museum of Northern Arizona's Hopi Craftsman Exhibition, and she avoids gallery exhibitions. Even so, she cannot keep up with the demand for her pottery, for which she is well compensated.

Edwin and Dextra cooperated with each other in maintaining a comfortable home in Polacca for themselves and Dextra's invalid father (Emerson Namingha) until his death in the spring of 1992. Shortly thereafter, the couple moved to a new home they built on the outskirts of Kykotsmovi near the foot of Third Mesa where Edwin established a new farm. (He is also a part-time artist who markets his work occasionally.) One of Edwin and Dextra's goals is to restore the Sand Hills Ranch buildings to a livable condition.

Dextra's two children, Dan and Camille, have successful well-established careers and reputations as outstanding Native American artists. Dan Namingha, now a resident of Santa Fe, is a contemporary painter whose costly works hang on the walls of museums and renowned galleries and are prized by discriminating collectors. His works have been featured in numerous art magazines and in educational television documentaries. Dextra's daughter, Camille, also is an outstanding artist whose ceramic pieces bring high prices. Her pottery shapes are often unique, her designs original. Each piece surpasses the last in delicate execution and near-perfect design application. She signs her work with her Indian name, Hisi, and to it then adds the symbol of her clan, an ear of corn.

The Quotskuyvas have five grandchildren. Dan's children are Ario and Michael; Camille's are Lowell, Erika, and Reid. The art world can expect much from these young people in the future; in fact, Lowell has already made some respectable pottery.

The Daisy Healing Naha Hooee Family

Born ca. 1905, Daisy led a rewarding, eventful, but sometimes tragic life. Endowed with an intellectual curiosity, she was attracted to schools, first attending Polacca Day School and the Phoenix Indian School. The Phoenix school, like many other Indian educational institutions, was desperately seeking to increase its enrollment and thereby fatten its federal support. Thus Daisy was admitted at an early age with a letter of permission from her parents.

In Phoenix, Daisy developed serious eyesight problems. Errors resulting from poor eyesight were mistaken for stupidity, and an impatient teacher beat her before the class, a terrible embarrassment. Daisy was transferred back to Polacca, but her learning there degenerated as her vision worsened. Learning of the child's plight through her friends the Healings, Anita Baldwin moved Daisy to her home in Anoakia, near Arcadia, California, and arranged for eye surgery. The surgery was successful, and after recovery Daisy enrolled in

Pasadena High School. She remained with Anita for several eventful years and returned to the Hopi reservation only during the summer.

Emry Kopta, a sculptor living in Polacca at that time, saw some of Daisy's work and wrote to Mrs. Baldwin to recommend that the young woman be given further art training. The California philanthropist responded generously and enrolled Daisy in the School of Fine Arts in Paris, where she studied many art forms and learned French. Later Mrs. Baldwin arranged a worldwide art study tour for Daisy.

Near the age of twenty, Daisy wanted to return to the land of her people, a desire not uncommon among Native Americans who have left their homeland. In Polacca she married Neil Naha. Daisy's absence from the reservation had come at a time in her life when most other Hopi women were learning how to run Hopi households and raise their children. Daisy soon found that she was unable to cope with the demands of her marriage to Neil Naha, nor was she then equipped to raise three children, handle household duties, or participate in the demanding ceremonial and social life of her people, in addition to making pottery. She felt that her husband and in-laws were jealous of her world experiences and had become abusive toward her.

Despite all, Daisy accomplished two positive things which contributed to her recognition as a Hopi-Tewa potter worthy of applying the Nampeyo name to her work. She had worked with her blood relatives and strengthened her pottery-making skills, and she had collected, with the assistance of the members of the Peabody Museum's Awatovi Expeditions of 1935–1939, a myriad of designs copied from unearthed vessels and sherds.

This expedition was conducted during the height of the Great Depression in the 1930s. With few visitors and meager funds for scientific expeditions, excursions by photographers and artists to Hopi country had been sharply curtailed. Not only did the expedition bring employment for native workmen at a time when jobs were scarce, but it also brought money to the area. The outsiders were welcomed and thus benefited from a spirit of cooperation with the tribal elders, cooperation which they might not have received under more stable circumstances. The expedition studied extensively the vast

Awatovi ruin as well as other ancient ruins on Antelope Mesa and in the Jeddito Valley area. The scientists believed that "pottery typology, as presented in the various manuals, was the be-all and end-all of ceramic studies."[18] Assisting the group were Harold Colton and Barton Wright, both of whom were devoted to preserving, promoting, and sponsoring Hopi art and artists. Many First Mesa inhabitants related to famous artists were employed as excavators. The staff established an excellent rapport with the Hopi-Tewas, especially people such as Daisy Healing Naha who were interested in studying and reproducing the ancient ancestral murals and pottery designs being unearthed.

> Few archaeological excavations have had the good fortune to encounter such a wealth of material of the kind provided by the wall paintings in our prehistoric Hopi towns. One of the outstanding features of these finds was the extent of information supplied by them [the Hopis] which usually is denied to archaeologists. In the murals was depicted much that is ordinarily restricted to the field studies of ethnologists working among living peoples, but which has almost always fallen away into complete decay centuries before the spades and trowels of the archaeologist were brought into play.[19]

These murals provided inspiration to Hopi and Tewa potters as well as artists and writers such as Fred Kabotie, Wilson Tawaquaptewa, Don Talayesva, Jimmie Kewanwytewa, and Edmund Nequatewa, who had assisted the expedition members.

Pottery finds were considerable as well. Approximately eighty-five hundred pottery specimens were recovered and more than half a million sherds studied and cataloged. Daisy copied untold numbers of the unearthed designs on paper, which formed a stack as thick as a book. Although these designs unfortunately disappeared, many of them remained in her mind.

Following her divorce from Neil Naha, Daisy met and married Leo Poblano of Zuni. She left home once again and established residence at his pueblo, but because of its proximity she was able to return for frequent visits. Leo, a master jeweler and sculptor, proved to be a good husband and a good father to Daisy's three Hopi-Tewa children. Daisy learned to carve from Leo, and a local trader purchased their output, often paying them with used furniture. Daisy's and Leo's work was later sold for unbelievably high prices.[20] Leo Poblano was a firefighter by occupation, and in the late 1950s he was killed by a falling tree while fighting a blaze.

After a lapse of ten years and shortly before Leo's death, Daisy returned to pottery making. Finding Zuni clays difficult to work, she at first used Hopi materials and made Hopi-style pottery. She spent much time with her sister Rachel at Polacca. As Rachel's eyesight began to fail, Daisy took over much of her pottery decorating. Most of the decoration on Rachel's pottery made during the last few years of her life was executed by Daisy. As their reputations grew, they sold more and more of their work directly to collectors from Rachel's home, a situation Daisy understandably preferred to that of marketing through dealers.

Following Leo's death, Daisy married Sidney Hooee, a Zuni with a reputation as a fine silversmith who specialized in needlepoint and fine-channel work. Daisy continued to merge easily into Zuni social life, participating in their Olla Maiden Dance on special occasions such as the yearly Inter-Tribal Indian Ceremonial in Gallup, New Mexico. Daisy held rehearsals at her home, where the performers practiced perfect posture and smooth movements so necessary to carry the large jars on their heads.

Throughout her adult life Daisy was ever willing to teach pottery-making skills to others. To revive the art of fine pottery making by the women of Zuni, she began to teach at the Zuni High School in the 1960s and later established a school at her home. Daisy's pottery decoration at Zuni sometimes followed the Zuni tradition (fig. 4.22). In addition to her classes at Zuni she was willing to go anywhere for demonstrations. She remembered especially fondly a trip to the Honolulu Academy of Arts in Hawaii in 1974. After six days of demonstrating pottery forming and decorating, she spent a final day

Fig. 4.22. Daisy Hooee's classes in pottery making and design at Zuni Pueblo included work with the old established Zuni designs: representations of deer, deer hooves, antelope, dragonflies, mountains, and stars. Here Daisy holds one of her large decorated pots with a Zuni design made ca. 1975. J. R. Bloom, photographer. Collection of Daisy Hooee.

outdoors, teaching her students Hopi firing techniques.

In her later years, Daisy suffered a fall that left her unable to move about without the aid of a walker, but until her death in 1994, she and Sidney continued to enjoy the colorful dances at First Mesa as well as visits with family members.

Two of Daisy's children made their marks as Indian artists—son Raymond and daughter Shirley. Raymond Naha first showed promise as an artist while a student at Zuni High School. After attending Sherman Institute at Riverside, California, his art training began in earnest at the Hopi High School in Oraibi. There he studied under the famous pioneer Indian artist Fred Kabotie, who came to the school when it first opened in 1937. Raymond's paintings were awarded prizes at various Indian art exhibitions and sold through various dealer outlets including the one who marketed the carvings of Daisy and Leo Poblano. Unfortunately, Raymond died unexpectedly in 1975.

Shirley Benn first became a silversmith under the tutelage of her stepfather and later studied pottery making with Daisy (fig. 4.23— see p. XX). Shirley's children Marlin and Cheryl have also become artists of note. Shirley and Cheryl have sometimes made and jointly signed pottery pieces. Shirley makes pottery and also works with her husband Virgil on jewelry. Cheryl Naha is becoming a fine potter, and she markets her craft through Zuni dealers. Her innovatively shaped pottery, signed "C. Naha Nampeyo" is decorated with the classic designs used by most members of the Nampeyo family. She has also carved some small kachina figures.

Shirley's son, Marlin Pinto, is a recognized carver. His sought-after works can range in size from approximately two feet to as small as one and one-half inches. No matter the size of his renditions, all are unique and exquisitely detailed (fig. 4.24—see p. XXI).

The Dewey Healing Family

Annie and Willie's son Dewey and his family were never deeply involved in creative art. His special contributions toward supporting both the welfare of the Hopi people and the perpetuation of their art are worthy of mention. He is known for his political accomplishments, which culminated in the landmark *Healing* v. *Jones* decision. At the time the suit was filed, Dewey, named as plaintiff, was chairman of the Hopi Tribal Council and acted as tribe representative. As a result of the decision, a portion of land, formerly known as District 6 was expanded and officially named the Hopi Indian Reservation. In 1965, the new reservation was resurveyed and almost 20,000 acres added (to a total of some 650,000 acres). The Navajos living inside the new boundary were moved by the government in 1972, and the Hopis were given exclusive mineral rights to all of District 6. Navajos and Hopis had joint, undivided, and equal rights and interests to the remainder of the 1882 Executive Order Reservation.[21] Thus the Hopis had returned to them some of what was theirs in prehistoric times, but the dispute continues to this day as the U.S. government vacillates in its enforcement of its decision, just as it has in the past.

Although Dewey made no claim to artistic ability, he did much to assist his family in their constant search to uncover inspiring artifacts made by the prehistoric people who had settled the area. He alerted them when sites in the path of construction projects were about to be obliterated. As new sites were located, he accompanied family members to the area and assisted in recovering artifacts before they were lost. Ceramic production was always present in the Healing household, for Dewey's wife, Juanita, produced and sold ware of a very respectable quality.

Fig. 4.25.
Koshari clowns carved and painted ca. 1984 by Fletcher Healing, who specializes in making winsome clowns such as these. Collection of Erik Bromberg.

The Fletcher Healing Family

Annie's son Fletcher is a practicing Hopi-Tewa carver and is often assisted by his wife, Julia. His most famous carvings are of whimsical Hano or Rio Grande clowns portraying one of their favorite roles, that of the glutton (fig. 4.25). These clowns were masters of pantomime, and although classic comedy vignettes are not of Hopi origin, they were brought to the area by the Tewa when they left their Rio Grande Valley homeland to escape the Spanish in 1696.

Although Nampeyo's son William Lesou Komalestewa did not make pottery, he made an outstanding contribution of at least one of his

William Komalestewa Lesou

grandchildren, a potter who has gone practically unrecognized in the literature as a descendant of Nampeyo. Obtaining information on Komalestewa from interviews was at first unproductive. It was not until a photograph of him was found at Oxford University (fig. 2.9) and shown to people who had not been previously interrogated that his history began to be revealed.

William was born about fourteen years after Annie, around 1893. He is remembered as a retiring person who preferred to remain close to home in the company of his own people. About 1914 he married Vina Tahomana. They had their only child, Austin, in 1916. No records could be found of other children born to the couple nor of pottery or other native art produced by either William or his wife. Vina died during the flu epidemic of 1918.

William enjoyed ranching and raising animals (fig. 4.26). He supplemented his ranching income by driving a supply wagon for Tom Pavatea, thus joining other Nampeyo family members already associated with the trader. In the early winter of 1922, William drove Pavatea's eight-horse freight wagon to the railroad siding to pick up supplies, a distance of seventy miles. The route crossed flat country occasionally pierced by spectacular, vividly colored, volcanic extrusions that formed abrupt peaks incapable of supporting much vegetation and affording little protection from the elements. The delivery wagon was overtaken by a blizzard so severe that the horses were unable to proceed. William was forced to abandon the rig and proceed on foot through the driving snow in subzero weather to the nearest habitation, a distance of fifteen or twenty miles. Severely frostbitten, he never fully recovered and died a short time later.

Fig. 4.26. Nampeyo's son, William Komalestewa, during his days as a rancher. Wesley Lesou, photographer. Courtesy of Emily Komalestewa.

Austin Komalestewa (known as Austin Sr.), son of William and Vina Komalestewa, was born in 1916. He married Emily Shupla, and together the couple had twelve offspring. Emily, an adopted child of Edgar Shupla and Lela Twaownisie, was responsible for maintaining the tradition of pottery making in the Komalestewa branch of Nampeyo's family. She admits that she experiments with the use of commercial rather than reservation clays. Her stepbrother, Kenneth Shupla, married Helen Baca of Santa Clara Pueblo and moved to her home in the Rio Grande Valley. Helen, who died in 1983, was one of Santa Clara's outstanding potters and achieved particular recognition for her large, impressed melon bowls.

Austin and Emily spent a good portion of their married life in Tucson. A semi-invalid for the last seventeen years of his life, Austin passed away in 1987. He was a sometime kachina carver. As of this writing, Emily continues to maintain their home at Hano.

A close relationship between the Shupla and Komalestewa families continued. The youngest son of Austin and Emily, Alton, met and married Jeannie Shupla (no blood relation) when his family resided in Tucson. Owing to the fact that Alton's mother is a Hopi, not a Tewa, Alton's connection to Nampeyo is not often recognized. In addition, when he first became interested in pottery making, he was living at Santa Clara where his then mother-in-law, Helen Shupla, taught him the art at which he has become most proficient (fig. 4.27—see p. XXI). From the beginning he produced beautiful and uniquely formed ware in the Santa Clara tradition. In addition to large melon bowls, almost indistinguishable from Helen's, he has produced rainbow-shouldered water jars, pieces with impressed bear-paw designs, and other similar forms of Rio Grande Tewa tradition.

The untimely death of Alton's wife, Jean, in 1989, combined with the deaths of his father and mother-in-law all in less than four years of one another, left Alton devastated. He returned to Polacca and started making pottery from the clays, fuels, slips, and colors of that area, which differed widely from those he had used at Santa Clara. The results were gratifying. Although much of his work is presently shaped and decorated in the Santa Clara tradition, his highly polished works are sometimes of unusual color and texture. Alton has produced traditional Tewa blacks, tans, and reds, as well as rich chocolate colors. Some of his pottery is etched with delicate, geometric designs, and his pieces are purchased almost before they have cooled from the fire. In 1992 he married Pam Lalo, a Second Mesa resident, and settled into a new family life.

Nellie Lesou Douma

According to the 1913 census records, Nellie Lesou was born in 1894. We rely on census records because babies born at home in that era, often without the presence of a nurse or doctor, were not provided accurate birth dates. Nampeyo's children had no birth certificates; thus, when asked by census takers for a date of birth, the year given was arrived at, after some debate, by family conference.

As a child, Nellie accompanied Nampeyo to more pottery-making demonstrations and appearances than her siblings and was the only child to go to the Chicago Land Exposition of 1910. There, it is said, she acted as interpreter. She was removed from school at an early age to assist her mother with pottery making. Despite all, she never aspired to become a famous potter herself. Compared to her sisters, her output was low and her noninnovative decoration did not have the sophistication that theirs did (fig. 3.20B—see p. XIV). Although Nellie had the ability, she seemed to lack the necessary interest and didn't need the added income. For years Nellie's large, approximately twenty- inch-high jar, belonging to a private collector, was displayed at the Keams Canyon Trading Post along with one of similar size and decoration done by Fannie. The piece was as beautifully made as that of any of the Indian masters, but the decorative techniques were not comparable. Nellie was well aware of her shortcomings, but this never appeared to bother her. Credit is due this generous lady for the encouragement and lavish praise she bestowed on the work of others, particularly that of her younger sister Fannie.

Nellie married Douglas Douma, the manager of Tom Pavatea's enterprises, and in 1913 they established a home in Polacca near her siblings. Since the homes of most of Nampeyo's children were separated by only a few hundred yards, it was easy to maintain close contact. The exception was William, who lived with his Hopi wife atop the mesa in Hano. Jovial, easygoing Nellie was affectionately called Ta-We or Daway, which means "Grandmother" (fig. 4.28).

Nellie marketed most of her later work through the Keams Canyon Trading Post, then and now operated by the McGee family. The Pavatea Trading Post was sold to the owners of the Keams Canyon operation, and the interests of both enterprises were combined. In addition to retail selling, the Pavatea Trading Post became a collection point for materials to be sold by the hub post at Keams Canyon. At one point, some of the McGees established residence in a home close by the old Pavatea store at Polacca.[22] The McGees established a close relationship with the Nampeyo descendants, particularly with daughters Nellie and Fannie who often baby-sat for the McGee children.

Nellie and Douglas had ten children and at least thirty-four grandchildren, many of whom either make pottery or carve. Daughters

Fig. 4.28. *Nellie and Douglas Douma with three of their children at Polacca. Probably taken by Walter Hough around 1920. No. 94-1445, NAA-SI.* **Inset:** *Nellie and Douglas Douma's home in 1989, where Nellie's descendants continue to live. L. Blair, photographer.*

Fig. 4.29. Left: Classic polychrome bowl made by Zella Douma Ray in 1975. It was overfired, as revealed by the dark reddish-brown discoloration on the right shoulder. The work is signed "Zella Nampeyo" and is accompanied by a drawing of an ear of corn. 3 in. by 5 in. Right: A bowl decorated with Sikyatki-style design elements, with some stippled area, made by Marie Douma Koopee just prior to her death in 1982. Signed "M. Nampeyo." 2¹/₈ in. by 3¹/₂ in. Private collections.

Augusta Poocha and Zella Ray are potters. Zella's deceased son, Buddy, and his wife, Charlene, both made pottery. Daughter Marie Koopee (fig. 4.29), while not well known for her work, has two daughters (Emma Lou and Betsey) who make pottery and two sons (Jacob and Richard) who carve kachina dolls. Son Douglas is also a part-time carver.

Wesley, the youngest boy of Nampeyo and Lesou, was born in 1900 (fig. 4.30). He first went to a reservation school and then graduated

Wesley Lesou

from the Phoenix Indian School. He found work in Phoenix, and there he met his first wife, Ida Russell, a member of the Pima tribe. Ida, before her premature death, bore him four children—Edgar, Louella, Eloise, and Wesley. Wesley's second wife, Cecelia, was also a member of the Pima tribe. The couple remained childless until they adopted a girl named Lynette.

Like most, Wesley had a strong attraction for his boyhood home, and after living for most of his professional life in Phoenix, he returned and took up residence in the Polacca home that Lesou had built for Nampeyo (fig. 4.30). Wesley did not contribute to the arts.

Fig. 4.30. Left: *Wesley Lesou with Ellsworth Polacca, ca. 1942, taken near Keams Canyon.* Courtesy of Ellsworth Polacca. **Right:** *View in 1989 of Nampeyo's home, built by Lesou and later used as a permanent residence by Wesley Lesou. The addition on the right was not a part of the original structure.* L. Blair, photographer.

Fig. 4.31. *Nampeyo's daughter Fannie noted that this photograph of her at Hubbell's Trading Post was taken around 1921, rather than 1925 as recorded. Her attire, including the high-laced shoes, came from a mail-order catalog available at the trading post and was purchased with her wages.* C. N. Wood, photographer. Neg. No. 1116, AZSM. **Inset:** *The Hubbell Trading Post in Ganado, Arizona, in 1920 while Fannie was employed there.* Courtesy of Hubbell Trading Post National Historic Site.

His wife Cecelia made pottery that was not up to the standards of her in-laws. Her Pima traditions are not evident in her work; her methods of pottery forming and design are strictly Hopi. It is interesting to note that she was not discouraged in her pottery making as were others outside the tribe who married into the family. Daughter Lynette forms small pieces of pottery.

Fannie Lesou Polacca

The stoic, strong, and talented Fannie is credited by most researchers of Hopi pottery as being one of the foremost in perpetuating the ceramic art of her mother, Nampeyo.[23] Unknown to many outsiders is the fact that she also maintained a Corn Clan house, so important to Hopi-Tewa ceremonial life. Both Nampeyo and Fannie assumed the position of clan matriarch: "Men may roam about, work the fields or hold their religious ceremonies, but it is the clan matriarch, forever at home, who is the real power. She controls lives through the branching lines of female descendants and the land through their husbands and sons. She is the caretaker of the most religious objects, a director of thought and a participant of many ceremonies. She is the ultimate conservative, the cohesive focus of the Hopis and their way of life."[24]

Fannie was told that she had probably been born in February 1904, near the time of the Bean Dance (*Invanyu* to the Hopi-Tewa or *Powamu* to the Hopi). The 1919 U. S. census gives her birth year as 1902, however. Other sparse information indicates that the correct year might be closer to 1900; Fannie's earliest memories seem to support 1900 as the correct year.

Fannie was first named Popongua or Popong-Mana (Picking Piñons), a name given to her by the older women of her father's family, women who were members of the Coyote-Fire clans. It is said that the name "Fannie" was later bestowed upon her by either missionaries or health-care workers. Born late in her parents' lives (she was their last girl child), Fannie had no memory of her grandparents or other elder relatives. Her earliest recollections were of the Grand Canyon in 1906, where Nampeyo was demonstrating her craft. Above all, the colorful Hopi dancers made an impression on Fannie that remained with her throughout her life. Her most enjoyable tasks were setting a table to feed the kachinas between performances. She also said that one of her greatest pleasures was to attend kachina dances, including those given by people of the other mesas. When kachina dancers from her town were asked to dance for the people of the neighboring villages, Fannie was always present and usually involved.

Fannie's brief education began at Polacca Day School, where she completed the third grade. She recalled, with some bitterness, being transferred the next year with brother Wesley to the Indian boarding school at Keams Canyon while the Lesous, with sister Nellie, went to Chicago to attend the 1910 land exposition. She could not understand why she was not included in the party.[25]

Fannie was fortunate that her stay at the boarding school was relatively short. Living conditions there were reported to be almost unbearable. The children were:

> ...herded into inadequate, unsanitary, and horribly over-crowded school facilities. The living conditions for the children at the Keams Canyon boarding school were vile. The result was the spread of many diseases....
>
> Children who developed tuberculosis could not be adequately cared for and were simply sent home to die. Trachoma, that serious eye infection which so often results in blindness, became rampant. In those pre-sulfa and antibiotic days, the treatment available to the Hopi children and a few adults consisted in washing out the eyes with a copper sulfate (bluestone) solution. In severe cases doctors sometimes subjected the patient to a painful operation....When this operation was performed it was essential that the eyes be kept clean and the wounds sterile until healing was complete. Such post operative care was difficult to secure in the boarding school and impossible in the villages. As a result, a tragic number of Hopi became blind.[26]

Within five years after Fannie's sojourn at the Indian school, it was judged to be in a dangerous condition and closed. Little information could be wrested from Fannie about her activities at school, but she did participate in at least one activity—drama (fig. 2.12). Upon their return from Chicago, the Lesous withdrew Fannie from school. Her formal education came to an abrupt end.

Fannie did not rush to join the ranks of the pottery makers of her day. She emphasized that she began ceramic work relatively late compared to many Hopi women, at first limiting her efforts to decorating her mother's clay forms. Her initial contributions to family support came from outside employment, such as her work as a maid at the Hubbell Trading Post (fig. 4.31). Others from her reser-

Fig. 4.32. *Family gathering on Sand Hills Ranch.* **Standing, left to right:** *an unidentified church associate; Elsie Polacca (wife of Vinton's brother Starlie) holding an unidentified baby; Vinton Polacca; Fannie Polacca holding her youngest son, Ellsworth; and an unidentified woman.* **Sitting in the front row, left to right:** *an unidentified child of Elsie and Starlie Polacca; Fannie and Vinton's daughters Elva and Tonita and sons Thomas and Harold; Nampeyo; and Leah Polacca. The monument was dedicated to Tom Polacca in 1940, two years before Nampeyo's death. This may be the last photograph taken of Nampeyo.* Starlie Polacca, photographer. Courtesy of Ellsworth Polacca.

vation were also employed at the post, in particular her friend Sadie Adams.[27]

After returning from Hubbell's, Fannie married Vinton Polacca, whom she had known most of her life. Since Vinton was not a frequent visitor to Polacca and Hano, the couple undoubtedly became acquainted at Sand Hills Ranch. Fannie spent much time on the ranch due to her family's relationship with Tom Polacca. Although annoyed at the time, Fannie later laughed when she recalled her marriage ceremony. Vinton arrived to take his vows at the Polacca Baptist Church dressed as a cowboy, resplendent in boots, spurs, and chaps.

Moving to a new home that Vinton had built at Sand Hills, Fannie easily adapted to ranch life and soon became a skilled equestrian. Her attachment to horses remained constant throughout her life; she tended animals of her own or those of her children in a corral behind her Polacca home, almost to the time of her death.

Vinton Louis Polacca was born at the ranch on 27 November 1898 to Aw-Kung, his mother, and Tom Polacca.[28] Vinton had no memories of his mother, who died when he was a small child. At age thirteen, he lost the father who had provided him with the training that qualified him more as a hard-working rancher than a typical Hopi-Tewa. Remarkably, Vinton also developed reading, writing, and arithmetic skills in addition to becoming fluent in the Tewa, Hopi, Navajo, and English languages, with a lesser knowledge of Spanish. Adding to his other accomplishments, he learned modern agriculture, construction, and building maintenance so necessary to keeping up the ranch. These skills he would later teach his sons. The family cultivated fruit trees and raised fowl for their own consumption and trading purposes, but most of their efforts were directed at raising cattle.

Through his father, Vinton and members of his family became involved with Christianity. Tom had passed on to his children the Hopi tradition that true religion would come through young men, "arriving from the south wearing white shirts, dark ties, and pants." Vinton was first sent to a Roman Catholic school in Santa Fe, but he returned home after a short time feeling discrimination since he was neither Hispanic nor Catholic. He later permanently affiliated him-

Fig. 4.33. *Nampeyo and Fannie. This photograph was taken in 1935, when the two artists had reached the peak of their work produced together.* Tad Nichols, photographer. Neg. No. 74-1655, Fred Harvey Collection, MNAZ.

self and his family with the Church of Jesus Christ of Latter-day Saints after being proselytized by Mormon missionaries arriving from the south "dressed in white shirts, dark ties, and pants." Affiliation with the Mormon church was strengthened when its spiritual leader, Spencer Kimball, became an occasional guest at the ranch; once he even recuperated there from an illness. He considered the area ideal for this purpose since it was "a quiet, clean place to live" (fig. 4.32).

Fig. 4.34. *The picture for this postcard was taken ca. 1922 and published by Frasher's Fotos Incorporated of Pomona, California. Fannie remembered that she resisted posing at the time because of a severe cold and sore throat. Nampeyo dressed for the photographer, wearing borrowed clothing and jewelry. The decorations on the pottery were all executed by Fannie; the often photographed grinding stone is immediately in front of her.* Courtesy of Iris Polacca Youvella, photographer unknown.

Shortly after Vinton and Fannie's marriage, pottery making became an important part of Fannie's life. Increasingly, she worked with Nampeyo, first in decorating the pottery and then with forming it (figs. 4.33, 4.34, 4.35, and 4.36—see pps. XXII-XXIII). According to John Anson Warner: "Nampeyo, and in the beginning her daughter Fannie, cream slipped their vessels with the finest kaolin clays. This trait was a hold-over from the earlier tradition of Hopi pottery known as Polacca polychrome."

Referring to a large, unsigned piece in the Gilcrease Collection (fig. 4.35), Edwin Wade evaluated the work of mother and daughter stylistically:

Daughters typically assisted their mothers in the potter's trade, learning the art as they worked. The celebrated commercial illustrator William Leigh, original collector of this jar, maintained that it was made by Fannie but this is suspect. Such meticulously designed jars, featuring historic systems, were favored by Nampeyo, and irrespective of the degree of work Fannie may have done on the piece, the conception is stylistically her mother's. The final stage of Nampeyo's stylistic experimentation, during which her daughter Fannie took an increasingly commanding role, emphasized an angular Art Decoesque refinement that reduced the vitality and spontaneity of the designs to a handsome, but less forceful decoration.[29]

Early cooperative works by Fannie and her mother were signed "Nampeyo;" we can assume the signatures were by Fannie as her

*Fig. **4.35.** Decorated pottery formed jointly by Nampeyo with a daughter. **Left:** The decoration on this jar has been applied over a cream slip. The piece is dated 1912, long before Fannie began to decorate for her mother, substantiating Warner's conclusion that daughter Annie, in spite of the documentation, was the maker, not Fannie. 10 1/2 in. by 13 in. No. 5437-7774. GIAHA. **Right:** This is possibly one of the last complicated decorations applied by Nampeyo; another possibility is that it was formed by Nampeyo and decorated by another. Although similar to Nampeyo's earlier work, the design lacks the freedom of movement so characteristic of her designs. No. 5437-4413. GIAH&A.*

mother could not write. Later, according to Fannie, signatures on the jointly crafted pieces changed to "Nampeyo Fannie". Pottery made solely by Fannie was signed "Fannie Nampeyo," usually with a drawn figure of corn. Fannie's decorating was unsurpassed, and her forms, seldom duplicated by the best of present potters, were large, symmetrical, smooth, and thin-walled. Fannie's style was meticulous, though not as free flowing as her mother's. An example of this is the way the two potters fill space between lines—Nampeyo's spaces appear hurriedly scrubbed, while Fannie's are parallel strokes (4.36—see pps. XXII-XXIII).

Of Fannie and Vinton's thirteen children, five (Duran, Presley, Leslie, Milton, and Milford) died soon after birth. The other children lived to excel as pottery makers.

Fig. 4.37. A set of twenty-four decorated polychrome tiles, each signed "Fannie Nampeyo," sold through the Keams Canyon Trading Post. The base tile upon which the decorations were painted are a square and uniform 6 by 6 inches, indicating they were formed in a mold. The angle of the photographs gives the illusion that the tiles are not square. There were originally twenty-eight designs. Nos. 47.P.94—121, SWMLA.

Vinton developed very good skills as a carpenter-contractor and found work outside the ranch at trading posts on the nearby Navajo Reservation, including Smoke Signal and Bidahochi. His biggest job was at Bidahochi, the old established post located midway between the Holbrook railway station and Keams Canyon. For three years, beginning in 1934, the Polacca family lived at the post in a building with a hogan attached to one end. Fannie continued making pottery at the site and began to teach pottery making to their daughter Elva when she was eleven years old.

By 1942 Vinton had developed such crippling pains from the many broken bones and other physical abuse suffered while running cattle and breaking horses, that he moved the family to Keams Canyon where he could find less strenuous work in the government school. He worked first as a cook's helper and then as head baker. The family was provided with a home in a nearby government complex. The two oldest boys, Harold and Thomas, ages twelve and seven, were able to keep the ranch operating during the summer months, though at a much slower pace.

Vinton and Fannie were soon overwhelmed with work and family obligations. They obtained some relief by placing Tonita and Thomas in the Keams Canyon boarding school during winter residence. Not understanding the reason for being sent away, both children deeply resented the situation. They remembered looking out the school windows and seeing their home, which they were not allowed to visit.

Although Fannie entered a new and more Anglicized phase of her life at Keams Canyon, she kept up her work as a potter. The time at the canyon was one of her most productive and commercially active periods. She established close business and personal relationships with the McGees, who established primary retail and wholesale markets for her work. The children of the two families were classmates and friends. Both families were members of the Mormon church (Vinton and Fannie were one of the first families from First Mesa to join), and both were deeply involved in church activities. Vinton, who had been selected as a priest in 1939, became a church elder in 1948.[30]

Fannie participated in church life, enjoying covered-dish suppers and active in the relief society in the 1950s. She quilted, sang, and gave testimonials, partly in English and partly in Tewa. On occasion during visitations of church members to her home, she would suddenly leave the room if no other women were present and not return until the last guest departed.

Fannie founded her own tamale business while at Keams Canyon. She prepared as many as seventy large tamales a day, all made from scratch, and her children sold them for ten cents each. They were so popular that all the children had to do was situate themselves at the hospital entrance where traffic was heavy, and they sold everything quickly. Seven dollars a day from tamale sales was a helpful supplement to Fannie's income in the early 1940s. Some remember her tamales as too hot; others considered them gourmet items, and they were so remembered even twenty-five years after she closed the business when an old customer called and wanted to buy some of her tamales.

The Polaccas lived at Keams Canyon for eighteen years. All of the children except the youngest, Iris, completed their educations there and became self-supporting. Retirement with an acceptable pension then allowed Vinton and his family to take leave of the canyon and move to Hano. With her reputation as an outstanding potter well established and bolstered by an upturn in the economy, Fannie was able to command an acceptable price for her work. At the start of her career she accepted special orders (fig. 4.37), but she later found that she could sell all that she produced without taking special orders. Her works during these years showed infinite variation in shape and design (fig. 4.38—see pps. XXIV-XXVI).

After Vinton died in 1965 Fannie assumed the role of both parents. One of her children stated that she was "rock hard, strong, and tough physically, mentally, and emotionally—ready to work for the present, plan for the future, and not live in the past. She kinda took up where our father left off." They expected her to live forever (fig. 4.39).

Following Nampeyo's death, the Corn Clan house remained vacant for a period, and despite its important role in Hopi-Tewa ritual, it deteriorated to the point that it was unfit for occupancy. Regardless of the fact that Fannie had now become the clan mother, she could not live in the old house. To compensate for her losses she began a

Fig. 4.39. Left: *Fannie's Polacca home in 1987. The cinder block structure, with the firing shed to the rear, was often visited by both family members and customers for her pottery. The firing shed to the rear of the home was torn down shortly after Fannie's death, indicating the abandonment of traditional firing.* **Right:** *Fannie Polacca holding a fine sample of her work made ca. 1972. It displays several motifs she handed down to her descendants.* Courtesy of Ellsworth Polacca.

tireless drive to restore the old clan home. She organized and participated in work parties with her children and related Corn Clan members or with any other Hopi-Tewas she could press into service. All gathered building materials or helped in some way with the reconstruction. During this period, she gained a reputation for carrying heavy loads up and down the mesa, an ascent of some five hundred feet. All the spare money Fannie could raise was donated to the cause. From the beginning of reconstruction, and for a period of twenty years, she assumed responsibility for the upkeep of the home, the preservation of the ceremonial paraphernalia, and support of the activities of the kachinas.

Conditions can be harsh on the mesas during winter, and the nearest trading posts and necessary medical services are always difficult to reach. By 1970, when she was past normal retirement age, a new and final home was provided for Fannie in Polacca by her family; it had a view of her ancient mesa top home. Nestled in a sheltered area across the road from her sister Nellie, it was near Nampeyo's old Polacca home, which was by this time occupied by brother Wesley. Both homes were within an easy walk of Annie's residence.

By this time pressure to earn money from her art had eased. Her children took turns in tending to her needs. They stabled their animals and fired their pottery in areas adjacent to her home and saw to it that the family's pottery-making supplies, stored at the home, were replenished for themselves and their mother. There, Fannie's children and grandchildren studied pottery making with her. Many of the pieces produced were the result of joint efforts but were either signed by Fannie alone or by one other family member.

As with many older Indian women, she became a television enthusiast in her later years. She was so skilled at pottery making that many of the difficult operations had become routine; she could do them and instruct her grandchildren while following the soap operas. A rough calculation indicates that seven of her children and seventeen of her grandchildren are excellent potters as a result of her training. Unlike some other older potters, she did not insist that they follow all the classic forming and decorating techniques but instead encouraged most of their departures from the classic styles.

Remarkably, she continued making pottery almost to the time of her death. Her last work, completed two weeks before her final hospitalization, was made jointly with daughter Tonita. Despite age and severe pain, the forming and decoration of her work remained unparalleled, showing no deterioration from the magnificent creations she produced at the pinnacle of her career.

Aware that her life was nearing an end, she told of visions of two unidentified people introducing her to a beautiful place where Vinton was waiting for her. Characteristically, her funeral services embraced both the Christian and Indian faiths. The services began in the Church of Jesus Christ of Latter-day Saints at Keams Canyon, where Bruce McGee rendered the eulogy. Fannie was then accorded Indian burial rites and laid to rest in a grave next to Vinton in the Polacca family burial ground at Sand Hills Ranch.

Both Vinton and Fannie agreed with Tom Polacca that their children should receive the best academic and religious educations to prepare them for coexistence with whites. All of their children completed high school, and most of them went on to higher education.

Neither Fannie's children nor grandchildren were required to make and sell their artwork under the adverse conditions their predecessors had known. Notwithstanding, their careers have often been marred by problems, some self-inflicted, some due to ill health, and many resulting from cyclic economic conditions.

At first all the children signed their pottery in the style initiated by Fannie. They used their Anglo first names followed by Nampeyo and a drawing of the clan corn symbol. Thus, Fannie Lesou Polacca signed Fannie Nampeyo, and Elva Polacca Tewaguna signed Elva Nampeyo, and so forth. They claim that they continue to use the Nampeyo name since they are proud of being her descendants and wish to honor "the Old Lady." A few admit that the Nampeyo name also brings higher prices. Some of the children are confident that their outstanding work will be accepted on their own merit, and they prefer to sign their real names. All agree that they owe their pottery-making skills to the instruction given them by their mother.

The Elva Polacca Tewaguna Family

The oldest of Fannie's children to survive more than a few years was Elva, born in 1926 in the Corn Clan house, which was inhabited by Nampeyo at the time. As a child Elva played with her grandmother Nampeyo's clay. Unlike many potters, her grandmother was always generous with this important commodity. Although Elva absorbed ceramic knowledge from Nampeyo, it was not until her parents were living at Bidahochi Trading Post in the late 1930s that Elva became interested in making pottery.

In her prime Elva routinely formed an average of eight pieces of pottery a day. She experienced great pleasure in her work, claiming that should she again have the opportunity, she would choose pottery making over all other professions. Decorating and painting pottery, at which she was so expert, were the most absorbing aspects of her work. Her skill was such that only a few small pencil marks (which burned out during firing) were required to complete her designs. Like her siblings close in age, she specialized in classic fine-line and eagle motifs, reminiscent of the works of her mother and grand-

Fig. 4.40. Thin-walled bowl made by Elva Polacca Tewaguna in 1978. Elva made this unusual piece with ten flute players encircling the exterior when a friend encouraged her to break with tradition and try designs of her own invention. 3 1/2 in. by 7 1/2 in. Private collection.

mother. Her work was innovative, however, only when well-meaning outsiders pressured her to greater activity (fig. 4.40).

Elva formed pottery until the end of her life. Some of the forms were quite large. When she was no longer able to do the finishing work, her daughter Adelle polished, decorated, and fired her pottery for her. Elva's husband, Richard Tewaguna, never became involved with Elva's pottery production, and her children took no credit for their contributions. No works bearing dual signatures were ever made. Elva is survived by five children, four of whom—Neva, Elton, Miriam, and Adelle—are potters (fig. 4.41—see p. XXVII). All of them sign their work with their first names, followed by "Nampeyo" and an ear of corn.

Neva, the oldest daughter, has been making pottery intermittently since 1970. She says that she finds little pleasure in it, however, and considers it a chore. She must "set her mind to make" meaningful form, for she professes that she finds forming difficult; nonetheless her shapes are often complicated and original. She can coil two medium-sized pieces in an hour and produce as many as forty-five items in one week. Like others in her family, Neva enjoys designing and decorating more than other pottery-making. At first she concentrated on fine-line design and then decided to try more original work. In 1986 she moved to Tuba City for work and, unfortunately, has all but abandoned pottery making. Her son Bobby Choyou Jr. has made a few plain pieces of pottery and has been encouraged by the family to continue his work.

Following his graduation from Phoenix Indian High School in 1979, Elva's son Elton served in the United States Army and then returned to Polacca to help his ailing parents and render assistance to the Tewaguna potters. Elton digs, cleans, and mixes clay for his sisters just as he once did for his mother. He sells surplus refined clay to potters outside the immediate family who have neither the skill, inclination, nor time to prepare their own. Not only can he form pots, but he also helps the family with firing, taking little credit. Only recently has he begun to sign his pottery. (None of his works could be located for illustration in this volume.) A rather stern appearance masks his soft-spoken, considerate manner. In 1986 he married Georgianna Webster and then announced that he would begin in earnest his own career as a potter.

Although learning pottery-making techniques early on by watching her mother and grandmother, Miriam Tewaguna Ami developed no real interest in the art until after her marriage to Delmar Ami when she discovered the economic advantages of pottery making to help care for her growing family. Her early work was limited mostly to the formation of vases with square openings, decorated primarily with eagle designs. She likes to paint but considers sanding a dirty, unpleasant chore. In addition to raising a family and making pottery, Miriam has worked as a teacher's aide at the Polacca Day School.

Adelle Tewaguna Lalo also learned pottery making by watching her mother and grandmother work. She enjoys painting traditional designs, characteristic of the art of her predecessors. During a productive week, she is capable of forming about nine pieces of pottery. Adelle makes her own dark brown paint from the wild spinach that grows in Polacca Wash behind her home; this is a departure from her mother and grandmother's practice of producing a similar color from boiled tansy mustard plants. Raising five children has to this point limited Adelle's opportunity to expand or to experiment with her art.

The Leah Polacca Garcia Family

Born in 1928, Leah was a woman of small stature and mild disposition, remembered as a kind and generous person who encouraged everyone in their pottery making. Leah married Lewis Garcia, a native of Laguna Pueblo, in 1958. Lewis died ten years later, leaving her with the responsibility of raising three children between the ages of six and nine years. With help from Fannie, she supported them primarily by making pottery. Leah passed away six years after her husband, leaving the children, by then young teenagers, in Fannie's care. Without hesitation Fannie raised them as her own and became their full-time ceramic art instructor, helping the three develop into master potters (fig. 4.42).

The hallmarks of Leah's work were vessels of excellent quality and large size. Leah's husband, Lewis, never became involved in what he considered Leah's work, and the children were too young to be of much practical help during her productive years. Her pottery pieces are often compared with those of her sister Elva. Both women limited their designs to variations of the classical motifs used by their family predecessors. Leah was noted for her fine-line work, producing many classical migration designs and adaptations similar to those of her mother. She decorated a fair portion of her work with graceful eagle themes. Following the pattern of most Nampeyo descendants, Leah's children sign their ware with their given names followed by "Nampeyo" and the corn symbol.

The oldest child of the Garcia family, James, was born at Keams Canyon in 1958. His secondary education at Phoenix Indian School was interrupted by the death of his mother; he returned to the Hopi Reservation to live with Fannie and to complete high school at Keams Canyon. He then lived in the Corn Clan house in Hano during most of the year and at Sand Hills Ranch during the summers. A potter and kachina carver, he credits his mother with instilling in him an early interest in pottery and his uncle Thomas Polacca with providing much inspiration for his kachina carving. But the person mainly responsible for teaching him pottery work was Fannie. He cherishes a canteen which Fannie made and presented to him as a high school graduation gift.

Fig. 4.42. The Leah Polacca Garcia family and their work. **A.** Like the old master potters, Leah was able to fire many pieces at the same time. This jar was made by Leah in 1973 and decorated with outstanding fine-line applications reminiscent of Nampeyo's. The work is signed "Leah Nampeyo" with an accompanying ear of corn. $5^5/8$ in. by $7^1/2$ in. **B.** Rayvin Garcia made this jar in 1985 under the supervision of Fannie. Well formed with a fine-line migration design, it is signed "Rayvin Nampeyo" with an accompanying drawing of an ear of corn. $4^1/8$ in. by $4^1/2$ in. Private collection. **C.** This bowl by Melda Garcia Navasie has deceptively simple interior and exterior abstracted designs. Made in 1985, it was her largest work to date. It is signed "Melda Nampeyo" with a drawing of an ear of corn. $4^1/2$ in. by $11^5/8$ in. Private collection.

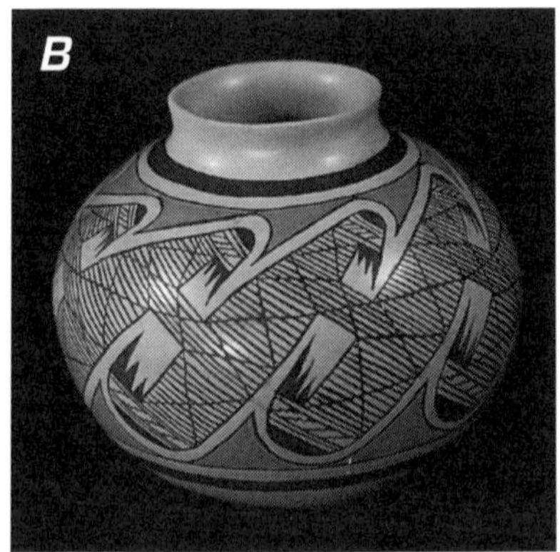

James married an excellent potter, Little Fawn Navasie, a granddaughter of ceramic artist Paqua (Frog Woman). The marriage has had a positive influence on his work. The union of these two families can be expected to result in unusual works of pottery art. By 1987 James was making large, well-decorated pottery that commanded high prices. His decoration follows classical patterns, which are applied over limited areas to produce a more open design (fig. 4.43—see p. XXVIII). Late in 1984 James abandoned construction work to devote himself fully to his art. He uses only the fine gray clay from Antelope Mesa in his creatively shaped pottery and derives his decorative colors almost solely from yellow clay slips and tansy mustard plant extracts. He applies his excellent painting skills both to his well-executed kachina dolls and his pottery.

Melda, born in 1959, is the second Garcia child. She graduated from a Riverside, California, high school and then attended Phoenix College. She married Elroy Navasie, a soldier in the U.S. Army, and the couple lived at Fort Bliss, Texas, and then Fort Carson, Colorado, before Elroy was assigned duty in Germany. Melda returned to Polacca to settle close to Fannie and her brothers when Elroy went overseas, and she began to make pottery. Her well-executed vessels, which measure up to twelve inches in diameter, are decorated in traditional styles (fig. 4.42C). She has mastered the fine-line decorating techniques taught to her by Fannie.

While it is standard practice for young potters to be helped by the more experienced in firing, Melda mastered the technique quickly (fig. 3.26). Her husband assists with routine and less critical chores of preparing fuel and lifting and adjusting heavy wind barriers when needed. They are a well-coordinated team. Melda is quiet and modest, busy with the domestic work of raising a family of four young children. She aspires to become a master potter. Her pottery is sold almost exclusively through local outlets.

Rayvin Garcia, the youngest of Leah's children, was born in Keams Canyon in 1961. Like his siblings, he received his primary education locally. He began high school at Tuba City, Arizona, but upon the death of his mother transferred to the Laguna-Acoma Reservation school. He spent the remainder of his growing-up years in Fannie's household. Rayvin was a constant attendant at his grandmother Fannie's home during her frequent pottery-making sessions. As a result of these instructions and of observing his grandmother, Rayvin endeavors to emulate her work. Forming pottery is difficult for him, but painting and firing are more to his liking (fig. 4.42B). He has concentrated on perfecting fine-line decoration and prefers to work with tansy mustard ink rather than beeweed since "it sticks better than spinach." His wife, Jody, helps sand and polish his pottery, as well as producing her own. At first he sold his work locally but now finds better outlets off-reservation.

The Harold Polacca Family

The oldest of Fannie's boys, Harold, was born on First Mesa in the Tewa village in 1930. He attended local schools and then completed his education at the Phoenix Indian High School where he met his Pima Indian wife-to-be, Alice Cassa. Harold began his career in Phoenix, devoting two years to leather work and specializing in saddle making. He abandoned this trade when his father located work for him in the Keams Canyon Hospital kitchen. Through a series of promotions, he ultimately retired in 1985 from the hospital dietary department where he had supervised all food preparation.

In his youth, Harold assisted his mother with her pottery chores and made a few small vessels of his own. With her urging, in the mid 1970s he found time to form a few traditional pottery pieces and became the first male Hopi-Tewa to sign his work. In the 1980s, he made traditionally shaped but nontraditionally incised, red-slipped pottery similar to that of the Tewa artists of the Rio Grande area. His largest piece was a bowl, which during formation grew to a height of twelve inches. Like others have done, he claimed the clay had a mind of its own and had assumed control. He preferred forming to decorating. He was an intense person, interested in helping perpetuate pottery making at Hopi, both traditional ware and more innovative pieces. He did not, however, produce a lot of pottery himself.

Strongly supportive of Tewa culture, Harold devoted much time and energy to clan and village ceremonial activities. During December of each year, he retreated to the inner court kiva to participate in singing songs of the history of and motives for the migration of his ancestors from the Rio Grande area to their present home. The chants consist of more than forty songs that are repeated over and over to ensure that an exact oral record of them will be passed on to future generations and yet be protected from prying outsiders.

Harold kept cattle at the family's Sand Hills Ranch and specialized in raising colored Indian corns by traditional Hopi dry farming methods. Though self-sustaining farming is no longer possible, others like Harold continue to raise traditional corn and a few vegetables for ceremonial use.

Alice and Harold had seven children, four of whom showed interest in pottery making (fig. 4.44). All in the household speak fluent English, the common language because of a mixed tribal marriage. Beneath Harold's somber face and piercing dark eyes was a surprising and delightful sense of humor.

*Fig. 4.44. Harold Polacca family and their work. **A.** Harold claims to be the first male Hopi-Tewa potter to sign his work. He produced only a few pieces. This bowl is signed "Harold Nampeyo 1975," with an accompanying drawing of an ear of corn. 3^1/$_8$ in. by 3^1/$_2$ in. **B.** Vernida Polacca Adams was trained by her grandmother Fannie. Vernida made this seed jar in 1988 and decorated it with the eagle design. It is one of many she has produced for the trade. Signed "Vernida Polacca Nampeyo" with two lines under "Nampeyo." 3^3/$_4$ in. by 4^3/$_4$ in. **C.** Pottery piece by Clinton, the latest member of the Harold and Alice Polacca family to begin making pottery. This well-shaped, fine-line work was made in late 1991 and signed "Clinton Polacca, '91, Tewa." 5^1/$_2$ in. by 5^1/$_2$ in. Private collections. **D.** Polychrome jar formed by Clinton and decorated by his younger sister Reva in 1993. Reva's design is meticulous. Signed "Reva Ami '93." 7^1/$_4$ in. by 10 in.*

Clement, born in 1953, was the oldest of Harold's sons. He produced a few small pottery pieces shortly before his untimely death. The few surviving pieces indicate that, had Clement lived, his pottery would probably have been made in the traditional style.

Vernida Polacca was born at Keams Canyon in 1955. She studied data processing at Eastern Arizona University for two years and then worked as an accountant at the San Carlos Apache Indian Reservation. She returned to Hopi, worked for the tribe for a year as a teacher's aide, and then, beginning in 1979, managed the Hopi Cultural Center Motel on Second Mesa. This very intelligent, efficient, and attractive person made good use of an incentive program offered by the cultural center to fund travel to Spain, Germany, Hawaii, and China.

On her return to Polacca, her interest in pottery was kindled by both her father and her grandmother. She industriously practiced the skills for three years, but work and family responsibilities limited her output. In 1988 she began producing pottery of fine quality in greater quantity. She finds forming difficult but enjoys decorating, using either beeweed or mustard for black and brown colors. Her traditional designs include fine-line and eagle motifs. She signs her work "Vernida Polacca Nampeyo" but omits the drawing of an ear of corn, undoubtedly due to the fact that her clan affiliation, if any, would originate from her mother's side of the family (fig. 4.44B).

Marvin Polacca was born in 1961. He is married to Delaine Tootsie, also from a family that produces pottery. She makes vessels with innovative decorations and signs them "Delaine Polacca." Marvin prefers kachina-doll carving to working with clay. The first of his pottery work appeared in 1982, after a period of close association with aunts and uncles who made pottery. He fancies the skill of forming pottery, dislikes decorating, and remains with the traditional designs used by other in the family. (No example of his work could be located for illustration.)

Clinton Polacca, born in 1958, is married to Angelita Tawayamptewa and has two children at this writing. He started making pottery about 1990. Considering the short period of time that he has made pottery, his work is remarkably well formed and decorated (fig. 4.44C).

A relatively recent potter descended from Nampeyo is Reva, the youngest child of Harold and Alice Polacca. Like many contemporary artists, she showed little or no interest in pottery until after her marriage to Lloyd Ami Jr. in the early 1980s. At the time of this writing, the young couple are the parents of three children. Although her first pieces were small in size, they are increasing in size and her fine-line decorations are among the best (fig. 4.44D).

The Thomas Polacca Family

Thomas was born in 1935 in the village of Polacca in the Nampeyo home originally built by Lesou. He lived with his uncle Wesley while attending Polacca Day School and spent his summers at the family's ranch, where he became an expert cattleman. He married Gertrude Lomasnewa, a Second Mesa Hopi from the village of Shungopovi.

Thomas followed several occupations before restricting his primary efforts to making pottery. In addition to his early years as a rancher at Sand Hills, he worked as an automobile mechanic in Gallup, a general handyman at Keams Canyon Trading Post, a maintenance worker at Keams Canyon Boarding School, and a dishwasher at Grand Canyon Lodge. Gertrude and Thomas also served as dormitory parents at the Inter-Mountain School in Brigham City, Utah. A transfer to Tuba City, Arizona, as supervisors of dormitory aides brought the Polaccas closer to their ancestral homes. Throughout Tom's school career he involved himself with educational art projects.

During the years in Tuba City, Thomas began to create innovative pottery sculptures and vessels. Although he had observed his relatives at work and had made clay marbles as a boy, it was not until 1972, at the urging of his sister Leah, that some vessels made by Gertrude inspired Thomas to try decorating. Gertrude has never decorated pottery but has shaped many of Thomas's pottery bases. She never signs them. By 1974 Thomas had broken with tradition to produce remarkable, forceful works of great beauty (figs. 4.45—see p.XXIX, and 3.18). He became so engrossed in working with clay that he resigned his school position to devote more time to his ceramic art.

Thomas admits to an unpredictable nature, though perhaps mellowed and matured by both age and life's hard knocks. In spite of personal problems, he has always returned to his work to reach for new artistic heights. He possesses a tremendous urge to create, often deriving inspiration from the unsurpassed vistas of his environment. His carved creations appear to spring from their clay backgrounds, as though emerging from the earth. His works assume an ever-changing variety of shapes and decoration, some almost Oriental in feeling. When a design is complicated and difficult to visualize, he sketches, erases, and re-sketches several times on the clay surface before carving; he uses the sharp blades employed by model makers. His brown paint, produced from tansy mustard, is skillfully applied to the clay surfaces and often gives them the appearance of wood. He creates a variety of red colors from fine suspensions of yellow and red clay to which he may add small amounts of inorganic ingredients that he obtains locally. The red clays are obtained from the Hualapai people. Thomas claimed that firing made him nervous, but he had been observed turning his back on his blazing manure kiln and casually practicing roping while the fate of a valuable work of art hung in the balance.

His work first received national recognition when he was awarded both Best in Class for pottery and a First Place for sculpture at the Gallup Inter-Tribal Indian Ceremonial competition in 1980. He has used the signature "Nampeyo" on his work out of respect for the "Old Lady" to whom he feels he owes a great debt. Near the end of 1988, in order not to be accused of relying on the Nampeyo name to market his work, he began to sign his pieces with his family name.

An interesting progression is apparent in his design work. Starting as a protégé under his mother's tutelage, he formed traditional pottery with traditional painted designs. He next began to incise around the traditional designs. Incising gave way first to shallow carving, then deepened into bas-relief. Thomas has inspired many who have followed him in breaking the ties of tradition with innovative forms and decoration. The inspiration for their pottery, however, comes from nature and Hopi-Tewa historic and religious traditions. He is also credited with founding a new school of Hopi ceramic art as he continues to experiment with locally obtained raw materials and new forming and firing techniques.

Other outstanding potters who acknowledge Thomas for exposing new horizons include his son Gary, daughters Carla and Elvira, nephew Eugene Hamilton, and brother-in-law Wallace Youvella. Each has a distinctive style that nonetheless reflects his influence.

Thomas has always been involved with the ceremonial life of his people; his commitment has grown in recent years and has intensified since the death of his mother, Fannie. Shortly after her death, he and his family moved to her Polacca home. Sadly, he removed Fannie's firing area and is using an electric kiln.

Thomas and Gertrude's oldest son, Gary, was born at Keams Canyon and received his primary and secondary education at Tuba City. At Eastern Arizona College, he received an associate teaching degree and did two more years of study at the Northern Arizona University. He taught in the Hopi Head Start Program at Second Mesa Day School and states that his educational career, family, and accompanying ceramic avocation have provided him with a full and satisfying life. He spends some time at the ranch tending cattle. Gary observed his father's creations and decided to emulate him. His meticulous decorative style differs somewhat from his father's, and his colors are more subdued (figs. 4.46—see p. XXX, and 4.47A). Not having spent his boyhood on the reservation, Gary feels that his efforts to make pottery express a yearning to return to his people. His mother, Gertrude, is Hopi, and as a result he claims Hopi rather than Hopi-Tewa allegiances, despite the fact that he uses the Nampeyo name in his signature.

Carla was born at Brigham City, Utah, began school in the Head Start Program at Tuba City, and finished high school there as well. Following two years at Northern Arizona University, she was first employed as a secretary and later as a bank teller at Tuba City. In her youth, summers were spent at Sand Hills Ranch with her grandmother Fannie and her cousins. She gleefully recalls a protective grandmother who kept interested boys away from her attractive young granddaughters. She is married to Ral Claw, a Navajo, and lives in Tuba City.

Carla began making pottery in 1982 under the tutelage of her father. She prefers the gray clay from First Mesa for forming and covers it with a thick slip pigmented with beeweed, using a stone on the slipped pieces to produce an unusual, highly polished, rich brown surface. She executes incised designs with a nail punch and a small knife and fires by placing the objects in a metal pan and covering them with the prescribed protective pottery sherds and sheep dung fuel. Initially, her pieces were small, but they have since increased in size and sophistication (fig. 4.47B). Her forms are both spherical and ovate. Although some of her pieces appear to be completely closed, she employs various means to conceal a small hole that must be present in the pot wall to allow for the release of expanding gasses during firing. A few of her works resemble pieces made by her father.

Carla leads a busy life, maintaining a home and raising children while working at her art. She often averages one piece of pottery per day. Her work received almost immediate acceptance, and in a short time she developed marketing outlets as far away as California. Her husband Ral is enthusiastically supportive of her efforts and assists with much of the work and his name sometimes appears with hers in the signature. Her signature usually appears as "Carla C. Nampeyo."

Elvira Polacca, born in 1968, was also raised and educated in Tuba City. Shortly after her marriage to Marty Naha, she temporarily occupied her Hopi mother's home on Second Mesa but soon relocated to Fannie's home in Polacca. Elvira and her husband jointly form pottery that follows patterns established by her parents (fig. 4.47C). Because Thomas now fires in an electric kiln, Elvira has never learned to fire traditionally.

The Tonita Polacca Hamilton Family

Tonita Hamilton is a friendly and industrious successor to the Nampeyo legacy. Born in Polacca in 1936, she completed her secondary education before her marriage to Eugene Hamilton. Both Tonita and Eugene became teacher's aides and then enrolled at Northern Arizona University to earn Bachelor's degrees in education. Prior to retirement, they taught for several years in the Keams Canyon school system. Presently, their time is divided between supporting ceremonial affairs and making pottery.

As far back as Tonita can remember, she nurtured a desire to make pottery and studied long hours with her mother Fannie. While quick to become an expert at pottery forming, her painting and decorating

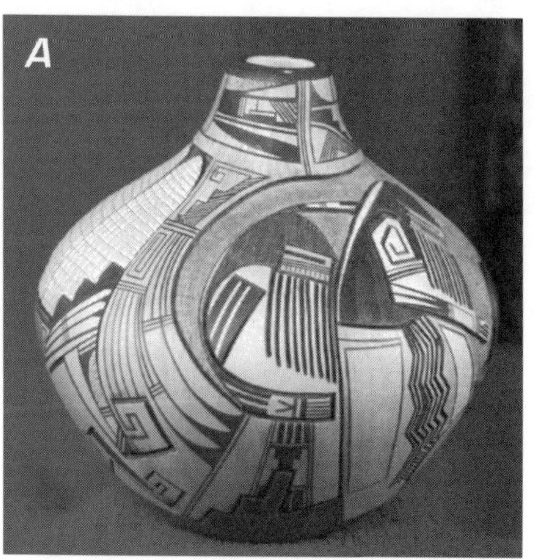

Fig. 4.47. The work of the Thomas Polacca family. **A.** This intricately decorated, narrow-necked jar by Gary Polacca made in 1988 features four Long Hair Kachinas, stylized ears of corn, clouds, and other elements. A tansy mustard stain fired onto the carved design is similar to those applied by his father Thomas. The work is signed "G. Nampeyo." $6^3/4$ in. by $6^1/2$ in. Private collection. **B.** Carla Polacca Claw made this pot in 1986. The kachina design is nicely incised through a dark, highly polished slip and is characteristic of much of her work. Other designs feature realistically portrayed animals. $6^1/2$ in. by 5 in. KCAC. **C.** Elvira Polacca Naha's small, deeply carved, ovate-shaped ceramic piece is colored and decorated in a style reminiscent of her father. It is signed "Marty & Elvira Naha Nampeyo." Made in June 1992. 3 in. by $2^1/2$ in. Private collection.

techniques took more time to perfect. Originally, Tonita's decoration followed classic patterns, but more recently she has produced mixed styles, some old and some new (fig. 4.48A—see p. XXXI). She looks upon her craft as a means of supplementing her income. Admittedly, much of the work involved is hard and dirty, but she feels fortunate since it pays her well and gives her such a deep sense of satisfaction. She will not release a piece of pottery until she is certain that it is artistically correct. Her work has been well recognized at the Southwest American Indian Association's Santa Fe Indian Market and at other Indian art competitions. She signs her work "Tonita Nampeyo" along with the drawing of an ear of corn.

Eugene Hamilton has also become a fine potter, adept in both incising and carving. He skillfully applies his stylized, bright, clean-colored Hopi designs to geometric backgrounds (fig. 4.48B—see p. XXXI). He spends most of his time that would be devoted to making his own pottery to assisting Tonita; thus, his individual output is limited. Eugene signs his work with a deer track symbol.

Tonita worked closely with her mother, Fannie. Near the end of Fannie's life, the two were inseparable. Without doubt, some works were formed that represented the efforts of both, yet Tonita refused to cosign the pieces, ignoring the entreaties of collectors and traders who, realizing their ultimate value, were willing to pay inflated prices (fig. 3.21B).

Although making pottery is Tonita's profession, the Hopi-Tewa and Corn Clan ceremonial activities are more important to her. Following Fannie's death, the Hamiltons moved into the Corn Clan home where Tonita assumed the full duties of clan matriarch. She became the caretaker of the home and of the religious objects housed there; her work included organizing feasts as well as participating in many ceremonies. In addition, the revered grinding stones for the colored slips and those for polishing, used by both Nampeyo and Fannie, came into her possession. These artifacts and tools now reside in the old clan home where they originated. Upon receiving these ageless tools, Tonita passed on the stones that Eugene had made for her to her niece Melda.

The Hamiltons' son, Loren, was born at the Seventh Day Adventist Hospital near Gouldings in Monument Valley on the Navajo Indian Reservation. He attended preschool in Mexican Hat, Utah, where his parents were employed. He attended school at Polacca, Tuba City, and finally Winslow, Arizona, where he graduated from high school. For some time he was an employee of the housing arm of the Hopi Tribal Authority, the agency that administers federal grants for HUD.[31]

Although Loren acquired pottery-making skills from his mother, he learned some decorating skills from his uncle Thomas. Initially, Tonita decorated for Loren, but he soon developed his own carved, innovative, contemporary style. He applies designs to surfaces that have been prepared by smoothing them with a special sandpaper, coarse on one side, fine on the other, and more durable than most abrasive papers. He first draws in pencil on the smooth unfired clay and then highlights by carving and incising his complicated decorations in delicate detail with razor-sharp blades. His carving subjects are often animals or birds, but he also portrays kachinas, designs from pottery sherds, and countless other themes (fig. 4.48C—see p. XXXI). His work, like that of the Polacca male relatives, received immediate recognition and is valued by collectors. He signs his work "Loren H. Nampeyo" and uses a drawing of a stalk of corn next to his signature.

The Ellsworth Polacca Family

Born in Polacca, Ellsworth first attended school in Keams Canyon. In 1955 he was sent to Centerville, Utah, to participate in a Mormon-sponsored relocation project. Feeling that his role was that of an unpaid farmworker rather than a member of the sponsoring family, he ran away and returned to his family. His parents, upset with this behavior, sent him to school in Stuart, Nevada. His father, Vinton, reasoned that Stuart was so far from Polacca that Ellsworth would find it impossible to return. Fortunately, Ellsworth enjoyed the new school. After graduation, Vinton's illness prompted the youth to return to Sand Hills Ranch to help the family and learn ranching, a profession that suited him well. He also worked for the U. S. Forest Service as a firefighter, as a night attendant at the Inter-Mountain School in

Brigham City, and then served in Vietnam in the U. S. Army. He studied at Northern Arizona University and then took a job as a juvenile probation officer. In 1973 he became a junior officer in the Hopi Police Force, but always helped Fannie with pottery making, as well as making a few pieces himself (fig. 4.49).

In 1981 a restless Ellsworth abandoned his ceramic work completely to become a Hopi ranger.[32] In 1987 he was promoted to the position of director of Range and Livestock Services for the Hopi Tribe. One of his responsibilities was to prevent artifact theft from the many prehistoric ruins located within the reservation. During off-duty hours, he continued along with his relatives to maintain a cattle herd at the family ranch. Proud of his inheritance, he collected family photographs and history. Following his marriage to Mary Lou Yoyokie, also employed by the Hopi tribe, the couple established residence in the village of Kykotsmovi, located below Third Mesa.

Eventually Ellsworth missed the quietude of pottery making, which he considered all-absorbing. Beginning with conventional polychrome painting, he expanded his field of expertise by incising designs on a polished, red-slipped pottery base. He considered polishing very tedious, but he found the task made easier by utilizing slips containing a small portion of the same white clay that his grandmother had used. He was able to produce a very few pieces a year. His sole motivation for working with clay was a desire to create;

Fig. 4.49. Ellsworth Polacca formed and decorated this bowl in 1975 in a style reminiscent of that of his mother, Fannie. The piece is signed "Ellsworth Nampeyo" with an accompanying drawing of an ear of corn. 5¹/₂ in. by 6¹/₂ in. *Private collection.*

the family income was such that there was no need to augment it with pottery sales. He signed his pottery "Ellsworth Nampeyo," which was accompanied by a drawing of an ear of corn. Ellsworth agreed with the philosophy of his grandfather, Tom Polacca, that "to improve, the Hopi should selectively adopt from the white man's culture only that which is good." In the mid 1980s he was stricken with diabetes, the scourge of Native American peoples, and suffered a fatal heart attack in 1993.

The Iris Polacca Youvella Family

The youngest of Fannie's living children, Iris, was born in Polacca and attended schools at Keams Canyon, Provo, Utah, Tuba City, and, while living with her brother Thomas, at Phoenix Indian High School. She continued her education as a nurse in Albuquerque and worked in a hospital on Staten Island, New York, for a time but found little in favor of city life, so returned to the West to practice nursing in Brigham City, Utah.

Iris molded some pottery as a child, but not until 1973 did she seriously pursue working in clay. A meticulous person in her appearance, habits, and ceramic work, Iris enjoys forming the clay but not the dusty job of sanding. She is known for pottery with delicate, sculpted ears of corn rising from the surface. Her pieces often fire to a rosy blush color, creating a warmth absent in electric kiln-fired pottery. She is intrigued with the delicate hues intrinsic in different clays, and her work reflects these differences. She will, on special order, paint traditional designs, but most of her production is sculptured (fig. 4.50A and C—see p. XXXII). Iris does not enter competitions; several pieces have been submitted as dealer entries, however, and have earned prizes, including Best of Class at the 1985 Gallup Inter-Tribal Indian Ceremonial. Iris inscribes her signature as either "Iris Nampeyo" or "Iris Y. Nampeyo" and does not include the corn symbol with her signature.

Iris is married to Wallace Youvella (figs. 4.50B—see p. XXXII), who also comes from a Hopi-Tewa pottery family. Informed collectors prize the work of his mother, Susie, a classmate and friend of Fannie.

Wally has been an outstanding potter since 1975, and occasionally this gifted couple collaborate. Wally and his mother-in-law, Fannie, shared a deep mutual affection. The Youvellas often supplied Fannie with clay and transported her as needed. Near the end of her life, Iris and Wally nursed Fannie in their home. Having spent so much time in Fannie's company, Wally credits her with teaching him much of his basic pottery know-how. He also credits Thomas with instilling in him the drive to differ creatively. As a student of prehistoric pottery decoration, his work demonstrates imaginative designs based on the art of the ancients.

The Youvellas' four children, Wallace Jr., Charlene, Nolan, and Doran, all produce and market a limited amount of pottery (fig. 4.50D—see p. XXXII). In 1986 Nolan began producing a few small float-polished bowls and pipes made from his mother's clays. The bowls were similar to those produced by his brother Doran at a later date. The pottery of the Youvella offspring has increased in sophistication. All are inscribed with their given names followed by "Nampeyo."

✤ In July 1989 we attended a Mixed Kachina dance held in Tewa around the shrine in the plaza. Just as they were important to Nampeyo, such dances continue to be important to the Hopi-Tewa way of life, to the various clans (including the Corn Clan), and to Nampeyo's many descendants. Family members continue to participate to this very day in the celebrations. The dance of the regal and powerful kachinas, the complicated rhythms of drummers and singers, the antics of those masters of comedy the koshari, the beautifully executed masks and brilliantly colored attire, and huge quantities of food—all these elements merge under the dazzling Southwest sun into an unforgettable occasion of community exuberance and spiritual affirmation.

Admirers of Indian ceramic art, after attending such a celebration at the Corn Clan home, cannot fail to realize that pottery making is a flourishing form of artistic expression undeniably strengthened by this culture and belief system. Five generations of Nampeyo descendants have now been nurtured and taught by their faith and cultural values; and numerous members of these five generations have become outstanding potters. Such a sustained artistic inheritance is uncommon in any culture. The people presented in this book have been and continue to be dedicated to preserving their cultural inheritance by maintaining this inherited art form, a way first explained by a small quiet woman over a century ago. Their art is not likely to die. Rather, a safe prediction would be that it will continue to flourish and assume new and beautiful dimensions in the future.

Notes

Notes to Chapter One

1. Rohn 1985, 3-10.

2. Harrington 1916, 336.

3. Dickson 1979; Kelley 1980; Palkovich 1980; Rose, Dean and Robinson 1981; and Lange and Harris 1984.

4. To attempt other than a brief summary of these dramatic historic events would be presumptuous. For interested readers the following sources are recommended: Rohn 1985; Cordell 1985; Blair and Blair 1986; Nelson 1916; Reed 1943a and 1943b; and Schroeder 1979.

5. Schroeder and Matson 1965.

6. Forrest 1979, 107-109; and Reed 1943a, 73-76, 119-120.

7. Warren n.d., 184-197.

8. Harrington 1916, 483.

9. Ryan 1907, 42-43.

10. Yava 1978, 16-28.

11. Fewkes 1900, 614-616; Yava 1978, 144; and Freire-Marreco, 1913. Versions of this Corn Clan story can be attributed to the Corn Clan in Zuni, the Akokwes, the Pi Kiac Clan in Oraibi, and others.

12. Espinosa 1988, 275.

13. Yava 1978, 28-29.

14. Stanislawski 1979, 589; and Fewkes 1900, 614.

15. Dozier 1966, 56-57.

16. Yava 1978, 32-33.

17. Dozier 1966, 25.

18. Bloom 1931, 204-205.

19. Dockstader 1954, 166.

20. Adams and Chavez 1956, 303.

21. Spicer 1962, 195-196.

22 & 23. James 1974, 75 and 78.

24. Calhoun 1915, 172. For further information concerning Calhoun's problems with the military, see James H. Simpson 1964, 175-181.

25. Stegner 1954, 137.

26. The authors are indebted to H. L. Douch, curator of the Royal Cornwall Museum, for providing personal and written information concerning Keam's life.

27. Bullen 1905.

28. For a summary of Keam's life in the West see McNitt 1962, and Van Valkenburgh 1940 and 1946.

29. Arny 1873, 13-28.

30. McNitt 1962, 153.

31. There was some confusion as to the relationship between Thomas and William Keam. (H.C. James 1974). From a search of birth and census records as well as the epitaph on their mother's gravestone, there can be no doubt that they were brothers.

32. Information concerning William's death was obtained from the inscription on the tombstone of Grace Keam, located in the Kenwyn churchyard in Truro. The Fort Wingate cemetery is practically abandoned. The remains of the soldiers buried there have been removed to the National Cemetery at Santa Fe, New Mexico. The whereabouts of the remains of William are not known, but they may have been moved along with those of the soldiers, may still be at the old fort, or they may have been returned to England by Keam.

33. Stephen's middle name remains a mystery, not even known to Keam, who in 1896 wrote to Washington Matthews, "You asked of our late lamented friend 'dear old Steve'. His middle name I never learned, all we ever knew was Alexander Stephen." One year later Keam remarked that a person named Phillips told him that it was Middleton, but nothing in the records verifies the claim as accurate. Dellenbaugh 1884-1885, quoted in Parsons 1936.

34. Bourke 1984, 80.

35. Culin 1901-1905, 10.

36. Anonymous 1865-1866.

37. Stephen 1889.

38. Information provided by Lucy M. Rios, postmaster at Keams Canyon, Arizona, from 1971 to 1987.

39. Donaldson 1890.

40. Gallaher 1887.

41. Parsons 1936, 799.

42. The Hopi word for butterfly is *poli*, not *polacca*.

43. Farrish 1915-1918.

44. Culin 1901-1905, 11.

45. Personal communication with Byron Harvey III.

46. James 1974, 109 and 110.

47. Wade and McChesney 1980, 12.

48. Anonymous n.d.

49. Fletcher 1979, 66 and 361.

50. At the start of World War II the Berlin collection was carefully crated and stored in nearby mine shafts and suffered little, if any, shell or bomb damage. During our attempt to study it, a curator missed our appointment and did not delegate a substitute to assist us. The collection was housed in large locked, unlighted, glassed door cabinets for which no keys could be found. Articles were stacked so as to obscure lower items from view. The few pieces located outside the cabinets were undergoing a crude and destructive form of over-restoration. Provenance of the collection was not available, and record books, in Stephens writing, gave little information except for comparing dimensionless shapes with numbers on the pottery.

51. Lange, Riley, and Lange 1984, 654.

52. Ibid., 442.

53. Brunius 1985, 2.

54. Fewkes 1898a, 648-649.

55. Fewkes 1919, 279.

56. Ibid., 218.

57. Wade and McChesney 1980, 9-10.

58. Courlander 1982, 121-122.

59. Colton 1943, 44-45.

60. James 1974, 114.

61. Anonymous, *Journal of the Royal Cornwall Museum,* 1907, ix-xi.

62. Keam 1894.

63. Keam 1896.

64. Information courtesy of Mrs. Lise Michelman, research associate of the Brooklyn Museum, who in a personal communication stated that the original papers may be an entry #1563 in the society's *Freeman Guide.*

65. Bourke 1984, 276-277.

66. Anonymous, 1885-1902; and Brugge, 1993.

67. Interviews with members of the McGee family, owners of Keams Canyon Trading Post and McGee's Indian Arts, reveal that the records had been stored at the post until they became so cumbersome that they were buried under the shoe department and covered with concrete.

68. Dozier 1966, 67.

69. Yava 1978, 11.

Notes to Chapter Two

1. W. H. Jackson 1929, 250; Douglas 1942, 233. Douglas gave Jackson no credit for first establishing the approximate year of Nampeyo's birth even though Jackson's writings are a part of the Douglas Library, Denver Art Museum, which was then under the supervision of Douglas.

2. Dockstader 1954, 161-172.

3. Mindeleff 1886-1887, 61. "Bahana" is a Hopi term meaning "white outsider." The word is also a derivation of the Hopi word "Pahana," meaning "people of the water," possibly a reference to the old Hopi belief that whites came from across the water to become ceremonial leaders (Hough 1915, 81).

4. Keam continued for as long as he lived in the United States to prevail upon the U. S. government to respect the basic rights of the Hopis. G. A. Dorsey, in a letter to H. Voth dated January 15, 1901, (on file in the Mennonite Archives at North Newton, Kansas) wrote: "Mr. Keam passed through here yesterday and paid a visit to the Museum. He is very enthusiastic over your work on the altars, etc. and is frank to say that it is of the very highest order. As you probably know he has been to Washington to secure Burton's [Charles E. Burton was then the unpopular acting Hopi school superintendent] scalp and claims that he will have it dangling from his belt within a few months or at least have him transferred."

5. Collins 1974, 9; Parsons 1936, 1020-1021; and Kramer 1996, 13 and 189.

6. H. C. James 1956, 158.

7. Hough 1915, 75-77.

8. Jackson 1947, 239-240. The works identified by Holmes included Smithsonian specimens bearing the catalog numbers 158.143, 158.146-158.148, 158.151 and 158.152.

9. Bunzel [1929] 1972, 5.

10. Schweizer 1942. Records do not verify that this fair ever took place. Kramer (1988, 47) states: "The mythical exhibition was created during a confusion of correspondence between an elderly and ill Herman Schweizer . . . and Harold S. Colton, director of the Museum of Northern Arizona."

11. Information provided dated February 2, 1988, by Diane D. Dittermore, Ethnological Collections Curator, Arizona State Museum, Tucson. She stated that "Dr. Miller was a medical doctor who came to Arizona in 1888 from Kansas. He lived in Prescott. Through connections to Governor Murphy, he was appointed head of the Arizona Insane Asylum in Phoenix during the 1890s. In 1895, he founded the Arizona Antiquarian Society [which later became the Arizona Archaeological and Historical Society]. He worked at the ruin of Pueblo Grande near Phoenix in 1901. He spent much time at Hopi; among other things, he was interested from a medical standpoint in the Snake Dance, and of snake bite. He died on his way to a Snake Dance in Flagstaff in 1901. The Museum purchased his collection from his widow in 1916."

12. Freire-Marreco 1913, 45.

13. Webb and Weinstein 1973, 15 and 25.

14. Schwartz 1969, 116-121.

15. Personal communication, 17 April 1986.

16. Churchill 1904-1907. The purpose of the 1904 Churchill visit was to investigate complaints against Hopi School Superintendent Burton lodged by Keam and others. After a short stay during which Churchill interviewed a few witnesses friendly to Burton, Churchill concluded in his report to Washington that all charges against Burton were unfounded. Notwithstanding, Burton was transferred the next year. Keam did not live to enjoy the end results of his crusade against Burton, which finally succeeded through the assistance of Charles Lummis.

17. The reports of John Huckel are among the Hubbell papers, which are located in the Special Collections Section of the University of Arizona Library, Tucson.

18. McNitt 1962, 76, 210-211, 233 and 235; Anonymous 1910.

19. Bunzel 1972, 41.

20. Smith 1971, frontispiece and 115-125. Smith, Woodbury, and Woodbury (1966, 168) caution about arriving at a refined chronology for pottery-type manufacture. "Of course it must not be supposed that in discussing the increase or decrease of the occurrence of the shards of varying types we are dealing exactly with periods of pottery manufacture, but of pottery breakage. Yet Indian earthenware vessels were constantly made and constantly broken, like those of other people, so the greater the number manufactured the greater the number that met with accident. Some vessels, no doubt, survived for several generations, and finally meeting disaster, contributed to the refuse deposited later than that of the period in which they were made."

21. Two different sources (one an Indian art dealer and one a Nampeyo family member) reported that copies of designs on paper by Lesou were wrapped in cloth and stored in Nellie's house for safekeeping. Efforts to locate these, through inquiries made of the descendants now living in her home, have been unsuccessful. In the 1960s Barton Wright was told that this document was in Fannie's possession and that it was a book. In all probability it does not exist.

22. The Tiwa people are one of several Pueblo language groups and are divided into two branches. The northern branch now occupies the pueblos of Taos and Picuris, and the southern branch lives in the present pueblos of Sandia and Isleta. The Tigua Pueblo of El Paso also identifies itself as a Tiwa group forced to flee with the Spanish.

23. Wade and McChesney 1981, 84.

24. Euler and Dobyns 1971, 48.

25. Wade and McChesney 1981, 84.

26. The war continues between artifact looters and Hopi rangers and police over the theft of antiquities from archaeological sites. Acting on information that an area is targeted by looters, the rangers may stake out the site for several days in hopes of catching the thieves. Looters have even gained access to sites by helicopter, which provide fast and less detectable entry as well as escape from the law. Nampeyo's grandson Ellsworth Polacca, formerly chief of the Hopi Rangers, participated in armed "ruin skirmishes" with looters.

27. Fewkes 1898a, 642.

28. Fewkes 1895, 634-636.

29. Waters 1970, 122-123.

30. Mooney (1893, 283-284) reported that Keam had excavated portions of the ruin called Kawaika-a. Initially, it was thought that the people of this village were the first contacted by the Spanish explorers, but recent evidence indicates the contact was made at Awatovi. The residents of Kawaika-a had left before the Spanish arrival.

31. Daifuku 1961, vii, 46-51.

32. Tanner 1976, 120.

33. Laird 1977, 562.

34. Bunzel [1929] 1972, 79.

35. Benavides 1916, 207.

36. Brew 1979, 18.

37. Fewkes 1893, 363.

38. Smith 1971, 574-576.

39. Anonymous 1984. This is a custom among many Native American groups who share special locations. Another example is the Pipestone Quarries National Historic Sites in Minnesota, which is still actively quarried for catlinite to carve peace pipe bowls and fetishes.

40. Kramer 1996, 158.

Notes to Chapter Three

1. Polacca 1972, 24.

2. Kabotie and Belknap 1977, 67. The claim of the First Mesa people that they have inherited the sole right, by tradition, to make pottery is subject to challenge. Donaldson (1893, 45) records that in 1891, of a total of 366 recorded potters on the Hopi Reservation, 37% resided on First Mesa, 43% on Second Mesa, and 20% on Third Mesa.

3. Wyckoff 1990, 81.

4. Granzberg 1973, 48.

5. Information about availability of clays was provided by master potter Fawn Navasie, Frog Woman's daughter.

6. Hough 1915, 77.

7. Hough 1917, 78.

8. Curtis 1922, 26.

9. Ries 1927, 181.

10. Freire-Marreco 1913, 43; Curtis 1922, 26; and Applegate 1930, 4.

11. Tierney 1976, 50; Whiting 1939, 77.

12. Curtis 1922, 7; Chapman 1970, 47; Blair and Blair 1986, 127-128; and Whiting 1939, 77-78.

13. Ral Claw, husband of potter Carla Polacca, notes that this material is also used by Navajo women to protect themselves from sunburn.

14. Peterson 1980, 17; Curtis 1922, 26.

15. Granzberg 1973, 49-50.

16. Applegate 1930, 3; Stephen, as quoted by Parsons 1936, 617, 1021 and 1190; Wade and McChesney 1980, 444-447; and Freire-Marreco 1913, 42.

17. Barry 1981, 80; Wright 1979, 71.

18. Voth 1912, 5.

19. Personal communication with Porter Timeche from the village of Shungopovi. Parsons quotes Alexander Stephen's description of how a canteen is formed in Parsons 1936, 728 and 1188; O'Kane 1950, 142.

20. Grammer 1930, 190-191.

21. Freire-Marreco 1913, 44; James 1956, 159. Personal observation and conversation with Daisy Hooee at her home in Zuni.

22. Applegate 1930, 2.

23. Incising is also referred to as "graffito."

24. Freire-Marreco 1913, 37-38.

25. Traugott 1983, 6; Link 1985, 8.

26. Frank and Harlow 1974, 151. An example of Sikyatki work, no. 11019/12, is located in the University of New Mexico's Maxwell Museum of Anthropology.

27. Smith 1971; Wade and McChesney 1981; Stephen 1890 [Parsons 1936]; and Stephen and Fewkes 1919; Stephen and Fewkes in Appendix.

28. Stanislawski, Hitchcock, and Stanislawski 1976, 47-65; with additions by Barton Wright from conversations with the Coltons.

29. As recorded by Stanislawski, Hitchcock, and Stanislawski 1976, 64, and Wright 1989, 110.

30. Parsons 1936, 1189; Curtis 1922, 26; and Freire-Marreco 1913, 53. In 1986, Joy Navasie added corncobs to a dung fire to increase heat.

31. Shepard 1956, 78-80.

Notes to Chapter Four

1. Pueblo Indian Julian Martinez was hired as a maintenance man some time before his wife Maria was encouraged to join him to develop their pottery skills at the School of American Archaeology. The following letter from Julian illustrates the mutual tolerance required by both the artist and the institution in these situations.

San Ildefonso, N.M.
Feb. 4, 1911

Mr chapman [*sic*].

In answering your letter I will tell you that I am sorry because I dint go soon I would not like to leave my work so long but I could help it. You know that we have to do what the governor says. And now we are busy working on the ditch. But I am sure that I will be there by the first of March. So you tell Pablo to work this month.

Your Truly
Julian Martinez

2. Santana Gutierrez produced trains made from clay to sell from the Española platform. She was joined by Andreita Baca who sold small pipes conveniently shaped for holding in the hand (Freire-Marreco 1913, 101-102). Freire-Marreco also noted that thirty-cent pottery ladles in the shapes of kachinas were sold by an unknown Hopi woman at the station in Winslow, Arizona.

3. Peterson 1984, 38.

4. Ibid.

5. Freire-Marreco 1913, March 13.

6. Culin 1901, 31, and 1905, 5 and 26.

7. Anonymous 1905.

8. The films disappeared for a time but were later located in a small motion picture theater in Wisconsin by Dr. Paul Vanderbilt of the State Historical Society. In 1965 the film was donated to the Smithsonian Institution with Dr. Vanderbilt's statement, "It was in storage. The owner has no more idea than I have as to the source."

9. In 1988 Tad Nichols told us that at the time he was a member of a field trip or tour, part of which included a visit to the Corn Clan home.

10. Peterson 1980, 17. Any Nampeyo pottery with "wonderful painting" in 1922 probably had designs applied by Nampeyo's children.

11. Dozier 1966, 85.

12. We found no pottery pieces attributable to Annie in Clara Churchill's extensive Nampeyo pottery collection at Dartmouth College's Hood Museum of Art.

13. Information about the Baldwin camp was supplied by Dextra Quotskuyva and Daisy Hooee.

14. A history of the Phoenix Indian School and the evolution of its educational policies until its closing are impartially presented in R. A. Trennert's book *The Phoenix Indian School: Forced Assimilation in Arizona, 1891–1935*.

15. Ryan 1907, 55-56.

16. Kramer 1988, 46-53.

17. Hartman, Musial, and Tanner 1987, 91-93.

18. Smith 1971, xvii.

19. Smith 1952, vii.

20. Sotheby Parke Bernet Catalogue, November 1975, 97, 113, 130 and 191.

21. Redhouse 1985, 11.

22. While in residence, the McGees employed a carpenter to make improvements. The man was Alvin James, the kachina-doll carver whose work now brings prices in four figures.

23. There is a strong emphasis on Fannie in this book, mainly because she was the one surviving daughter of Nampeyo at the time this project began. She provided more information about the family than was available from any of the other Nampeyo descendants.

24. Wright 1975, 34.

25. If the 1904 birth date is accurate, it would have been impossible for her to be in the fourth grade at this time, another indication that she was born closer to 1900.

26. James 1974, 162.

27. Sadie, a lifelong friend of Fannie, became a recognized artist, particularly for her decorating abilities (Collins 1977, 11). At the request of Dr. Colton, Sadie made a set of decorated tiles which were set in the walls at the entrance to the Museum of Northern Arizona (Trimble 1987, 101).

28. Fannie recalled that she and Vinton were almost the same age. If correct, this information also supports her birth year more correctly as 1900 rather than 1904.

29. Wade 1986, 181 and 183.

30. Many Native Americans find it quite natural to accept multiple and often widely divergent religions. First Mesa converts explain that the Hopis and the Hopi-Tewas accept Mormonism because of its similar elements. Hopis and Gamilis (the Tewa name for Mormons) both have suffered persecution; therefore, they share much in common and are comfortable with one another.

31. The Hopi Tribal Authority is responsible for erecting and maintaining housing for the Indian people between Keams Canyon and Moencopi—an area measuring approximately thirty-three hundred square miles.

32. Ellsworth's Tewa forebears had defended First Mesa against marauding tribes after the Pueblo Revolt. Today many Hopi-Tewas are hired by the Hopi tribe for security jobs.

Appendix A

NAMPEYO
FAMILY DESIGNS

Hopi and Hopi-Tewa decorators use simple geometric forms in abundance on their pottery. These include squares, triangles, semi-circular or U shapes (said to be either water or feather symbols), scrolls (important in the migration design), stipples (often used as a filler within outlined areas in place of solid colors), crosses, and swastikas. Barbara Freire-Marreco noted that by 1910 the meaning of most designs had been lost. "For the most part they give merely the descriptive names to parts of the design." (1911 Collection Notes)

Kenneth Chapman (Transfile 34 at the School for American Research) stated that crosses represented stars. The swastika, found only occasionially on Nampeyo's pottery, is used by many tribes in both forward and reverse forms. To the Navajo it represents whirling wind or whirling logs. In 1907 Ryan (36, 37) said of the symbol: "It means different things to different lands, and has been known in all of them. It is found in prehistoric carvings, and is claimed alike by the Oriental and the Indian medicine singer, or chanter of healing songs of their faith....I like best the Apache reading of the symbol. To him it is a sign for the Spirits of the Air who reveal the unseen in visions."

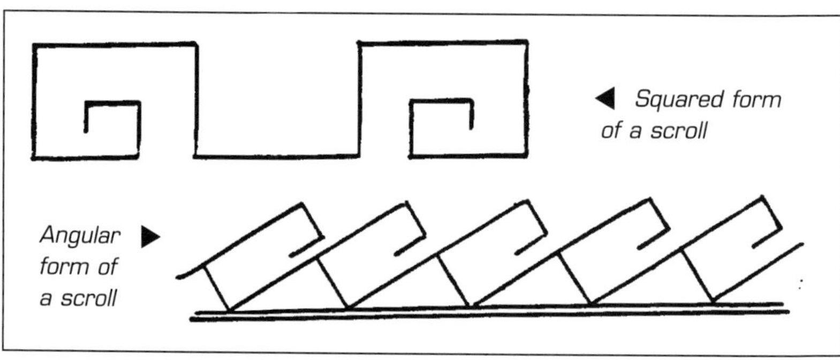

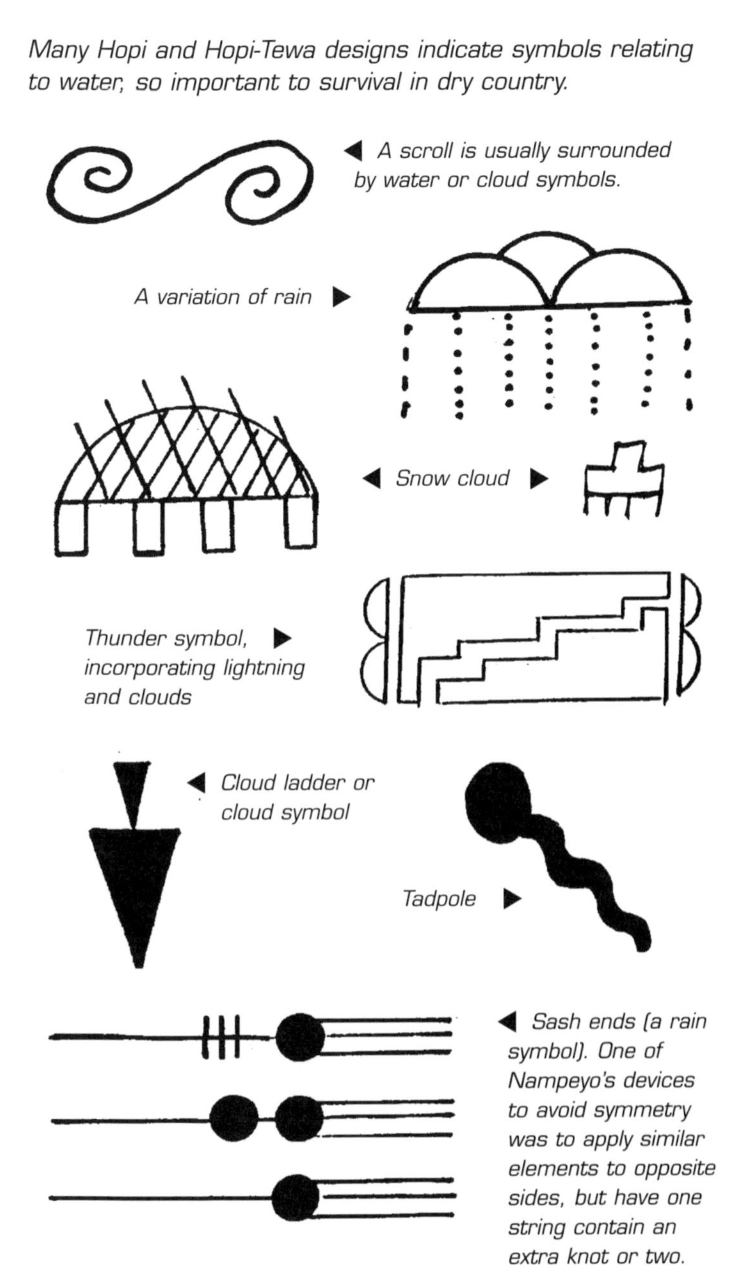

Many Hopi and Hopi-Tewa designs indicate symbols relating to water, so important to survival in dry country.
A scroll is usually surrounded by water or cloud symbols.
A variation of rain
Snow cloud
Thunder symbol, incorporating lightning and clouds
Cloud ladder or cloud symbol
Tadpole
Sash ends (a rain symbol). One of Nampeyo's devices to avoid symmetry was to apply similar elements to opposite sides, but have one string contain an extra knot or two.

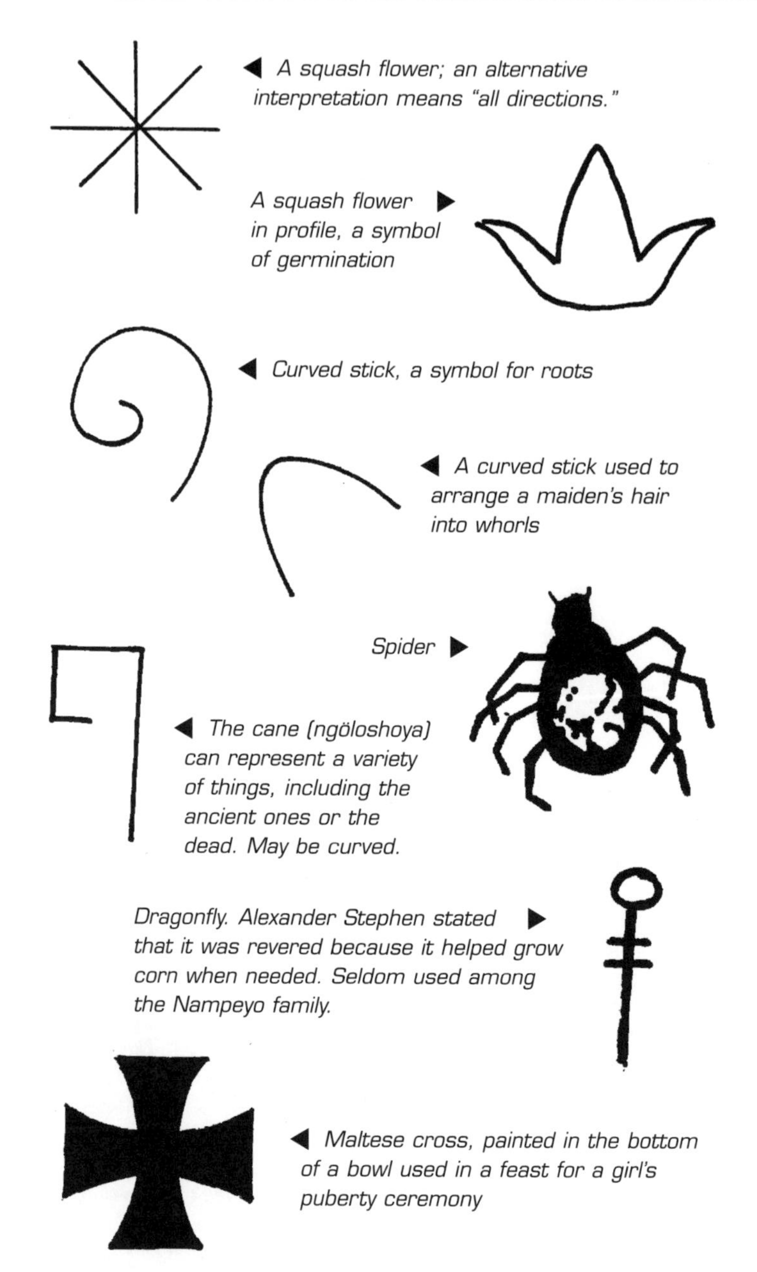

◀ *A squash flower; an alternative interpretation means "all directions."*

A squash flower in profile, a symbol of germination ▶

◀ *Curved stick, a symbol for roots*

◀ *A curved stick used to arrange a maiden's hair into whorls*

Spider ▶

◀ *The cane (ngöloshoya) can represent a variety of things, including the ancient ones or the dead. May be curved.*

Dragonfly. Alexander Stephen stated that it was revered because it helped grow corn when needed. Seldom used among the Nampeyo family. ▶

◀ *Maltese cross, painted in the bottom of a bowl used in a feast for a girl's puberty ceremony*

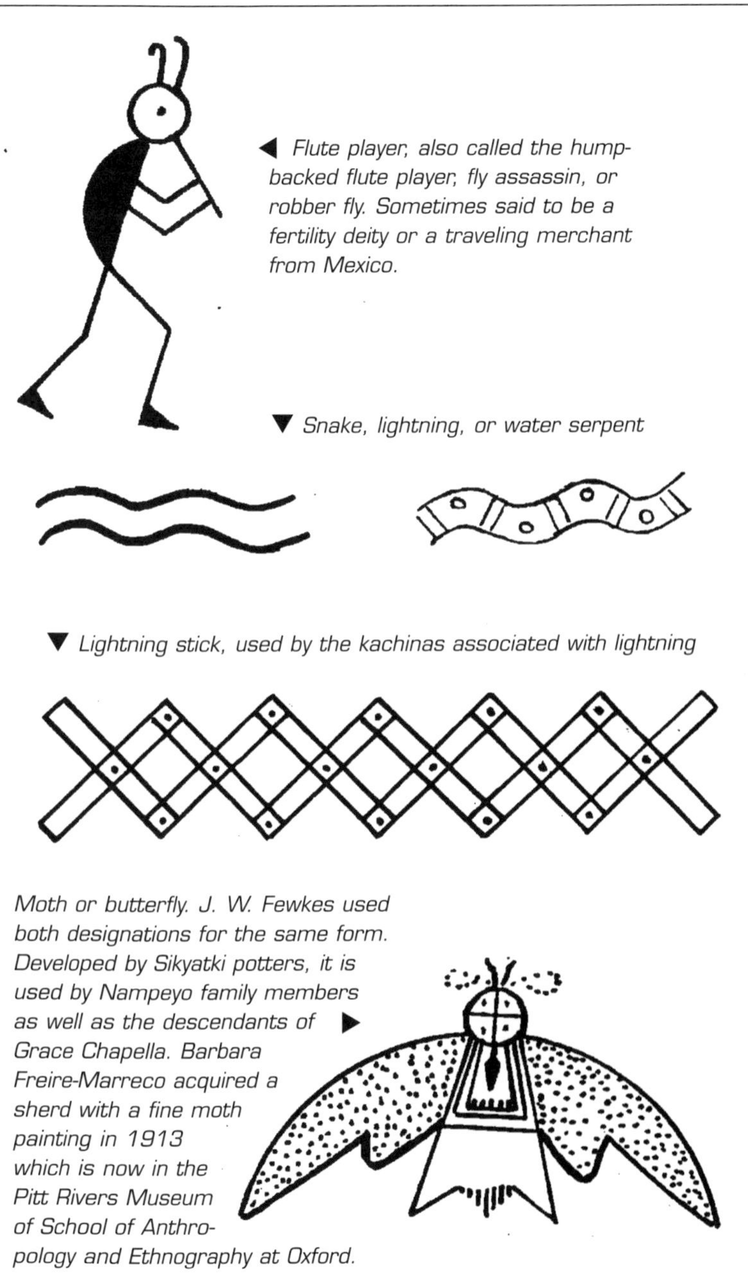

◀ Flute player, also called the hump-backed flute player, fly assassin, or robber fly. Sometimes said to be a fertility deity or a traveling merchant from Mexico.

▼ Snake, lightning, or water serpent

▼ Lightning stick, used by the kachinas associated with lightning

Moth or butterfly. J. W. Fewkes used both designations for the same form. Developed by Sikyatki potters, it is used by Nampeyo family members as well as the descendants of ▶ Grace Chapella. Barbara Freire-Marreco acquired a sherd with a fine moth painting in 1913 which is now in the Pitt Rivers Museum of School of Anthropology and Ethnography at Oxford.

◀ Symbols of the horns of the kachinas Sotuknangu or the Aahltu

Bird, insect, or deity? The Nampeyos who use this decoration offer different interpretations. ▶

Kokle or Oögöle

Polik Mana

Konin or Supai Kachina

▲ Three of many kachina designs painted by Hopi-Tewa potters. Sikyatki potters adapted kachina symbols as did potters of the Little Colorado Red Ware traditions before them.

◄ An assemblage of design elements: triangles, beaks, eyes, scrolls, feathers, etc. Often used by the Nampeyo potters and others. The design is applied in two units on either side of the piece and is topped by a cloud band.

▲ This popular Nampeyo family design is derived from an Awatovi design developed by potters under the influence of Franciscan fathers during the Mission period (Wade and McChesney 1981; 44, 66). The top and bottom segments of the design are often divided and placed at the top and bottom of the piece. Usually two complete elements encircle the vessel.

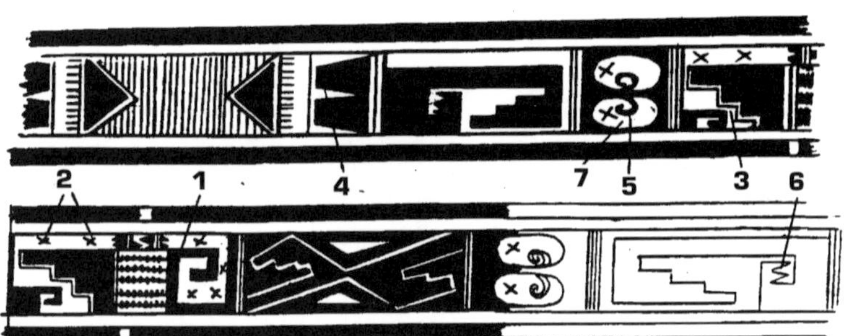

▲ Designs adapted from a drawing in Alexander Stephen's catalog of the Keam's Collection in the archives of the National Anthropological Archives. Identification by Barton Wright. 1. Bean sprout 2. Stars 3. Rain cloud with stars and bean sprout 4. Stylized mountain below rain clouds 5 & 7. The mask of the dawn kachina, Ahöla 6. Geometric filler. The entire panel contains all of the attributes assigned to Ahöla.

The illustrations above are by no means complete but do point out the variety of traditional design elements available to Hopi and Hopi-Tewa decorators and artists.

Appendix B
FAMILY GENEALOGY

It is difficult, and at times impossible, to construct an accurate genealogy chart for many Native American families. This fact applies particularly to the extended Hopi-Tewa family groups of which Nampeyo was a member. Were it not for the curiosity and enthusiasm of Hopi-Tewa art collectors and some religious organizations, the uses for such imperfect documentation would be strictly limited.

In most Native American cultures, lineage is traced by verbal recollection that usually goes back only two or three generations; and there are often discrepancies among these recollections. Were it not for Alexander Stephen and Jesse Walter Fewkes, who recorded the given names of a few individuals, we would not know that Nampeyo's father was Qots-Vema and her mother Qotea-Ka-O. Furthermore, determining the gender of historical names without accompanying explanation is all but impossible.

Birth names seldom survived because they were supplanted by others. Names by which adults became known were either of their own selection or bestowed on them by members of the community. Before the late nineteenth century, surnames were nonexistent in Hopi and Hopi-Tewa communities. Thus the famous potter was known simply as Nampeyo (translated as Serpent-with-No-Teeth or Snake Girl, among others), not Nampeyo Qots-Vema.

Intrusion of European mores into Hopi society brought change. The need to keep records and the bestowing of foreign names by teachers, who had neither the ear nor desire to learn the Tewa or Hopi language, dictated the practice of using surnames. Unpronounceable Hopi names were often modified with English pronunciation and converted into surnames, and new forenames of Christian origin were added. In his youth, the delightful man Porter Timeche, a Fred Harvey employee at the Grand Canyon for fifty years, had been known as Th-Me-Ha (closest English phonetic spelling for a name meaning "down feathers gently moving in a breeze"). On the first day of his enforced attendance at school, his teacher was unable to pronounce his name. After several attempts, the instructor blurted out, "Timeche." When no one responded, the man repeated it several times. Finally a friend nudged Porter and said, "That's you." Almost simultaneously his friends, for reasons unknown, began calling him Porter. For the reminder of his life, Down-Feathers-Gently-Moving-in-a-Breeze would be known as Porter Timeche. This is just one of the examples of name confusion that exists in many Hopi family records.

The Nampeyo-Lesou family is no exception. The three older children were first known by Indian names. The oldest girl, Kwe-Tea-We, was later given the Anglo name Annie by reservation missionaries. When she married Willie Healing, she became Annie Healing on the records. Only death allowed Nampeyo's oldest boy, Kalokun, to follow ancestral traditions. He is known only by this name, not Kalokun Lesou. The third child, Komalestewa, was forenamed William by either a missionary or teacher. He retained the designation Komalestewa by adopting it as surname. His only son went by the name of Austin Komalestewa Sr. and not Austin Lesou Sr. A grandson, an outstanding pottery artist and direct descendant of Nampeyo and Lesou, is Alton Komalestewa. It is for this reason that Alton is seldom recognized as a direct descendant of Nampeyo.

Census records were of help in constructing the following charts. The first census record was attempted by William Ross Mateer, Agent to the Hopis, on 1 July 1878. Theoretically, this included all of the population except for the hostile residents of Oraibi village. On review, this consists of a list of only male Hopis and Hopi-Tewas whose names were reproducible with English sounds. Lesh-sho (Lesou) and Nampeyo's brother Pu-lac-ca (Polacca) are recorded. The next census was made by T. Donaldson in 1890. It was similar to the earlier one, but it also provided an excellent historical and pictorial record of the area and its people at that time. Detailed census reports of the Hopis began a little over a quarter of a century later and for a few years were published almost annually. While providing valuable data, these records occasionally included different ages and name spellings for the same person. The apparent motive for frequent updating of records between 1915 and 1925 was to monitor the success of the policy of sending Native American children to off-reservation boarding schools. The records also served as evidence for the mortality rates of epidemics that struck the Hopi people during that period. The last available and most valuable Hopi-Tewa census was compiled in 1937.

Genealogical information since 1937 is best obtained from time consuming and often contradictory personal interviews. Migration away from the reservation and marriages outside the tribe have scattered many reliable sources over great distances, making it extremely difficult for us to construct charts for this book.

The exemplary custom of rearing the children of others within the extended family often leads to errors in registration. Children are accepted, nurtured, and loved without a trace of stigma and become completely integrated into the adopting family. Without an understanding of these practices, outsiders who attempt to construct family trees often err. Different approaches in constructing family trees would account for differences between those included here and those in other publications. We made no attempt to distinguish between adopted and blood-related wards, listing children with the parents who reared them.

Hence, our charts are not intended as a true record of descent. Strictly interpreted, they only show relationships between members of one extended family group, loaded with intrinsically inherited artistic talents coming from their ancestor Nampeyo.

We first thought that the charts would be of more value if they included only known Nampeyo family artists. However, experience has shown that an unrecognized person could and does suddenly win artistic acclaim. Also, the charts make no distinction concerning the quality of an artist's work. It is probable that some doing ordinary work now will develop into outstanding artisans.

In the time taken to write this book, there have been births, deaths, and changes in marriages and occupations. And most fortunately, several new talented artists have appeared, extending the great legacy of Nampeyo even further.

GENEALOGY CHART 1
Nampeyo Family

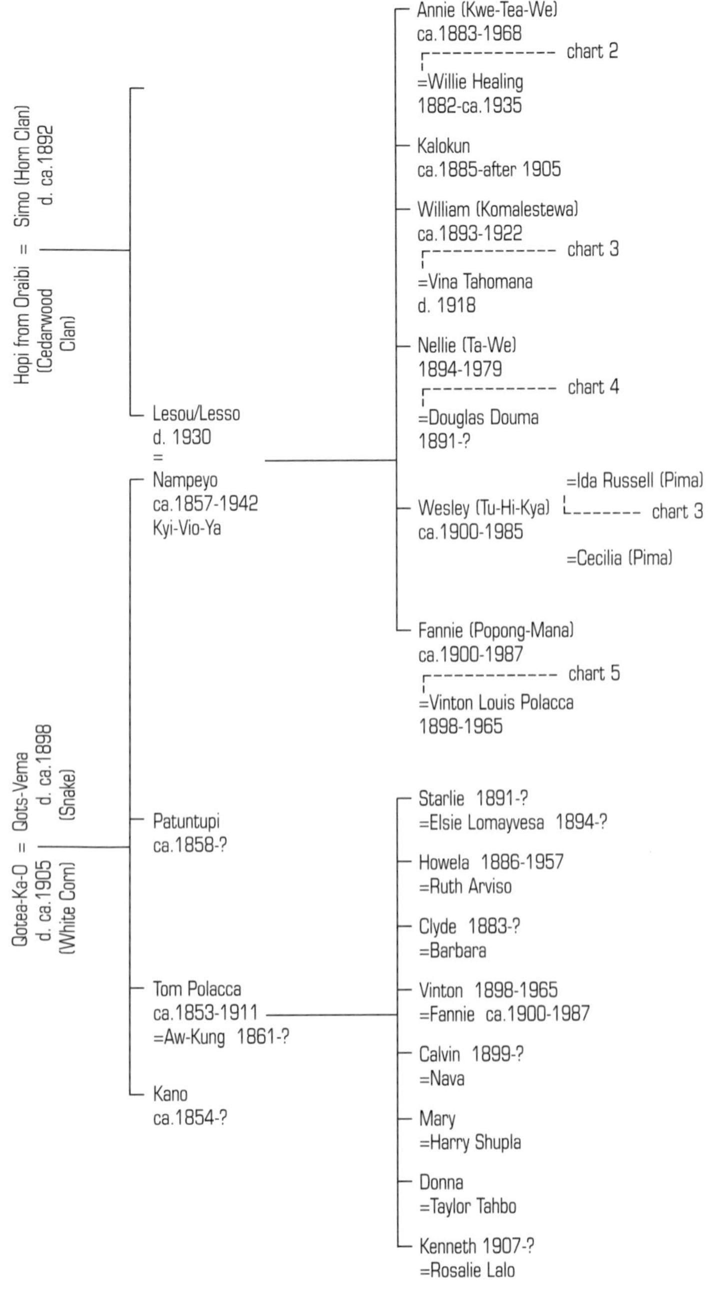

Marcella Ann
1922-1922
Dewey
ca. 1907-1992
=Juanita
=Martha
1916- ——— Alexander
1935-

Ami
Tyree

Priscilla
1924-
=Donnelly Sahmie

Foster

Andrew
1960-
=Ida Sahmie
(Navajo)
— Andrea
— Andrew Jr.
— Donally

Bonnie
1958-
=Earnest Chapella
— Doyle
— Sahmie
— Nikie

Jean
=Gordon Tom
=Elmer Tootsie
——— Donella

Randall
1950-
=Alicia
— Lisa
— Randy Jr.

Finkle
=Anita
— Daryl
— Emerson
— Debbie
— Kathy
— Mel

Eleanor
1930-
=Leslie Lucas
1928-

Karen
ca. 1954-
Jannelle
ca.1958- ——— Christine

Steven
1955-
=Yvonne Analla
(Navajo-Laguna)
— Samantha
— Natasha

Lowell
ca. 1938-1973

Emerson Jr.
1937-ca. 1975
=Irene Vicenti (Zuni)

Emory
1964-

Les
1967-
=Jocelyn Quam (Zuni)

GENEALOGY CHART 2
Annie & Willie Healing

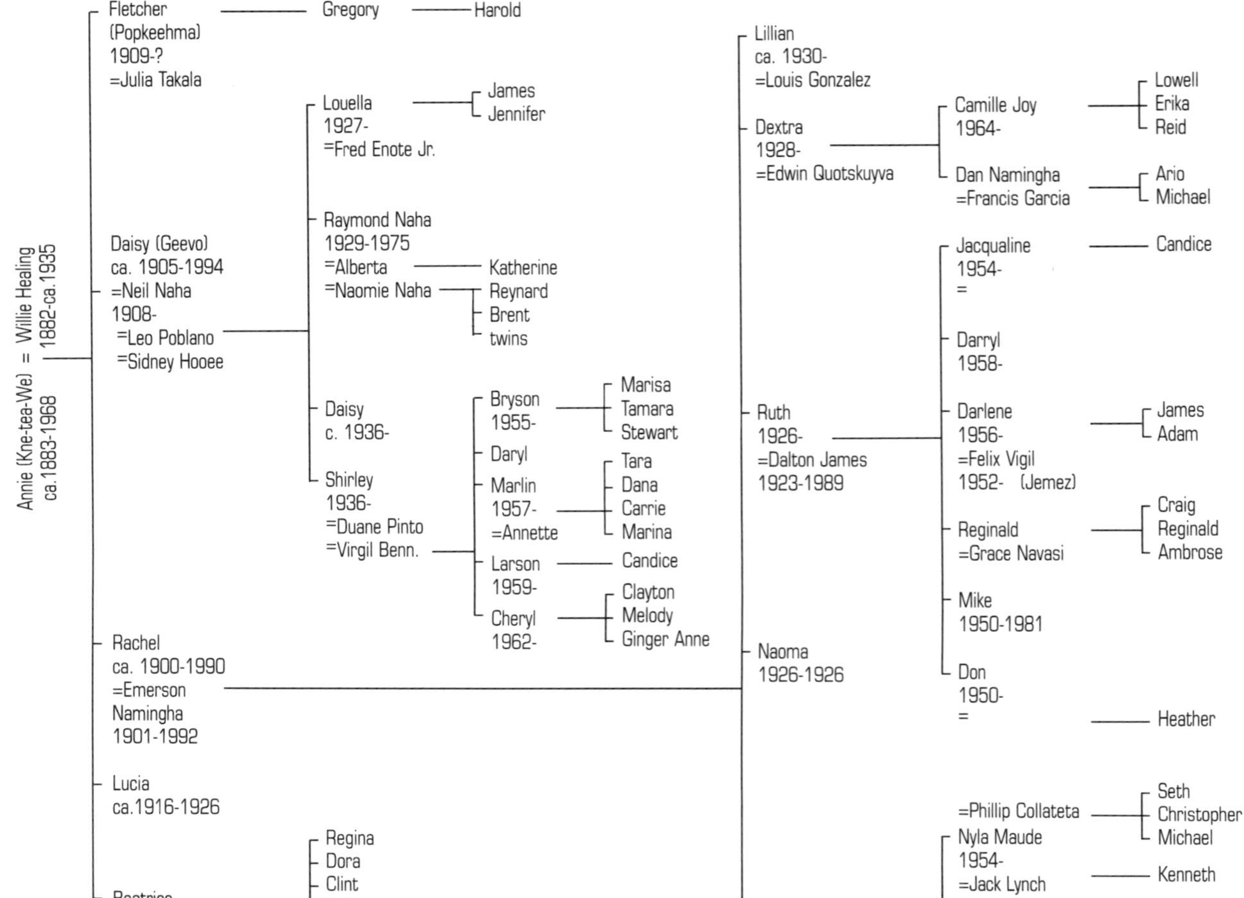

GENEALOGY CHART 3
Wesley Lesou & William Komalestewa

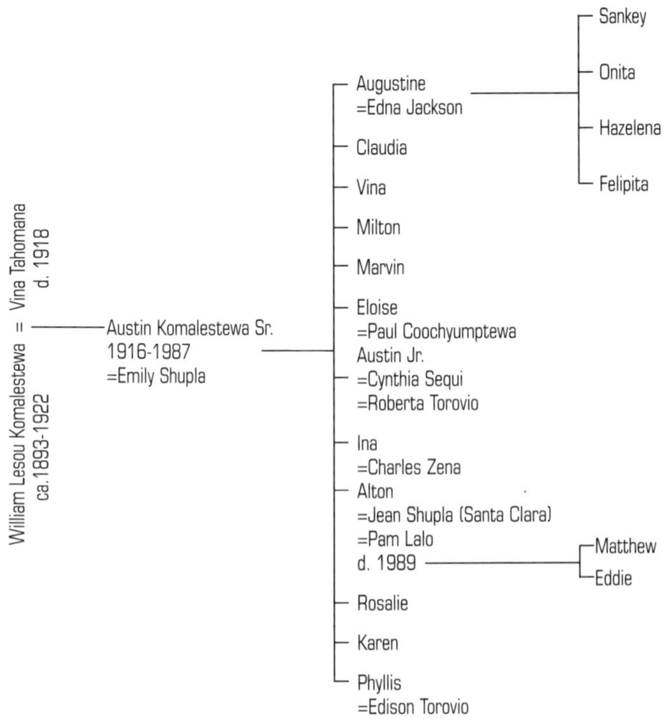

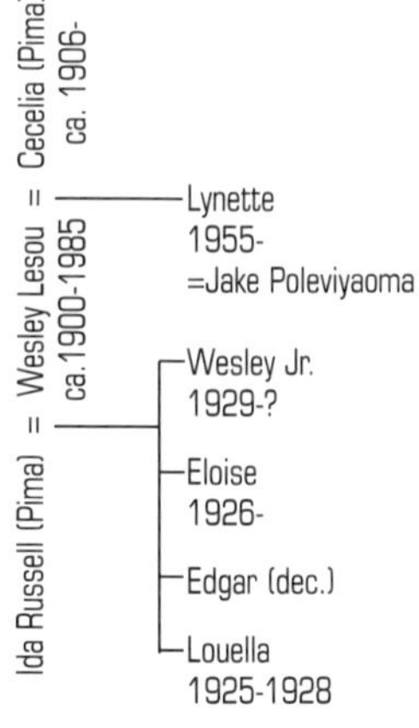

GENEALOGY CHART 4
Nellie Lesou & Douglas Douma

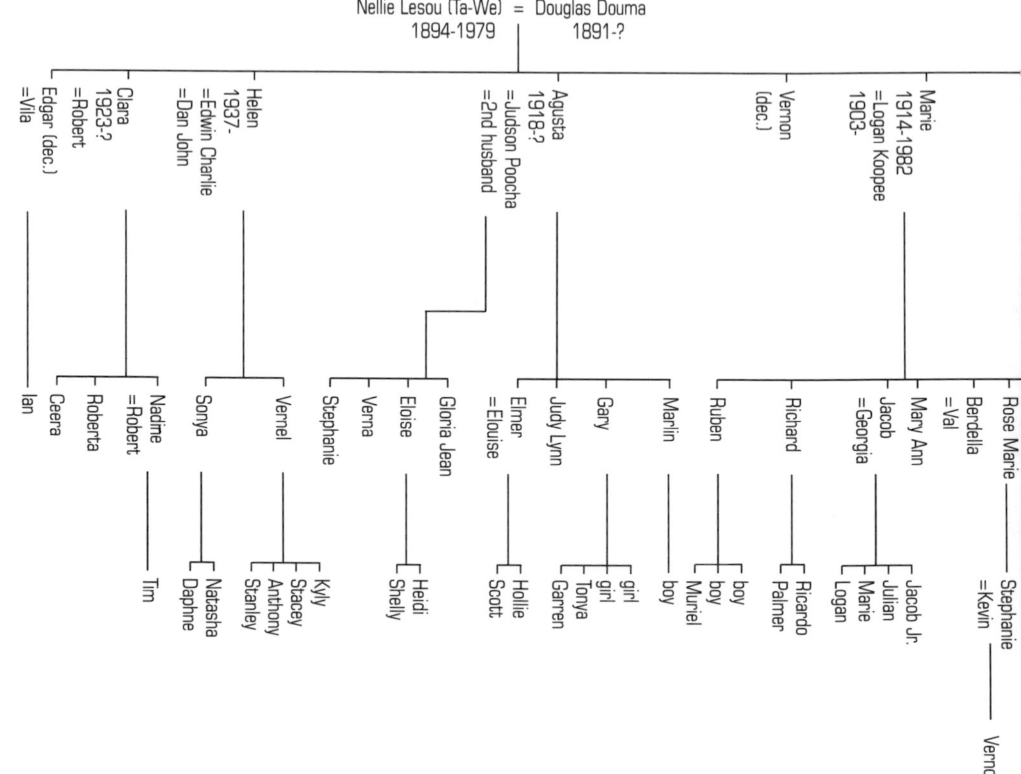

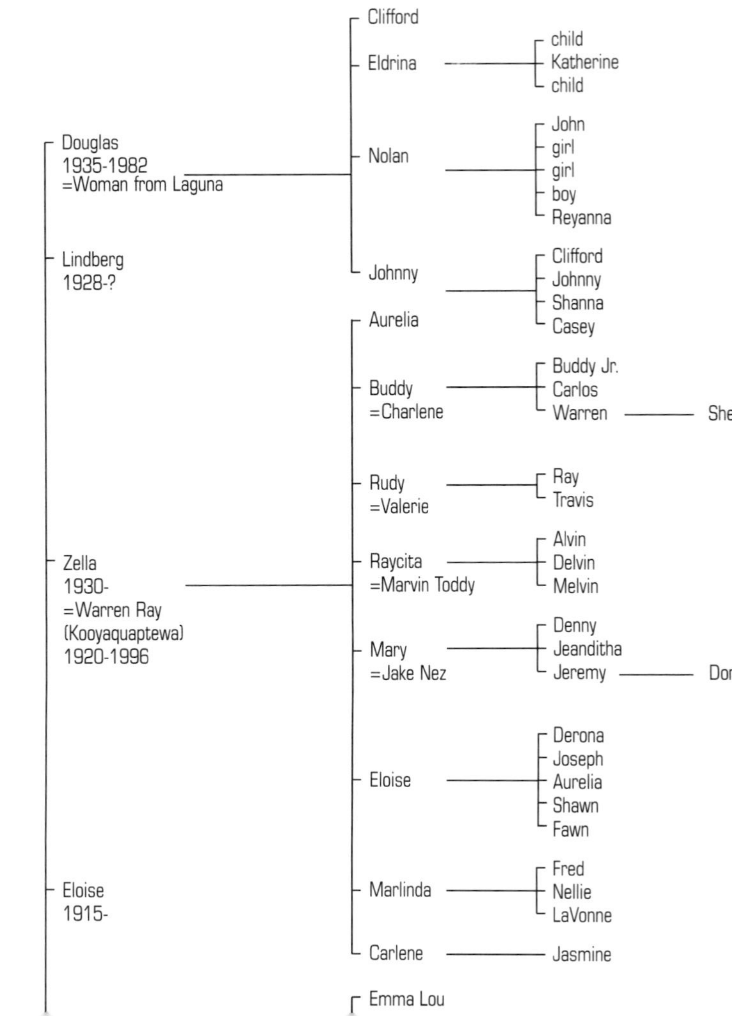

Douglas
1935-1982
=Woman from Laguna
Lindberg
1928-?
Zella
1930-
=Warren Ray
(Kooyaquaptewa)
1920-1996
Eloise
1915-
Clifford
Eldrina
child
Katherine
child
Nolan
John
girl
girl
boy
Reyanna
Johnny
Clifford
Johnny
Shanna
Casey
Aurelia
Buddy
=Charlene
Buddy Jr.
Carlos
Warren
Shelly
Rudy
=Valerie
Ray
Travis
Raycita
=Marvin Toddy
Alvin
Delvin
Melvin
Mary
=Jake Nez
Denny
Jeanditha
Jeremy
Doran
Eloise
Derona
Joseph
Aurelia
Shawn
Fawn
Marlinda
Fred
Nellie
LaVonne
Carlene
Jasmine
Emma Lou

GENEALOGY CHART 5
Fannie Lesou & Vinton Polacca

Fannie Lesou (Popong-Mana) = Vinton Polacca
ca.1900-1987   1898-1965

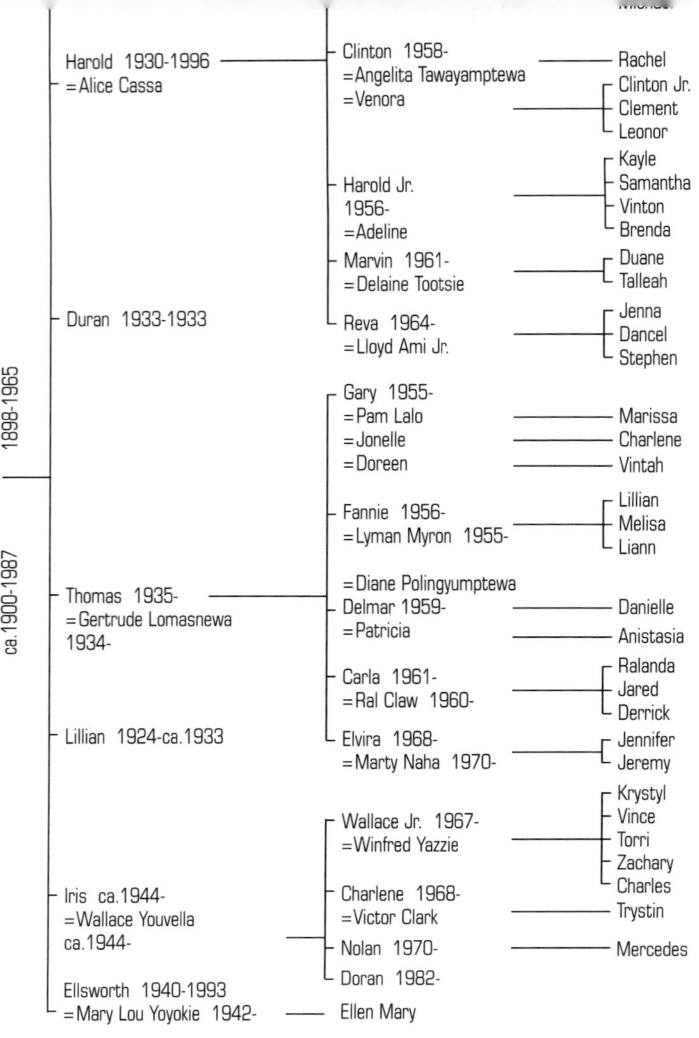

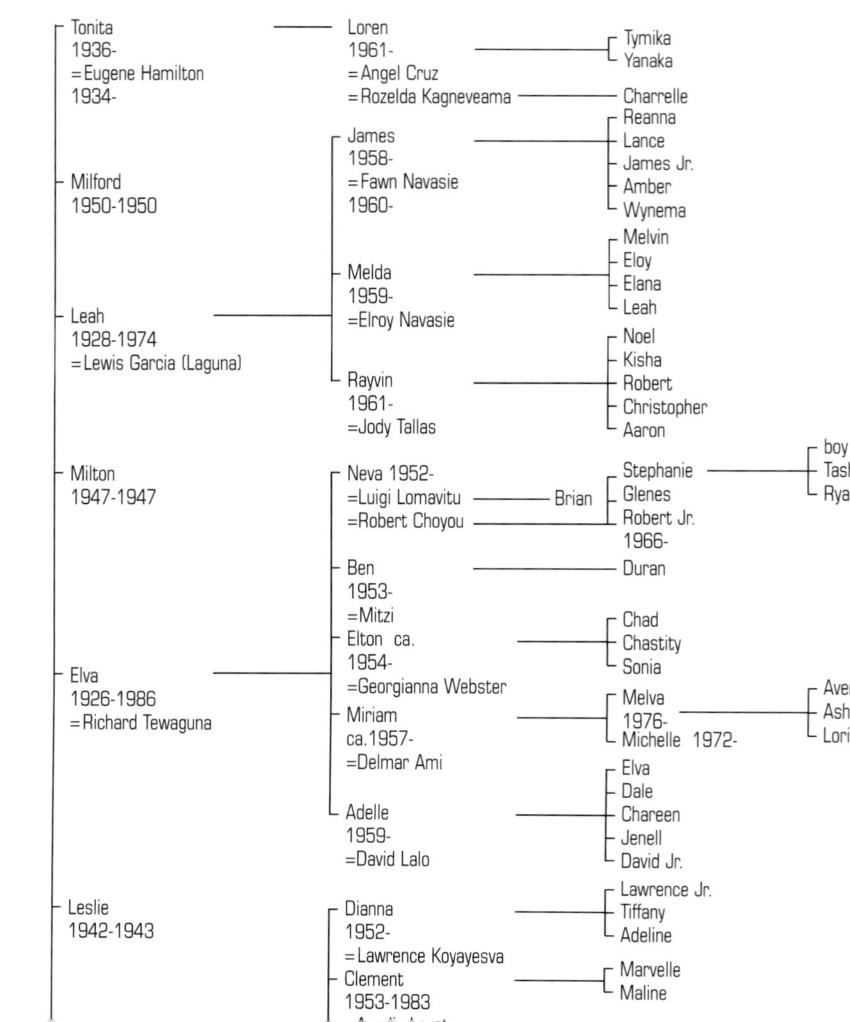

Tonita
1936-
=Eugene Hamilton
1934-

Loren
1961-
=Angel Cruz
=Rozelda Kagneveama
Tymika
Yanaka
Charrelle

Milford
1950-1950

Leah
1928-1974
=Lewis Garcia (Laguna)

James
1958-
=Fawn Navasie
1960-
Reanna
Lance
James Jr.
Amber
Wynema

Melda
1959-
=Elroy Navasie
Melvin
Eloy
Elana
Leah

Rayvin
1961-
=Jody Tallas
Noel
Kisha
Robert
Christopher
Aaron

Milton
1947-1947

Neva 1952-
=Luigi Lomavitu
=Robert Choyou
Brian
Stephanie
Glenes
Robert Jr.
1966-
boy
Tasha
Ryan

Ben
1953-
=Mitzi
Duran

Elton ca.
1954-
=Georgianna Webster
Chad
Chastity
Sonia

Miriam
ca.1957-
=Delmar Ami
Melva
1976-
Michelle 1972-
Avery
Ashley
Loriche

Adelle
1959-
=David Lalo
Elva
Dale
Chareen
Jenell
David Jr.

Elva
1926-1986
=Richard Tewaguna

Leslie
1942-1943

Dianna
1952-
=Lawrence Koyayesva
Lawrence Jr.
Tiffany
Adeline

Clement
1953-1983
Marvelle
Maline

References

Adams, Eleanor B., and Fray Angelico Chavez

1956   *The Missions of New Mexico, 1776: A Description by Fray Francisco Atanasio Domínguez with Other Contemporary Documents.* Albuquerque: University of New Mexico Press.

Adams, E. Charles

1979   Preliminary report of the ceramics recorded from the site of Walpi. Unpublished manuscript, Museum of Northern Arizona.

Ainsworth, Ed

1968   *The Cowboy in Art.* New York: Bonanza Books, Crown Publishers.

Allen, Laura Graves

1984   *Contemporary Hopi Pottery.* Flagstaff: Museum of Northern Arizona.

Anonymous

1862-1864   *Military Service Record. Thomas V. Keam.* National Archives, Washington, DC.

1864-1865   *Military Service Record. Thomas V. Keam.* National Archives, Washington, DC.

1865-1866   *Military Service Record. Alexander M. Stephen.* National Archives, Washington, DC.

1885-1902   *Rosters of Traders' Licenses.* Vol. 1. National Archives, Washington, DC.

1905   Untitled. *The Photographer.* New York, 21 November.

1910   Land show is on. *Chicago Sunday Tribune,* 20 November.

1937   *Hopi Reservation Census Report.* Washington, DC: U. S. Government Printing Office.

1947   Pottery makers used coal centuries ago in Arizona. *Science News Letter* 52, no. 8: 120.

1974   Nampeyo, Hopi potter: Her artistry and her legacy. *American Indian Crafts and Culture* 3, no. 5: 12-13.

1975   Interview with Daisy Hooee of Zuni, NM. *Many Fires.* Gallup, NM: n.p.

1975   *C. G. Wallace Collection of American Indian Art.* November. New York: Sotheby Parke Bernet.

n.d.   Svenska Man och Kvinnor. *Biografisk Uppslagsbok,* vol. 5 (Lindorm-O). Stockholm: Albert Bonniers Forlag.

1978   Hubbell Papers. Special Collections, University of Arizona Library.

n.d.   *List of Postmasters for Keams Canyon, Arizona 86034.* Keams Canyon, AZ, Post Office Publication.

1980   Hopi baby naming ceremony. *Arizona Highways* 9: 22-23.

1984   *Legend of the Quapaw Baths.* Reprint, Hot Springs, AR: National Park Service.

1988   Living the good life in old Keams Canyon: Life as son of a Navajo trader. *Indian Trader*. August.

Applegate, Frank G.

1930   Letter to F. H. Douglas. Douglas Library, Denver Art Museum.

Arny, William Frederick Milton

1873   Private land claims in New Mexico: Interesting items regarding New Mexico (Report to the Department of the Interior). In *Archives of the New Mexico Historical Society*. Santa Fe: New Mexico Historical Society.

Arrhenius, Olof W.

1984   *Stones Speak and Waters Sing: The Life and Works of Gustaf Nordenskiöld.* Mesa Verde, CO: Mesa Verde Museum Association.

Ashton, Robert Jr.

1976   Nampeyo and Lesou. *American Indian Art* 1, no. 3: 24-33.

Bacavi School

1987   *Passing the Moon: A Calendar.* Hotevilla, AZ: I. S. Productions.

Bailey, Lynn Robinson

1964   *The Long Walk.* Los Angeles: Western Lore Press.

1970   *Bosque Redondo: An American Concentration Camp.* Pasadena, CA: Socio-Technical Books.

Baird, W. David

1975   *The Quapaw People.* Phoenix: Indian Tribal Series, Publisher.

Bancroft, Hubert Howe

1888   *Arizona and New Mexico, 1530-1888.* San Francisco: The History Co.

Barber, Edwin Atlee

1875   Letter. Published in *The New York Times*, 1 October.

Barry, John W.

1981   *American Indian Pottery.* Florence, AZ: Books of Americana.

Bartlett, Katherine

1934   Spanish contacts with the Hopi, 1540-1823. *Notes, Museum of Northern Arizona* 6.

1951   How to appreciate Hopi handicrafts. *Notes, Museum of Northern Arizona.* Reprint Series, no. 3: 96.

1953   Twenty-five years of anthropology at the Museum of Northern Arizona. *Plateau* 26.

Bartlett, Katherine, and Francis H. Harlow

1978   *An Introduction to Hopi Pottery.* Flagstaff: Museum of Northern Arizona Press.

Bell, Barbara, and Ed Bell

1975-76   *Zuni: The Art and the People,* vols. 1 and 2. Dallas: Taylor Publishing Co.

Benavides, Alonzo de

1916   *The Memorial of Fray Alonso de Benavides, 1630.* Translated by Edward E. Ayer. Chicago: University of Chicago Press.

Blair, Mary Ellen, and Laurence Blair

1986   *Margaret Tafoya: A Tewa Potter's Heritage and Legacy.* Westchester, PA: Schiffer Publishing.

Bloom, Lansing B.

1931   A campaign against the Moqui pueblos under Governor Felix Martinez, 1716. *New Mexico Historical Review* 6, no. 2: 158-226.

Bourke, John Gregory

1984   *The Snake-Dance of the Moquis of Arizona.* 1884. Reprint, Tucson: University of Arizona Press.

Brandt, Elizabeth A.

1979   Sandia pueblo. In *Handbook of North American Indians,* vol. 9. Washington, DC: Smithsonian Institution.

Brew, John Otis

1939   Prehistoric use of coal by Indians of Northern Arizona. *Plateau* 12: 8-14.

1941   Preliminary report of the Peabody Museum Awatovi Expedition of 1939. *Plateau* 13, no. 3: 37-38.

1979   Hopi prehistory and history to 1850. In *Handbook of North American Indians,* vol. 9. Washington, DC: Smithsonian Institution.

Briggs, Lloyd Vernon

1932   *Arizona and New Mexico.* Boston: Privately published.

Briggs, Walter, and Wilson Hurley

1976   *Without Noise of Arms: The 1776 Domínguez-Escalante Search for a Route from Santa Fe to Monterey.* Flagstaff, AZ: Northland Press.

Brody, J. J.

1932   *Beauty from the Earth.* Philadelphia: The University Museum of Archaeology and Anthropology, University of Pennsylvania.

1971   *Indian Painters and White Patrons.* Albuquerque: University of New Mexico Press.

1979   Pueblo fine arts. In *Handbook of North American Indians,* vol. 9. Washington, DC: Smithsonian Institution.

Bromberg, Erik

1986   *The Hopi Approach to the Art of Kachina Doll Carving.* Westchester, PA: Schiffer Publishing.

Bullen, Nathaniel

1905   Letter to friends of Thomas Keam. 23 March. Culin Archival Collection, Brooklyn Museum Archives.

Bunzel, Ruth L.

1972   *The Pueblo Potter: A Study of Creative Imagination in Primitive Art.* 1929. Reprint, New York: Dover Publications.

Butterfield, Jody

1980   Daisy Hooee Nampeyo: Passing the tradition. *New Mexico Magazine* 58, no. 10.

Calhoun, James S.

1915   *The Official Correspondence of James S. Calhoun.* Edited by Annie Heloise Abel. Washington, DC: The U. S. Government Printing Office.

Ceram, C. W.

1972   *The First American: A Story of North American Archaeology.* New York: Harcourt Brace Jovanovich.

Chan, Roman Piña

1970   *A Guide to Mexican Archaeology.* México, DF: Minutiae Mexicana, S.A. de C.V.

Chapman, Kenneth M.

1970   *The Pottery of San Ildefonso.* Albuquerque: Published for the School of American Research by the University of New Mexico Press.

1977   *The Pottery of Santo Domingo Pueblo.* Albuquerque: Published for the School of American Research by the University of New Mexico Press.

Chapman, Kenneth M., and Bruce T. Ellis

1951   The line break, problem child of Pueblo pottery. *El Palacio* 58, no. 9: 251-289.

Churchill, Clara

1904-07   Journals. Archives of the Hood Museum, Dartmouth College.

Collins, John E.

1974   *Nampeyo, Hopi Potter: Her Artistry and Legacy.* Fullerton, CA: Muckenthaler Cultural Center.

1974   Nampeyo: Prestigious exhibition honors five generations of world-famous Hopi Pueblo potters. *Arizona Highways* 50, no. 5: 16-21.

1977   *Hopi Traditions in Pottery and Painting, Honoring Grace Chapella.* Signal Hill, CA: C. B. Hammonds Printing Co.

Colton, Harold S.

1939   The reducing atmosphere and oxidizing atmosphere in prehistoric southwestern ceramics. *American Antiquity* 4, no. 3: 224-231.

1951   Hopi pottery firing temperatures. *Plateau* 34, no. 2: 73-76.

1952   A guide to the description of pottery types in the Southwest. Paper presented to an archaeological seminar at the Department of Anthropology, University of Arizona, Tucson. Spring.

1953   Potshards: An introduction to the study of prehistoric Southwestern ceramics and their use in historic reconstruction. *Museum of Northern Arizona Bulletin*, no. 25.

Colton, Harold S., ed.

1955-1958   *Pottery Types of the Southwest.* Museum of Northern Arizona Ceramic Series, nos. 3A and 3D. Flagstaff, AZ: Northern Arizona Society of Science and Art.

Colton, Harold S., and Mary-Russell Farrell Colton

1943   An appreciation of the art of Nampeyo and her influence on Hopi pottery. *Plateau* 15, no. 1: 44-45.

Corbett, Pearson Hamblin

1952   *Jacob Hamblin, The Peacemaker.* Salt Lake City: Deseret Book Co.

Cordell, Linda S.

1985   Why did they leave and where did they go? In *Exploration: Annual Bulletin of the School of American Research.* Santa Fe: School of American Research.

Courlander, Harold

1982   *Hopi Voices: Recollections, Traditions, and Narratives of the Hopi Indians.* Albuquerque: University of New Mexico Press.

1987   *Fourth World of the Hopis.* Albuquerque: University of New Mexico Press.

Cox, Warren Earle

1945   *The Book of Pottery and Porcelain.* 2 vols. New York: Crown Publishing Co.

Craig, Lois A.

1943   Nampeyo, a famous Hopi potter. *Scenic Southwest* 15, no. 1.

Culin, Stewart

1901-1905   Stewart Culin Papers, Culin Archival Collection, Brooklyn Museum Archives.

Curtis, Edward S.

1922   The Hopi. In *The North American Indian,* vol. 12. Norwood, MA: Plimpton Press.

Daifuku, Hiroshi

1961   Jeddito 264: A report on the excavation of a Basket Maker III-Pueblo I site in northeastern Arizona with a review of some current theories in Southwest archaeology. *Reports of the Awatovi Expedition No. 7.* Papers of the Peabody Museum of American Archaeology and Ethnology 33, no. 1. Cambridge: Harvard University.

Dickson, D. Bruce Jr.

1979   *The Arroyo Hondo, New Mexico, Site Survey.* Arroyo Hondo Archaeological Series, vol. 2. Santa Fe: School of American Research Press.

Diehl, H. C.

1961   Letter to F. H. Roberts Jr. with enclosures. 5 September. Bureau of American Ethnology correspondence, National Anthropological Archives, Smithsonian Institution.

Dillingham, Rick

1994   *Fourteen Families in Pueblo Pottery.* Albuquerque: University of New Mexico Press.

Dittert, Alfred E., and Fred Plog

1980   *Generations in Clay.* Flagstaff, AZ: Northland Press.

Dockstader, Frederick J.

1954   *The Kachina and the White Man: The Influences of White Culture on the Hopi Kachina Cult.* Bulletin 35. Bloomfield Hills, MI: Cranbrook Institute of Science.

1961   Before and after Columbus. *Art in America* 49, no. 3: 24-43.

1979   Hopi history, 1850-1940. In *Handbook of North American Indians,* vol. 9. Washington, DC: Smithsonian Institution.

Donaldson, Thomas

1890   *Eleventh Census Report.* Washington, DC: U. S. Census Printing Office.

1893   *Moqui Pueblo Indians of Arizona and Pueblo Indians of New Mexico.* Extra Census Bulletin. Washington, DC: U. S. Census Printing Office.

Dorsey, George Ames

1899   Letter to Thomas Keam. 20 January. Archives of the Field Museum of Natural History.

1901   Letter to Henry Voth. 15 January. Mennonite Library and Archives, Bethel College.

Douglas, Andrew E.

1929   The secret of the Southwest solved with talkative tree rings. *National Geographic Magazine* 56, no. 6: 742-759.

Douglas, Frederick Hamilton

1942   The age of Nampeyo, the Hopi potter. *Masterkey* 16, no. 6: 223.

Dozier, Edward P.

1951   Resistance to acculturation and assimilation in an Indian pueblo. *American Anthropologist* 55, no. 1: 56-66.

1966   *Hano, a Tewa Community in Arizona.* New York: Holt, Rinehart, and Winston.

Eggan, Frederick R.

1950   *Social Organization of the Western Pueblos.* Chicago: University of Chicago Press.

1966   *The American Indian: Perspectives for the Study of Social Change.* Chicago: Aldine Publishing Co.

1979   Pueblos: Introduction. In *Handbook of North American Indians,* vol. 9. Washington, DC: Smithsonian Institution.

Ellis, Florence Hawley

1967   Where did the Pueblo people come from? *El Palacio* 74, no. 3: 35-43.

1974   *Hopi Indians.* New York: The Garland Press.

1979   Isleta pueblo. In *Handbook of North American Indians,* vol. 9. Washington, DC: Smithsonian Institution.

Emory, William H.

1848   *Notes of a Military Reconnaissance from Fort Leavenworth, in Missouri, to San Diego, in California, including part of the Arkansas, Del Norte, and Gila Rivers, made in 1846-1847.* 31st Congress, 1st sess., Senate Exec. Doc. 7, serial 505.

Espinosa, José Manuel

1988   *The Pueblo Indian Revolt of 1696 and the Franciscan Missions in New Mexico.* Norman: University of Oklahoma Press.

Euler, Robert C., and Henry F. Dobyns

1971   *The Hopi People.* Phoenix: Indian Tribal Series.

Farrish, T. E., ed.

1915-1918   *The History of Arizona.* Tucson: Arizona Historical Society.

Fewkes, Jesse Walter

1893   A-WA-TO-BI: An archaeological verification of a Tusayan legend. *American Anthropologist* 6, no. 4: 363-375.

1894   The kinship of the Tusayan villagers. *American Anthropologist* 7, no. 4: 394-417.

1895   Catalogue of the Hemenway Collection in the Historico-American Exposition of Madrid. In *Report of the Madrid Commission, 1892.* Washington, DC: U. S. Government Printing Office.

1896   Preliminary account of an expedition to the cliff villages of the red rock country and the Tusayan ruins of Sikyatki and Awatobi, Arizona in 1895. In *Sixteenth Annual Report of the Bureau of American Ethnology to the Smithsonian Institution for 1895.* Washington, DC: U. S. Government Printing Office.

1897   Tusayan katchinas. In *Fifteenth Annual Report of the Bureau of American Ethnology to the Smithsonian Institution for the Years 1893, 1894.* Washington, DC: U. S. Government Printing Office.

1898a   Archaeological expedition into Arizona in 1895-1896. In *Seventeenth Annual Report of Bureau of American Ethnology to the Smithsonian Institution.* Washington, DC: U. S. Government Printing Office.

1898b   Feather symbols in Hopi designs. In *Annual Report of the Bureau of American Ethnology to the Smithsonian Institution for 1897.* Washington, DC: U. S. Government Printing Office.

1898c   A preliminary account of archaeological field work in Arizona in 1897. In *Annual Report of the Bureau of American Ethnology to the Smithsonian Institution for 1897.* Washington, DC: U. S. Government Printing Office.

1899   The winter solstice altars at Hano Pueblo. *American Anthropologist* 1, no. 2: 251-276.

1900   Tusayan migration traditions. In *Nineteenth Annual Report of the Bureau of American Ethnology to the Smithsonian Institution for 1897, 1898.* Washington, DC: U. S. Government Printing Office.

1911   *Preliminary Report on a Visit to the Navajo National Monument.* Bureau of American Ethnology Bulletin 50. Washington, DC: Smithsonian Institution.

1919   Designs on prehistoric Hopi pottery. In *33rd Annual Report of the Bureau of American Ethnology to the Smithsonian Institution for 1911, 1912.* Washington, DC: U. S. Government Printing Office.

Field, Clark

1963   *Indian Pottery of the Southwest, Post Spanish Period.* Tulsa, OK: Philbrook Art Center.

Fierman, F. S.

1964   *The Spiegelbergs of New Mexico, 1844-1893.* El Paso: Texas Western College Press.

Fletcher, M. S.

1979   Nordenskiöld and the natives. *Journal of Arizona History.* Autumn.

Forde, C. Daryll

1931   Hopi agriculture and land ownership. *Journal of the Royal Anthropological Institute of Great Britain and Ireland* 41, no. 4: 357-405.

Forrest, Earle R.

1979   *Missions and Pueblos of the Old Southwest.* Glorieta, NM: Rio Grande Press.

Frank, Larry, and Francis H. Harlow

1974   *Historic Pottery of the Pueblo Indians 1600-1880.* Boston: New York Graphic Society.

Freire-Marreco, Barbara

1913   Unpublished notes of Hopi field investigations. Archives of the Pitt Rivers Museum, School of Anthropology and Museum Ethnology.

1914   Tewa kinship terms from the pueblo of Hano, Arizona. *American Anthropologist* 16, no. 2: 269-287.

1924   Letter to John Peabody Harrington. 16 January. National Anthropological Archives, Smithsonian Institution.

Frisbie, Theodore R.

1972   The influence of J. Walter Fewkes on Nampeyo: Fact or fancy. *Braud Book 1973*: 231-240.

Gallaher, James

1887   Letter to Commissioner of Indian Affairs. n.d. National Archives, Washington, DC.

Gifford, James C., and Watson Smith

1976   *Grey Corrugated Pottery from Awatovi and Other Jeddito Sites in Northwestern Arizona.* Papers of the Peabody Museum of American Archaeology and Ethnology 69, no. 10. Cambridge: Harvard University.

Gladwin, Harold S., Emil W. Haury, Edwin B. Sayles, and Nora Gladwin

1965   *Excavations at Snaketown: Material Culture.* 1937. Reprint, Tucson: Arizona State Museum, University of Arizona.

Grammer, Maurine P.

1930   Unpublished notes from Kenneth Chapman lectures at the University of New Mexico, in Grammer's possession.

Granzberg, Gary Robert

1973   Influences of the western economy on Hopi pottery making. *California Anthropologist* 3: 47-51.

Greenberg, Laura J.

1975   Art as a structural system: a study of the Hopi pottery designs. *Studies in the Anthropology of Visual Communication* 2, no. 1: 33-50.

Gumerman, George J., and S. Alan Skinner

1968   A synthesis of the prehistory of the central Little Colorado Valley, Arizona. *American Antiquity* 33, no. 2: 185-199.

Hack, John Tilton

1942   The changing physical environment of the Hopi Indians of Arizona. In *Reports of the Awatovi Expedition 1*. Papers of the Peabody Museum of American Archaeology and Ethnology 35, no. 1. Cambridge: Harvard University.

Hagen, K.

1903   *Jahrbuch der Hamburgishen Wissenschaftlichen Anstalten: XX Jahrgang 1902*, vol. 2. Hamburg, Germany: Museum fur Volkerkunde and Kommissionsverlag von Lucas, Grafe, & Sillem.

Halpern, Katherine S.

1985   *Guide to the Microfilm Edition of the Washington Matthews Papers*. Albuquerque: Published for the Wheelwright Museum by the University of New Mexico Press.

Hargrave, Lyndon Lane

1931   First Mesa. *Notes, Museum of Northern Arizona* 3, no. 8: 1-7.

1932   Guide to forty pottery types from the Hopi country and the San Francisco Mountains, Arizona. *Museum of Northern Arizona Bulletin*, no. 1.

1935   The Jeddito Valley and the first pueblo towns in Arizona to be visited by Europeans. *Notes, Museum of Northern Arizona* 8, no. 4: 17-23.

1937   Sikyatki: Were the inhabitants Hopi? *Notes, Museum of Northern Arizona* 9, no. 12: 63-66.

Harlow, Francis H.

1973   *Matte Painted Pottery of the Tewa, Keres and Zuni Pueblos*. Albuquerque: University of New Mexico Press.

1977   *Modern Pueblo Pottery, 1880-1960*. Flagstaff, AZ: Northland Press.

Harrington, John Peabody

1916   The ethnogeography of the Tewa Indians. In *29th Annual Report of the Bureau of American Ethnology for 1907, 1908*. Washington, DC: U. S. Government Printing Office.

Hartman, Russell P., Jan Musial, and Clara Lee Tanner

1987   *Navajo Pottery: Traditions and Innovations*. Flagstaff, AZ: Northland Press.

Harvey, Byron III

1981   *The Fred Harvey Company Collects Indian Art*. Phoenix: The Heard Museum.

Hay, Clarence L., et al.

1940   *The Maya and Their Neighbors*. New York: D. Appleton-Century Press.

Hayes, Alden C.

1985   Mesa Verde: A century of research. In *Exploration: Annual Bulletin of the School of American Research.* Santa Fe: School for American Research.

Hays, Kelly Ann, and Diane D. Dittemore

1990   Seven centuries of Hopi pottery. *American Indian Art Magazine* 15, no. 3: 56-65.

Hibben, Frank C.

1975   *Kiva Art of the Anasazi at Pottery Mound.* Las Vegas, NV: KC Publications.

Hillerman, Tony

1972   *The Boy Who Made Dragonfly.* Albuquerque: University of New Mexico Press.

Hinsley, Curtis M. Jr.

1981   *Savages and Scientists: The Smithsonian Institution and the Development of American Anthropology.* Washington, DC: Smithsonian Institution Press.

Hist, Pam

1980   On being a Hopi. *Arizona Highways* 56, no. 9: 16-27.

Hodge, Frederick Webb

1904   Hopi pottery fired with coal. *American Anthropologist* 6, no. 4: 581-582.

1942   Death of Nampeyo. *Masterkey* 16, no. 5: 164.

Holmes, William Henry

1882-83   Pottery of the ancient pueblos. *Fourth Annual Report of the Bureau of American Ethnology to the Smithsonian Institution.* Washington, DC: U. S. Government Printing Office.

Hooper, Mildred, and C. R. Hooper

1975   Awatobi: High Place of the Bow. *Outdoor Arizona* 47, no. 3: 18-19, 36-37.

Hough, Walter

1915   *The Hopi Indians: Mesa Folk of Hopiland.* Cedar Rapids, IA: The Torch Press.

1917   A revival of the ancient Hopi pottery art. *American Anthropologist* 19, no. 2: 322-323.

Hovland, Kenneth

1988   Undated taped correspondence to the authors.

Hubert, Virgil

1937   An introduction to Hopi pottery design. *Notes, Museum of Northern Arizona* 10, no. 1: 1-4.

Ilfeld Company (Charles Ilfeld)

1865-1907   Mercantile records.

Jacka, Jerry D.

1976   A Hopi baby naming ceremony. *Arizona Highways* 56, no. 9: 22-23.

Jacka, Jerry D., and Spencer Gill

1976   *Pottery Treasures.* Portland, OR: Graphic Arts Center Publishing Co.

Jacka, Jerry D., and Lois Essary Jacka

1986   Ancient traditions, new horizons. *Arizona Highways* 62, no. 5: 16-33.

1988   *Beyond Tradition: Contemporary Indian Art and Its Evolution.* Flagstaff, AZ: Northland Publishing.

Jackson, Clarence S.

1947   *Picture Maker of the Old West: William H. Jackson.* New York: Charles Scribner & Sons.

Jackson, William Henry

1877   *Descriptive Catalog of Photographs of North American Indians.* U. S. Geological Survey of the Territories Miscellaneous Publication No. 9. Washington, DC: U. S. Government Printing Office.

1929   *The Pioneer Photographer: Rocky Mountain Adventures with a Camera.* Yonkers-on-Hudson, NY: World Books.

1940   *Time Exposure: The Autobiography of William Henry Jackson.* New York: G. P. Putnams Sons.

James, George Wharton

1901   Indian pottery. *House Beautiful* 9, no. 5: 235-243.

1901   Indian pottery. *Outing* 39, no. 2: 154-161.

1912   *Grand Canyon of Arizona: How to See It.* Boston: Little Brown and Company.

James, Harry Clebourne

1956   *The Hopi Indians: Their History and Their Culture.* Caldwell, ID: The Caxton Printers.

1974   *Pages from Hopi History.* Tucson: University of Arizona Press.

Johnston, Bernice

1970   *Speaking of Indians: With an Accent on the Southwest.* Tucson: University of Arizona Press.

Josephy, Alvin M. Jr.

1961   *The American Heritage Book of Indians.* New York: Simon and Schuster.

Judd, Neil M.

1951   Nampeyo, an additional note. *Plateau* 24, no. 1: 92-93.

1954   *The Material Culture of Pueblo Bonito.* Reprints in Anthropology, vol. 23. Lincoln, NE: J & L Reprint Co.

1968   *Men Met Along the Trail: Adventures in Archaeology.* Norman: University of Oklahoma Press.

Kabotie, Fred, and Bill Belknap

1977   *Fred Kabotie: Hopi Indian Artist.* Flagstaff: Museum of Northern Arizona and Northland Press.

Kaemlein, Wilma R.

1967   *An Inventory of Southwestern American Indian Specimens in European Museums.* Tucson: Arizona State Museum and the University of Arizona.

Keam, Thomas Varker

1889   Letters to H. N. Rush. April and October. The Huntington Library.

1894   Letter to J. W. Fewkes. National Anthropological Archives, Smithsonian Institution.

1896-97   Letters to W. Matthews. Washington Matthews Papers, Wheelwright Museum of the American Indian.

1897   Letter to W. Sykes. Archives of the Arizona Historical Society.

1902-04   Letters to S. Culin. Culin Archival Collection, Brooklyn Museum Archives.

1904   Letter to W. Matthews. March. Archives of the Maxwell Museum, University of New Mexico.

Kelley, N. Edmund

1980   *The Contemporary Ecology of Arroyo Hondo, New Mexico.* Arroyo Hondo Archaeological Series, vol. 1. Santa Fe: School of American Research Press.

Koenig, Seymour, and Harriet Koenig

1976   *Hopi Clay-Hopi Ceremony: An Exhibition of Hopi Art.* Katona, NY: Katona Gallery.

Kramer, Barbara

1988   Nampeyo, Hopi House and the Chicago Land Show. *American Indian Art* 14, no. 1: 46-53.

1996   *Nampeyo and Her Pottery.* Albuquerque: University of New Mexico Press.

LaFarge, Oliver

1925   *Inventory of the George H. Pepper Collection of North American Indian Artifacts.* New Orleans: Tulane University.

Laird, W. David

1977   *Hopi Bibliography.* Tucson: University of Arizona Press.

Lang, Richard W., and Arthur H. Harris

1984   *The Faunal Remains from Arroyo Hondo Pueblo, New Mexico.* Arroyo Hondo Archaeological Series, vol. 5. Santa Fe: School of American Research Press.

Lange, Charles H., Carroll L. Riley, and Elizabeth M. Lange, eds.

1984   *The Southwestern Journals of Adolf Bandelier, 1889-1892.* Albuquerque & Santa Fe: University of New Mexico Press and the School of American Research.

Leakey, Richard E., and Roger Lewin

1977   *Origins: The Emergence and Evolution of Our Species and Its Possible Future.* New York: E. P. Dutton.

Lecomte du Nouy

1947   *Human Destiny.* New York: Longmans and Greenstreet.

Link, Martin

1985   Hopiland's famous Nampeyo family. *The Indian Trader* 16, no. 4: 5-8.

Linné, Sigvald

1946   Prehistoric and modern Hopi pottery. *Ethnos* 11, nos. 1 and 2: 89-98.

Lister, Robert H., and Florence C. Lister

1983   *Those Who Came Before.* Tucson: University of Arizona Press.

Lummis, Charles F.

1968   *Bullying the Moqui.* Prescott, AZ: Prescott College Press.

Lurie, Nancy Oestreich

1983   A special style: The Milwaukee Public Museum, 1882- 1982. *Publication 56,* Milwaukee Public Museum.

Mahood, Ruth I., ed.

1961   *Photographer of the Southwest, Adam C. Vroman 1856-1916.* Los Angeles: Ward Ritchie Press.

Mark, Joan

1976   Frank Hamilton Cushing and an American science of anthropology. *Perspectives in American History* 10, no. 5: 449-486.

Marriott, Alice Lee

1976   *Maria: The Potter of San Ildefonso.* Norman: University of Oklahoma Press.

Martinez, Julian

1911 Letter to K. Chapman. 4 February. Hewett files, Museum of New Mexico History Library.

McCoy, Ronald

1985 Nampeyo, giving the Indian artist a name. In *Indian Lives: Essays on Nineteenth- and Twentieth-Century Native American Leaders*. Albuquerque: University of New Mexico Press.

McGregor, John Charles

1965 *Southwestern Archaeology*. Urbana: University of Illinois Press.

McNitt, Frank

1962 *The Indian Traders*. Norman: University of Oklahoma Press.

Mera, Harry P.

1940 Population changes in the Rio Grande Glaze-Paint Area. *New Mexico Archaeological Survey, Laboratory of Anthropology Technical Series Bulletin* 9.

1970 *Pueblo Designs*, vol 2. ca. 1938. Memoirs of the Laboratory of Anthropology. Reprint, New York: Dover Publications.

Mindeleff, Cosmos

1900 Localization of the Tusayan clans. In *Nineteenth Annual Report of the Bureau of American Ethnology to the Smithsonian Institution for 1897, 1898*. Washington, DC: U. S. Government Printing Office.

Mindeleff, Victor

1886-87 A study of Pueblo architecture: Tusayan and Cibola. In *Eighth Annual Report of the Bureau of American Ethnology to the Smithsonian Institution for 1886, 1887*. Washington, DC: U. S. Government Printing Office.

Montgomery, Ross G., Watson Smith, and John O. Brew

1949 *Franciscan Awatovi: The Excavation and Conjectural Reconstruction of a 17th-Century Spanish Mission Establishment at a Hopi Indian Town in Northeastern Arizona*. Papers of the Peabody Museum of American Archaeology and Ethnology 36. Cambridge: Harvard University.

Monthan, Guy, and Doris Monthan

1977 Dextra Quotskuyua Nampeyo. *American Indian Art Magazine* 2, no. 4: 58-63.

Moon, Carl

n.d. Collection of Indian photographs. The Huntington Library.

Mooney, James

1893 Recent archaeologic find in Arizona. *American Anthropologist* 6, no. 3: 283-284.

Moses, Lester George, and Raymond Wilson, eds.

1985   *Indian Lives: Essays on Nineteenth- and Twentieth- Century Native American Leaders.* Albuquerque: University of New Mexico Press.

Muller, Florencia, and Barbara Hopkins

1974   *A Guide to Mexican Ceramics.* México, DF: Minutiae Mexicana S.A. de C.V.

Myers, J. Preston

1930   *The Oraibi Book of Indian Designs for Arts and Crafts or Decorative Work.* Oraibi, Arizona, School Project.

Nelson, John Louw

1937   *Rhythm for Rain.* Boston: Riverside Press for the Houghton Mifflin Co.

Nelson, Nels C.

1915   Pueblo Arroyo Hondo. Unpublished manuscript, collection of the American Museum of Natural History.

1916   Chronology of the Tano ruins. *American Anthropologist* 18, no. 2: 159-180.

Nequatewa, Edmund

1943   Nampeyo, famous Hopi potter. *Plateau* 15, no. 3: 40-42.

Nobles, A.

1978   A preliminary analysis of firing temperatures and selected paints and slips of historic Hopi pottery. Senior honors thesis, Harvard University.

Nordenskiöld, Gustaf

1991   *Letters of Gustaf Nordenskiöld.* Edited by I. Diamond and D. Olson, Mesa Verde, CO: Mesa Verde Museum Association.

Nunmaker, Harry G.

1969   Nampeyo of Hano: Evolution of modern Hopi pottery. *History of the Indians of North America.* Tucson: Department of Anthropology, University of Arizona.

O'Kane, Walter Collins

1950   *Sun in the Sky.* Norman: University of Oklahoma Press.

1957   Emry Kopta, sculptor of Indians. *Arizona Highways* 33, no. 8: 4-5, 34-37.

Olivera, Ruth

1981   Collection guide to the George Hubbard Pepper Papers (1873-1924). Latin American Library, Tulane University.

Ortiz, Alfonso

1969   *The Tewa World.* Chicago: The University of Chicago Press.

Owen, C. L.

1902   Recent explorations in prehistoric Hopi ruins, Arizona, by Stanley McCormick. Unpublished paper. Archives of the Field Museum of Natural History, Chicago.

Pabanale, Irving

1935   Hopi pottery. *Indians at Work* 2, no. 24: 21.

Packard, Al

1970   Trading to the Indians. *Donnelly Library Notes* (New Mexico Highlands University) 15, no. 2: 1-2.

Palkovich, Ann M.

1980   *The Arroyo Hondo Skeletal and Mortuary Remains.* Arroyo Hondo Archaeological Series, vol. 3. Santa Fe: School of American Research Press.

Parsons, Elsie Clews, ed.

1936   *Hopi Journal of Alexander M. Stephen.* 2 vols. New York: Columbia University Press.

Peterson, Susan

1980   *Master Pueblo Potters* (exhibit catalog). New York: ACA Galleries.

1984   *Lucy M. Lewis: American Indian Potter.* Tokyo, New York, San Francisco: Kodansha International Press.

Polacca, Vernida

1972   A visit with Grandmother. In *Arrow IV: Creative Writing Project of the Bureau of Indian Affairs.* (n.p.): Pacific Grove Press.

Powell, John Wesley

1961   *The Exploration of the Colorado River and Its Canyons.* 1879. Reprint, New York: Dover Publications.

Redhouse, J.

1985   *Geopolitics of the Navajo-Hopi Land Dispute.* Albuquerque: Redhouse/Wright Productions.

Reed, Erik K.

1943a   The origins of Hano Pueblo. *El Palacio* 50, no. 4: 73-76, 119-120.

1943b   The Southern Tewa pueblos in the historic period. *El Palacio* 50, nos. 11 and 12: 254-264, 276-288.

1952   The Tewa Indians of the Hopi country. *Plateau* 25, no. 1: 11-18.

Rice, P.

1987   *Pottery Analysis: A Source Book.* Chicago: University of Chicago Press.

Ries, H.

1927   *Clays: Their Occurrence, Properties, and Uses.* New York: John Wiley and Sons.

Robbins, Wilfred W., John Peabody Harrington, and Barbara Freire-Marreco

1916   *The Ethnobotany of the Tewa Indians.* Bureau of American Ethnology Bulletin No. 55. Washington, DC: U. S. Government Printing Office.

Rohn, Arthur H.

1985   Prehistoric developments in the Mesa Verde region. In *Exploration: Annual Bulletin of the School of American Research.* Santa Fe: School of American Research.

Rose, Martin R., Jeffrey S. Dean, and William J. Robinson

1981   *The Past Climate of Arroyo Hondo, New Mexico, Reconstructed from Tree Rings.* Arroyo Hondo Archaeological Series, vol. 4. Santa Fe: School of American Research.

Ryan, Marah Ellis

1907   *Indian Love Letters.* Chicago: A. C. McClure and Co.

Saunders, Charles Francis

1910   The ceramic art of the Pueblo Indians. *International Studio* 41, no. 163: lxvi-lxxi.

Schaefer, Paul D.

1969   Prehistoric trade in the Southwest and the distribution of Hopi Jeddito Black-on-yellow. *Kroeber Anthropological Society Papers* 41: 54-77.

Schmedding, Joseph

1951   *Cowboys and Indian Traders.* Albuquerque: University of New Mexico Press.

1984   *Arizona Memories.* Tucson: University of Arizona Press.

Schneider, Richard C.

1972   *Crafts of the North American Indian: A Craftsman's Manual.* New York: Van Nostrand Reinhold.

Scholes, France V.

1937   Notes on Sandia and Puaray. *El Palacio* 42: 57-59.

Schroeder, Albert H.

1973   *The Changing Ways of Southwestern Indians: A Historic Prospective.* Glorietta, NM: Rio Grande Press.

1979   Pueblos abandoned in historic times. In *Handbook of the North American Indians,* vol. 9. Washington, DC: Smithsonian Institution.

Schroeder, Albert H., and D. S. Matson

1965   *A Colony on the Move: Gaspar Castaño de Sosa's Journal, 1590-1591.* Santa Fe: School of American Research.

Schwartz, Herbert F.

1921   Spider myths of the American Indian. *Natural History* 21, no. 4: 382-385.

Schwartz, Stephen H.

1969   Nampeo and the origins of modern Hopi pottery. *Lore* 19, no. 4: 116-121.

Schweizer, Herman

1942   Letter to Harold S. Colton. Museum of Northern Arizona Library.

Shepard, Anna O.

1956   *Ceramics for the Archaeologist, Publication No. 609.* Washington, DC: Carnegie Institute of Washington.

1971   Ceramic analysis: The interrelations of methods. In *Science and Archaeology.* Cambridge: Massachusetts Institute of Technology Press.

Sides, Dorothy Smith

1936   *Decorative Art of the Southwestern Indians.* Santa Ana, CA: Fine Arts Press.

Sikorski, Katherine A.

1968   *Modern Hopi Pottery.* Monograph Series, vol. 15, no. 2. Logan: Utah State University.

Simpson, James H.

1964   *Navajo Expedition: Journal of a Military Reconnaissance from Santa Fe, New Mexico, to the Navajo Country Made in 1849.* Frank McNitt, ed. Norman: University of Oklahoma Press.

Simpson, W. H.

n.d.   El Tovar by Fred Harvey: A new hotel at Grand Canyon. Arizona Historical Society Archives, Tucson.

Smith, Mrs. White Mountain (neé Dama Margaret Langley)

1938   Tom Pavatea, Hopi trader. *The Desert Magazine* 1, no. 4: 4-6.

Smith, Watson

1952   *Kiva Mural Decorations at Awatovi and Kawaika-a: With a Survey of Other Wall Paintings in the Pueblo Southwest.* Papers of the Peabody Museum of American Archaeology and Ethnology 37. Cambridge: Harvard University.

1962   Schools, pots and potters. *American Anthropologist* 64, no. 6: 1165-1178.

1971   *Painted Ceramics of the Western Mound at Awatovi.* Papers of the Peabody Museum of American Archaeology and Ethnology 38. Cambridge: Harvard University.

1972   *Prehistoric Kivas at Antelope Mesa, Northeastern Arizona.* Papers of the Peabody Museum of American Archaeology and Ethnology 39. Cambridge: Harvard University.

Smith, Watson, Richard B. Woodbury, and Natalie F. S. Woodbury

1966   The excavation of Hawikuh by Frederick Webb Hodge: Report of the Hendricks-Hodge Expedition, 1917-1923. *Contributions from the Museum of the American Indian,* vol. 20. New York: Heye Foundation.

Spicer, Edward H.

1962   *Cycles of Conquest.* Tucson: University of Arizona Press.

Stanislawski, Michael Barr

1969   The ethno-archaeology of Hopi pottery making. *Plateau* 42, no. 1: 27-33.

1969   What good is a broken pot? An experiment in Hopi-Tewa ethno-archaeology. *Southwest Lore* 35, no. 1: 1-18.

1978   Pots, potters and potshards: The ethno-archaeology of Hopi and Hopi-Tewa pottery making and settlement. In *Discovery: Annual Publication of the School of American Research.* Santa Fe: School of American Research.

1979   Hopi-Tewa. In *Handbook of the North American Indians,* vol. 9. Washington, DC: Smithsonian Institution.

Stanislawski, Michael Barr, and Barbara B. Stanislawski

1978   *Hopi and Hopi-Tewa Ceramic Tradition Networks: Spatial Organization of Culture.* Pittsburgh, PA: University of Pittsburgh Press.

Stanislawski, Michael Barr, Ann Hitchcock, and Barbara B. Stanislawski

1976   Identification marks on Hopi and Hopi-Tewa pottery. *Plateau* 48, nos. 3 and 4: 47-65.

Stegner, Wallace

1954   *Beyond the Hundredth Meridian: John Wesley Powell and the Opening of the West.* Boston: Houghton Mifflin Co.

Stephen, Alexander M.

n.d.   Catalog of Keams Canyon Collection of the relics of the ancient builders of the Southwest Table-Lands. Unpublished manuscript at the Peabody Museum of American Archaeology and Ethnology, Harvard University.

1889   Letter to Major H. N. N. Rush. 25 April. The Huntington Library.

1893   Letters to J. W. Fewkes. 28 March, 19 October. National Anthropological Archives, Smithsonian Institution.

1898   Pigments in ceremonials of the Hopi. *Archives of the International Folk-Lore Association* 1: 260-265.

Stevenson, James

1883   Illustrated catalogue of the collections obtained from the Indians of New Mexico and Arizona in 1879. In *Second Annual Report of the Bureau of American Ethnology to the Smithsonian Institution for 1880, 1881.* Washington, DC: U. S. Government Printing Office.

Steward, Julian H.

1941   *Archaeological Reconnaissance of Southern Utah.* Bureau of American Ethnology Bulletin 128. Washington, DC: Smithsonian Institution.

Steward, Tyrone, Frederick Dockstader, and Barton Wright

1982   *The Year of the Hopi.* New York: Rizzoli International.

Stiles, Helen E.

1939   *Pottery of the American Indian.* New York: E. P. Dutton.

Stubbs, Stanley A.

1950   *Birds Eye View of the Pueblos.* Norman: University of Oklahoma Press.

Tanner, Clara Lee

1968   *Southwest Indian Craft Arts.* Tucson: University of Arizona Press.

1976   *Prehistoric Southwestern Craft Arts.* Tucson: University of Arizona Press.

Terrell, John Upton

1970   *Search for the Seven Cities: The Opening of the American Southwest.* New York: Harcourt, Brace, Jovanovich.

Thomas, Alfred Barnaby

1932   *Forgotten Frontiers.* Norman: University of Oklahoma Press.

Thomas, David H.

1978   *Southwestern Indian Detours.* Phoenix: Hunter Publishing.

Tierney, Gail D.

1976   Of pots and plants. *El Palacio* 82, no. 3: 48-52.

Titiev, Mischa

1944   *Old Oraibi: A Study of the Hopi Indians of the Third Mesa.* Papers of the Peabody Museum of American Archaeology and Ethnology 22, no. 1. Cambridge: Harvard University.

Toulouse, Betty T.

1977   *Pueblo Pottery of the New Mexico Indians.* Santa Fe: Museum of New Mexico Press.

Traugott, Joseph

1983   *Nampeyo of Hano and Five Generations of Her Descendants.* Exhibit catalog. Albuquerque: Adobe Gallery.

Trennert, Robert A. Jr.

1988   *The Phoenix Indian School.* Norman: University of Oklahoma Press.

Trimble, Stephen

1987   *Talking with the Clay: The Art of Pueblo Pottery.* Santa Fe: School of American Research Press.

Twitchell, Ralph Emerson, compiler

1914   *The Spanish Archives of New Mexico, Chronologically Arranged with Historical, Genealogical, Geographical, and Other Notations,* 2 vols. Cedar Rapids, IA: Torch Press.

Utley, Robert Marshall

1959   Special report on Hubbell Trading Post, Ganado, Arizona. Manuscript in Special Collections, University of Arizona Library.

Van Loon, Hendrick W.

1938   *The Story of Mankind.* New York: Garden City Publishing.

Van Valkenburgh, Richard F.

1940   Interview with Tom Keams, Jr. Archives of the Arizona Historical Society, Tucson.

1946   Tom Keam, friend of the Moqui. *Desert Magazine* 9, no. 9: 9-12.

Voth, Henry R.

1905   Traditions of the Hopi (including destruction of Awatovi and early Spanish missions at Oraibi). *Field Museum of Natural History Publication 96, Anthropological Series 8.*

1910   Catalogue of the Fred Harvey Hopi collection. Mennonite Library Archives, p 8, file 13, Bethel College.

1912   Brief miscellaneous Hopi papers. *Field Museum of Natural History Publication 157, Anthropological Series 11.*

1967   *The Henry R. Voth Indian Collection at Grand Canyon, Arizona.* 1912. Reprint, Phoenix: Byron Harvey, Publisher.

Wade, Edwin L.

1974   Change and development in the Southwest Indian art market. In *Exploration: Annual Bulletin of the School of American Research.* Santa Fe: School of American Research.

1980   The Thomas Keam collection of Hopi pottery: A new typology. *American Indian Art Magazine* 5, no. 3: 55-61.

1986   *The Arts of the North American Indian.* New York: Hudson Hills Press.

Wade, Edwin L., and Lea S. McChesney

1980   *America's Great Lost Expedition: The Thomas Keam Collection of Hopi Pottery from the Second Hemenway Expedition, 1890-1894.* Phoenix: The Heard Museum.

1981   *Hopi Historic Ceramics.* Cambridge: Harvard University Press.

Waldman, Carl

1985   *Atlas of the North American Indian.* New York: Oxford University Press.

Walker, Willard, and Lydia L. Wuckoff, eds.

1983   *Hopis, Tewas and the American Road.* Middletown, CT: Wesleyan University Press.

Warren, A. Helene

n.d.   Petrographic notes on glaze paint pottery: The Cochiti Dam archaeological salvage project, part I. *Museum Notes of New Mexico Research Records* 6: 184-197.

Waters, Frank

1970   *The Book of the Hopi.* Reprint, New York: Ballantine Books.

Watson, Don

1961   *Indians of Mesa Verde.* Ann Arbor, MI: Cushing-Malloy.

Webb, William, and Robert A. Weinstein

1973   *Dwellers at the Source: Southwest Indian Photographs from the A. C. Vroman Collection at the Natural History Museum of Los Angeles County.* New York: Grossman Publishers.

Welpley, Charles

1933   Pottery decorations among the Indians of the southwestern United States. Master's thesis, George Washington University.

Wheat, Joe Ben, James C. Gifford, and William W. Wasley

1958   Ceramic variety, type cluster and ceramic system in southwestern pottery analysis. *American Antiquity* 24, no. 1.

[Wheelwright Museum of the American Indian]

1985   *Guide to the Microfilm Addition of the Washington Matthews Papers.* Albuquerque: Published for the Wheelwright Museum of the American Indian by University of New Mexico Press.

Whiting, Alfred F.

1939   Ethnobotany of the Hopi. *Museum of Northern Arizona Bulletin,* no. 15.

Williams, Maj. Constant

1895-1898   Letters to Henry R. Voth. Mennonite Library Archives, Bethel College.

Wilson, Olive

1920   The survival of an ancient art. *Art and Archaeology* 9, no. 1: 24-29.

Wittick, Tom, and Terrence Murphy

1973   An 1883 expedition to the Grand Canyon: Pioneer photographer Ben Wittick views the marvels of the Colorado. *American West* X, no. 2: 38-47.

Wood, Nancy C.

1989   *Taos Pueblo.* New York: Alfred A. Knopf.

Woodbury, Richard Benjamin

1954   Prehistoric stone implements of northeastern Arizona. In *Reports of the Awatovi Expedition No. 6.* Papers of the Peabody Museum of American Archaeology and Ethnology 34. Cambridge: Harvard University.

Wright, Barton

1973   *Kachinas: A Hopi Artist's Documentary.* Flagstaff and Phoenix: Northland Press and the Heard Museum.

1975   *The Unchanging Hopi.* Flagstaff, AZ: Northland Publishing.

1977   *Hopi Kachinas.* Flagstaff, AZ: Northland Publishing.

1979   *Hopi Material Culture: Artifacts Gathered by H. R. Voth in the Fred Harvey Collection.* Phoenix: The Heard Museum.

1989   *Hallmarks of the Southwest.* Westchester, PA: Schiffer Publishing.

Wyckoff, Lydia L.

1990   *Designs and Factions.* Albuquerque: University of New Mexico Press.

Yava, Albert

1978   *Big Falling Snow.* New York: Crown Publishers.

Zimmerman, E.

1971   Daughter of famous Hopi artist continues Hopi pottery tradition. *Sun City-Youngstown, AZ, News.* 16 June.

Index

Other Titles from Treasure Chest Books

Books Of Special Interest

The Many Faces of Mata Ortiz The story of how a little village in Chihuahua, Mexico, has become the center of an unprecedented flowering in the art of pottery making. An introductory essay by Susan Lowell focuses on the unique background of the region and the people who made this phenomenon happen. Other contributors include Walter Parks, Jim Hills, and Michael Wisner. Biographical entries of over 100 artists. Approximately 200 photographs of the village, the potters, and their remarkable works of art by W. Ross Humphreys and Robin Stancliff. Available: Fall, 1999. Hardcover ISBN 1-887896-18-X, paperback ISBN 1-887896-08-2

Pueblo Stories and Storytellers by Mark Bahti. A popular book about storyteller figurines accompanied by a delightful selection of Pueblo Indian legends. Fully illustrated, paperback. ISBN 1-887896-01-5

Other Books On Native American Arts and Crafts

A Guide to Navajo Weavings by Kent McManis and Robert Jeffries. Heavily illustrated, paperback. ISBN 1-887896-07-4

A Guide to Zuni Fetishes & Carvings, Volume I: The Animals and the Carvers and ***Volume II: The Materials and the Carvers*** by Kent McManis. Heavily illustrated, paperback. ISBN 1-887896-14-7/ISBN 1-887896-11-2

Navajo Sandpainting Art: Where the Gods Gather by Mark Bahti. Completely revised edition of Bahti's fascinating look at Navajo ceremonial art. Fully illustrated, paperback. ISBN 1-887896-05-8

Spirit in the Stone: A Handbook of Southwest Indian Animal Carvings and Beliefs by Mark Bahti. An exhaustive new reference on fetishes and the many tribes who make them. Over 300 illustrations of the animals and other beings, along with the traditiional significance and legends associated with each. Plus a section on stones and and other materials, paperback. ISBN 1-887896-09-0